William Barton

The Book of Psalms in Metre

Close and proper to the Hebrew; smooth and pleasant for the metre ; to be sung in usual and known tune; newly translated with amendments, and addition of many fresh metres; fitted for the ready use, and understanding

William Barton

The Book of Psalms in Metre
Close and proper to the Hebrew; smooth and pleasant for the metre ; to be sung in usual and known tune; newly translated with amendments, and addition of many fresh metres; fitted for the ready use, and understanding

ISBN/EAN: 9783337317447

Printed in Europe, USA, Canada, Australia, Japan

Cover: Foto ©Lupo / pixelio.de

More available books at **www.hansebooks.com**

THE BOOK OF
PSALMS
IN METRE
CLOSE AND PROPER
TO THE HEBREW:
SMOOTH AND PLEASANT
FOR THE METRE;

To be sung in usual and known
TUNES.

Newly Translated with Amendments, and Addition of many fresh Metres.
Fitted for the ready use, and understanding of all good Christians.

By *William Barton* Mr. of Arts, as he left it finished in his life time.

PSALM 47. 7.
כִּי מֶלֶךְ כָּל־הָאָרֶץ אֱלֹהִים זַמְּרוּ מַשְׂכִּיל׃

To God with understanding praises sing,
For over all the earth he is the King.

Hezekiah commanded the Levites to sing praise unto the LORD, with the words of *David*, and of *Asaph* the Seer, &c. 2 Chron. 29. 30.

LONDON,
Printed for the Company of *Stationers*, 1682.

A PREFACE TO THE READER.

Courteous and Christian Reader,

IF the express commandment of God (who hath given all men voices) injoyning all to sing his praise aloud, Psal. 66. 1, 2. *especially his professed people to do this duty jointly and together*, Psal. 34. 3. 111. 1. 149. 1. *if this injunction even before the Levitical service was instituted*, Exod. 15. 1, 21. *and without any dependance on that service, while it stood*, 2. Chro. 23. 18. *and long after that service was abolished*, Col. 3. 16. *were duly considered; surely, singing of Psalms (even in mixt congregations) had never been spoken against: nor had occasion been given to so many learned men to Apologize and Dispute*

A Preface to the Reader.

things by meditation, then to nominate those whom we count God's enemies now on earth; imposing our shallow conceits upon the service of God and his Church, oftentimes according to the humours and corruptions of men? It was notably well hit indeed of the holy Martyr Barlam, that thrusting his hands into the burning flame, sang that of the Psalmist, Thou teachest my hands to war and my fingers to fight: But the false and erroneous interpositions and impositions of our own, I will spare to speak of for the credit of others. Only to know how to apply every Scripture passage of a Psalm, I refer and commend the Reader to the godly Sermons of Mr. FORD upon this subject, who gives no incouragement to compose any Psalms whatsoever besides Scriptural.

Do men say (still) that they can fit themselves better with expressions of their own, and need not the Scriptural? certainly the holy Prophets and Apostles, from Samuel (I may say) and after him to Christ, thought not so, but used these Psalms of David. See 1 Sam. 18. 6. Neh. 12. 42. Mat. 26. 30. Acts 16. 25. 'Tis true indeed, the Primitive Church immediately after Christ's Ascension, and
in

A Preface to the Reader.

in honour of that, Joh. 7. 39. *was endowed with rare gifts of Prophecy and Psalmestry, as also of Miracles and Tongues*, 1 Cor. 14. 26. *which long since ceast: and what manner of gifts men have now adays, that would obtrude their unscriptural raptures, or composures, we may see with shame enough: from whence we may undoubtedly conclude that the Scripture-Psalms, especially those of the sweet Psalmist of Israel*, 1 Sam. 23. 1. *ought as well to be translated into Verse for singing, as into Prose for reading*, 1 Cor. 14. 15, 19. *lest the Congregations should be wholly, or for the most part destitute of God's ordinance. As for the new songs spoken of in Scripture, these were the new songs*, Psalm 96. 1. & 98. 1. *which contained more gospel matters, and should be sung with new affections, as* Diodati *upon the place.*

And doubtless when once the Psalms of David *are translated to the life of Scriptures, (so far as a translation can go) and men can endure sound doctrine (for these Psalms bear so clear witness against heresy, apostacy, pride and prophaness, and all other fruits of the flesh that therefore many in these dayes so much dislike them) I may conclude with* David *Psalm* 141. 6.

A 4   Then

A Preface to the Reader.

Then shall they hear my words, for they are sweet.

Fourthly, if it were considered how exact and accurate the Scripture is in setting forth Psalms, as appears in the *Acrosticks*, where every verse, or half verse, or just part begins with the orderly procedence of the *Alphabetical* letter, one example whereof (but all are too hard to follow,) I have exhibited in the first *Metre* of the 111 Psalm, and two examples more in the first and last parts of 119. I say, if this and many other excellencies of the Hebrew verse were observed and considered, the delicacy of the best Poetical composure would never have been spoken against; I confess, I have found but few of that harsh humour; Nor do I count my labours hitherto worthy of the honour and favour they have found, when more than forty of the eminentest Scholars and Preachers of the Land, gave me their attest and approbation, and after them full forty more, among whom, the worthy Vice-Chancellor of the University of Cambridge, the learned Prolocutor of the Assembly, and divers eminent in Law and Physick, offered me their hands and helps to the further propagation and promotion of my Book. Nor can I omit an humble acknowledgment

of

their undeserved respects, that have taken notice of me in their Printed Books. In gratulation of whose noble incouragements, I have (in this my last Translation) corrected all the harsh passages, and added a great number of second Metres in choicest Tunes, having understood by learned Men that my last Edition had much sooner, and much more come into request, if it had not been deprived of those accommodations and accomplishments.

But now I have omitted none of the ancient Tunes, (but have added some new) except the 104. only, which is counted too crabbed, and if put into the same Measures too light; which therefore I have done in a Common Tune.

The Scots of late have put forth a Psalm-Book, most-what Composed out of mine and Mr. Rous his, but it did not give full satisfaction, for somebody hath been at Charge to put forth a new Edition of mine, and Printed some Thousands of mine in Holland, as it is reported; But whether they were Printed there or no, I am in doubt, for I am sure that 1500 of my Books were heretofore Printed by stealth in England, and carried over into Ireland.

Fifthly, If it be well consider'd how closely I have follow'd the Prose-Translation, I

A Preface to the Reader.

I trust I shall never be blam'd for varying so much from the old Psalms; for although they be very familiar to many, yet a just and due Correction would estrange them again, neither are men so well acquainted with them as with the Prose-Translation, nor do they hear them so often.

Considering also, that I have Compiled the whole Book (in all the first Metres especially) and in a great number of the second Metres as near as may be in the same order of words, and for the most part in as perfect Prose as Verse.

As for some second Metres which in part are done in Paraphrase; It's hoped that they are done very consonantly to the Text, and do not put in any thing but what is virtually if not verbally contained in it.

And I received this approbation and advise from a worthy Minister, viz. Mr. Rich. Baxter (which I have followed of mine own accord before his Letter came to my hand) in these words following, Sir, I thank you for affording me the sight of your Psalms. Those I saw (ad 26.) are very well done, and your various Metres will be grateful: I confess I could wish you had taken more liberty to make them Pleasant & Elegant, by expletive Epithets, as *Sandys* on *Job*, seeing such are oft not so much Paraphra-
stical

stical, as the very sense of the Hebrew words, which are hardly expressed by one in *English*, &c.

Sixthly and lastly, If it be considered that all the *Psalm-Translators* do of necessity add and alter, and sometimes explain and amplifie the *Prose-Translation*; yea, the Translators of the Prose it self, do oftentimes and of necessity do the same, as appears in a thousand places by the Or's, and Hebraisms *in the Margin*, and by the words inserted (*in a different Character*) into the Text : yea, the Scripture it self useth this diversity and latitude, as may appear by comparing parallel places, and in particular the 14 Psalm with the 53. and the 18 Psalm, with the 2 Sam. 22. &c. I trust I shall never be blamed for any liberty used in my Translation of the Psalms ; Especially considering that whatsoever is found therein, is either 1 The very words of the Prose-translation and (mostwhat) in the same order, or 2 Words to the same effect, or 3 An allusion to a parallel Scripture, or 4 An amplification of the plain scope of the Text, or 5 An explication of the sense of it, or 6 and lastly, A truer or (at least) a fuller exposition of the Hebrew. Allow me to insert a few instances.

Two

A Preface to the Reader.

Two famous examples are in Pſal. 78. v. 63. *And honourable marriage (alluding to* Heb. 13. 4.*) Their maidens might not have.* Heb. *their virgins were not praiſed,* viz. *with nuptial ſongs. And* v. 66. *A vile diſeaſe for vile deſerts*; *alluding to the ſtory* 1 Sam. 5. 9. 6. 4. *Vide* עפלו procidentia ani, mariſca, ficus ani, the piles, Aurei ani, *ſaith* Montanus, *in the Margin.*

A 2 *Inſtance is in* Pſ. 3. 5. *Becauſe I knew aſſuredly the Lord did me ſuſtain. Which being ſo eaſie and obvious for the ſcope, was choſen rather then an Hebraiſme in the room*: *Becauſe Jehovah from on high did ſtrongly me ſuſtain. Vide* סמך deſuper ſuſtinuit, fulcivit. Sch. *to under-prop and ſuſtain from above.*

3. *That inſtance* Pſal. 68. 63. Heb. *Their virgins were not praiſed, the Tranſlators render, Their maidens were not given in marriage, much better may I ſay, And honourable marriage,* &c. *Note here that the Tranſlators often give the ſenſe:* Pſal. 7. 10. *My buckler is upon God, they render, God is my defence*; *ſo in many hundred places both of the Old Teſtament and New. Yea, not only by alteration of the words, but by addition many times:* Pſalm 7. 11. Heb. *God is angry* ——— *every day, they put in,*

with

with the wicked, Pſalm 94. 10. *Heb. He that teacheth man knowledge, they add, ſhall not he know?* Ainſworth oftentimes makes the ſupplement divers wayes. The Septuagint *and* Chaldee *Paraphraſe go oft far wider, and add more to the Text, yet are followed in the quotations of the Old Teſtament by the New.*

4. *And laſtly to inſtance in a fuller Tranſlation of the* Hebrew, *take a few of many.* From the firſt word אשר *Beatitudines in the plural number*, I put in, Bleſſed, O bleſſed (*doubling is*) From חטאים *erravit to wander*, I take, Such as go aſtray, From יְרָע *approbavit, favit, to favour*, The Lord with favour knows From אבד *perdidit abolevit*, Periſh quite. *All theſe from the firſt Pſalm.* So Pſal. 7. 13. *from* חצץ *Sagitta dividens quod tangit*, Sharp arrows; Pſal. 34. From הלך *eſt ſedulitatis, ut ſeſſio pigritiæ,* &c. *Sch. it oft implies ſedulity,* Come children with alacrity : Pſal. 68. *from* בחור *Juvenis electus, ad militiam & negotia electus & idoneus, Sch.* their choice young men ſaith Ainſworth : Their young men brave. Pſal. 119. oftentimes from שכח *oblitus fuit, eſtque negligentiæ Sch.* And I will not through negligence, Thy holy word forget. *And truly when the* Hebrew *word is of larger extent then ordinary, although*

though otherwise I content my self in following the scope of the place, which is obvious to every vulgar eye (whereas Hebraisms are for Scholars only). I can hardly chuse but harp upon it, if I find it, and oftentimes it helps notably, to inlarge where the verse requires it. Psl. 119. 32. from רחב Dilatari, exhilarari, I take, When with thy sweet incouragements, Thou shalt my heart inlarge; Schindler upon this example gives this reason, In tristitia cor contrahitur, in lætitia dilatatur, In sorrow the heart is straiten'd, in joy enlarged, Psal. 143. ult. from עבד religiose coluit, Monachus, Mancipium, Servituti addictus, an humble godly servant, I take all this to be impli'd in it, For I serve thee religiously with all submissiveness, or attentiveness. In three places (viz. Psal. 17. 3. 26. 2. and 105. 19.) from צרף igne purgavit, excoxit, liquefecit, to melt in the fire, I express a trying by fire as Goldsmiths do. The comparison is followed in Psal. 66. 10. Thou hast tri'd us as silver is tryed, but more fully in the Translation both of the old Psalms and new. ——— Even as the skilful tryer doth prove his silver, casting it into the hottest fire. And now to dare an instance or two of truer Translation ראש Caput, fons, origo, Sch...

I.

A Preface to the Reader.

I translate the Wel-spring head, *Psal.* 106. 16. קדוש consecratus, consecrate, *I render,*---Who had the stamp of consecration: rather than *Jehovah*'s holy one. *Psal.* 105. 18. ברזל באה נפשו ferrum ingressum est animam ejus, *I render,* The iron pierc'd his soul. *These I count perfecter Translations, an amplification upon such an account doth rarely.* Psal. 119. 53. Horrour hath taken hold, &c. זלעפה. Schindler *expounds it* tempestas, tempestates, זלעבור, procellæ Buxt. *waves and tempests.* So *I render it,* Yet horror great, like storms that beat, Hath taken hold on me, &c.

I will end with one or two more that I have demurr'd upon, but follow the Translators Psalm 31. 23. עשה גאוה *the proud doer. A learned friend that was by at the translating, contended (as stoutly) that it was the stout doer, the couragious; and would have had me Translated it,* And the bold heart that never faints, He plenteously rewards. *Indeed coming from* גאה *eminuit,* strenuus fuit, strenue egit, *to do stoutly; not from* גור elatio, superbia, pride, *it sounds very like, and rarely well agrees with the context. Thus also* Psal. 2. 12. ותאברו דרך *may be construed from the path,* viz. *of grace and salvation*

(*and*.

A Preface to the Reader.

(and so be a Periphrasis with missing the way) or in the path, viz. of sin and destruction. (And perish in your path.) Ainsw. *The* Chaldee *and* Septuagint *adhere to the former which perhaps is the cause that ours do so: here I leave the Reader to his choice.*

Having

Several Tunes.

Have mercie, &c.

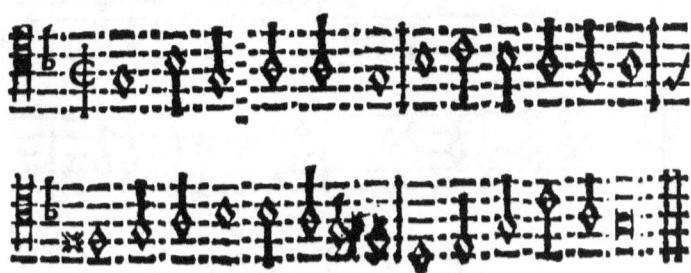

All people, &c.

Another for All people, &c.

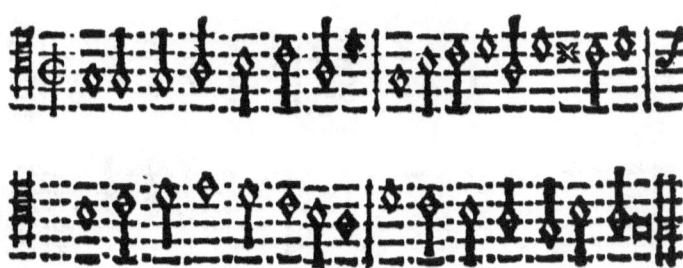

O Lord,

Several Tunes.

O Lord, consider, &c.

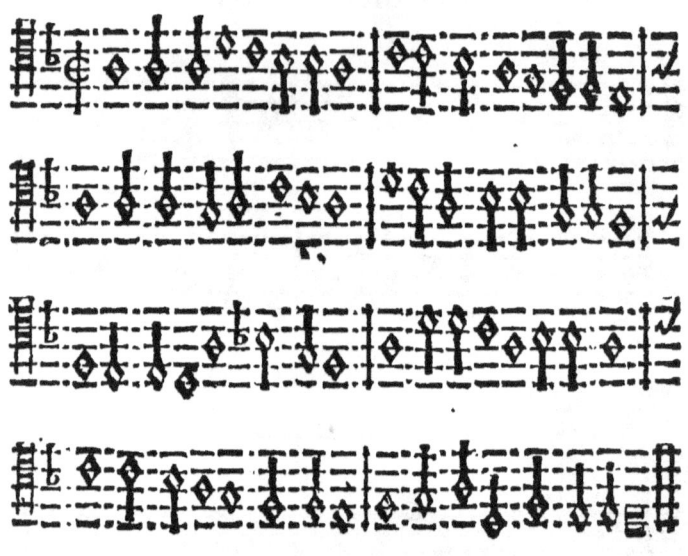

My God my God, &c.

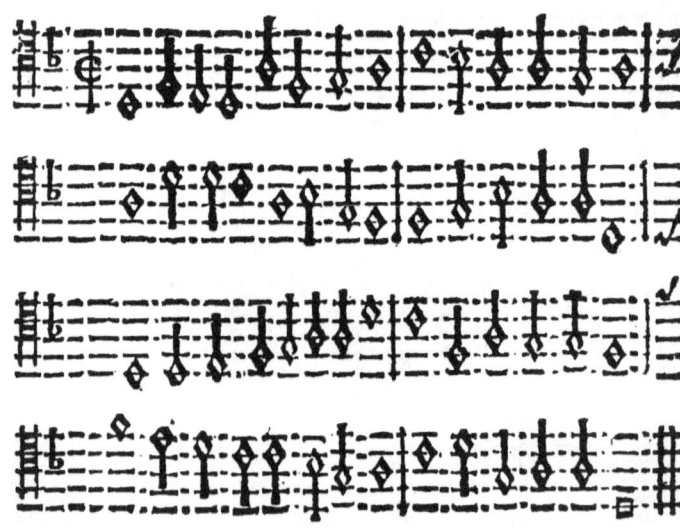

Ye

Several Tunes.

Ye Children which, &c.

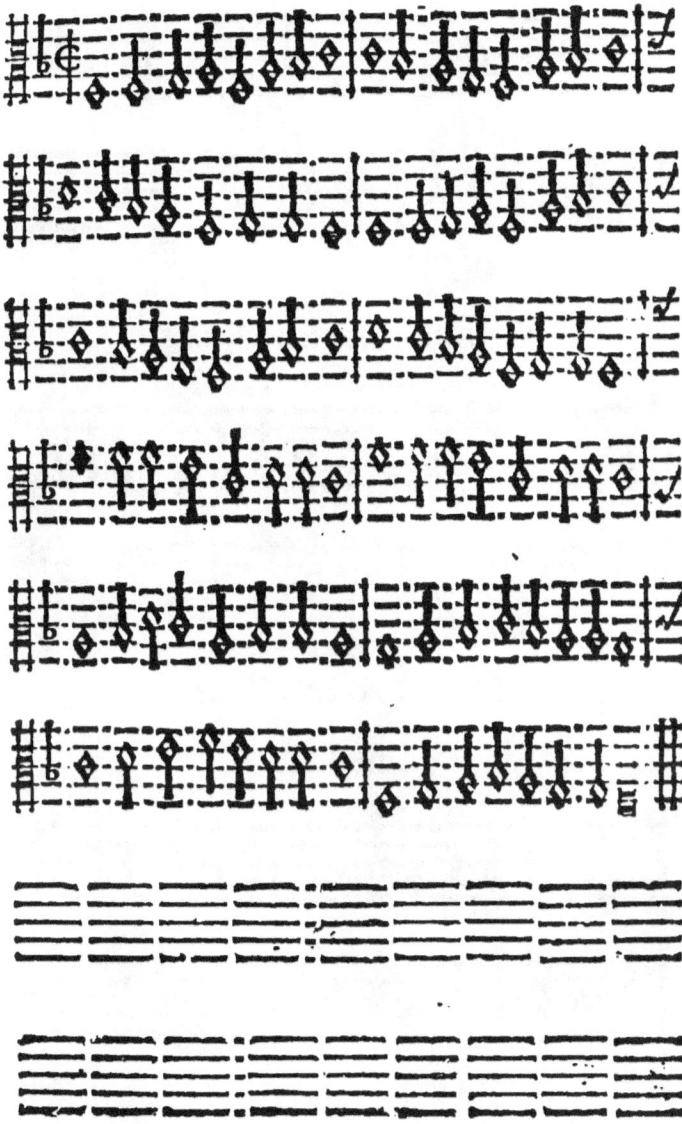

Give

Give laud unto, &c.

O praise the Lord, &c.

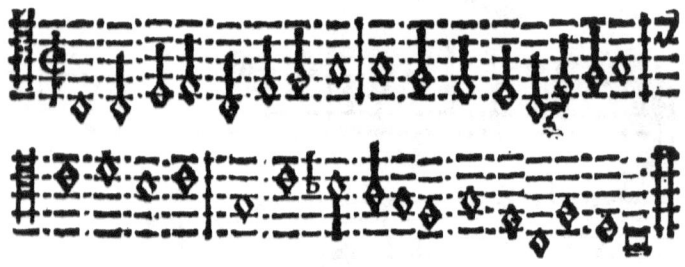

Several general Tunes.

The first.

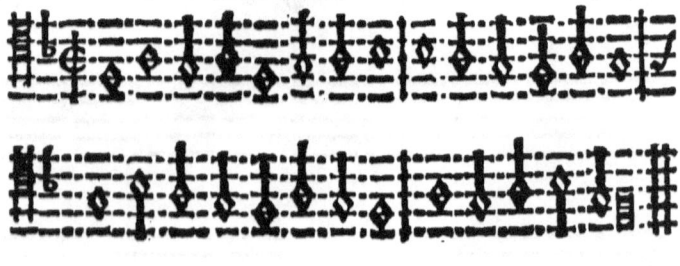

The

Several general Tunes.

The second.

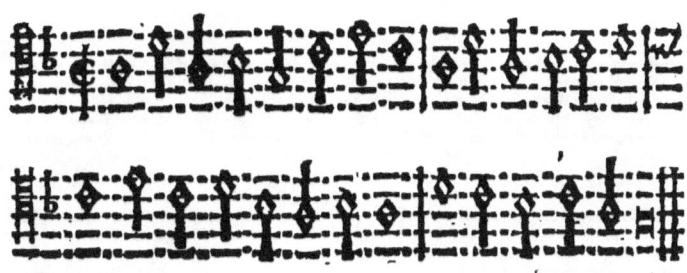

The third.

The fourth.

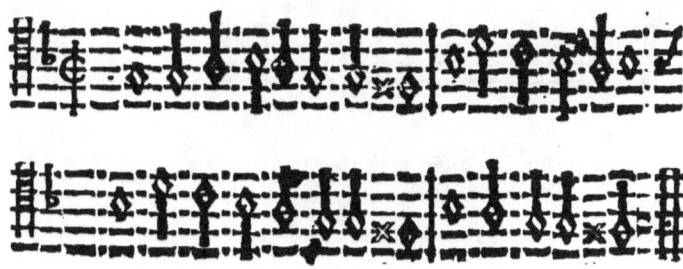

The

Several general Tunes.

The fifth.

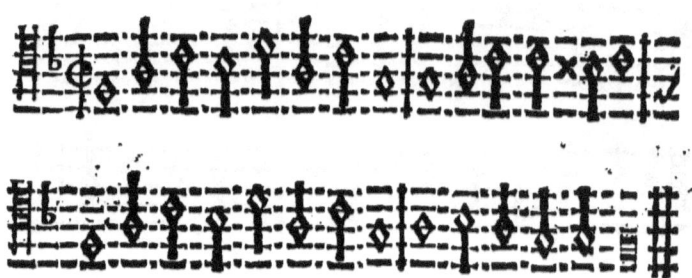

The sixth.

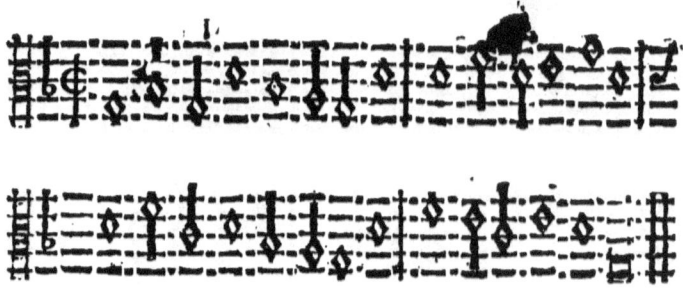

The seventh.

The

The eighth.

The ninth.

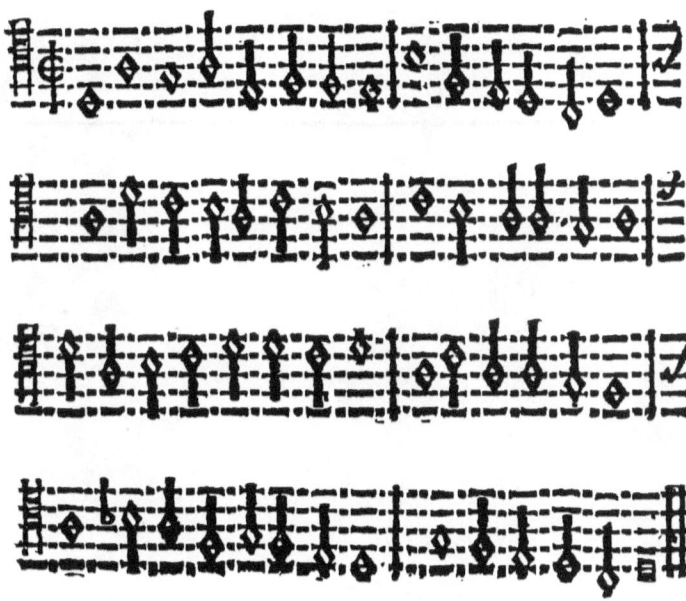

The

Several general Tunes.

The tenth.

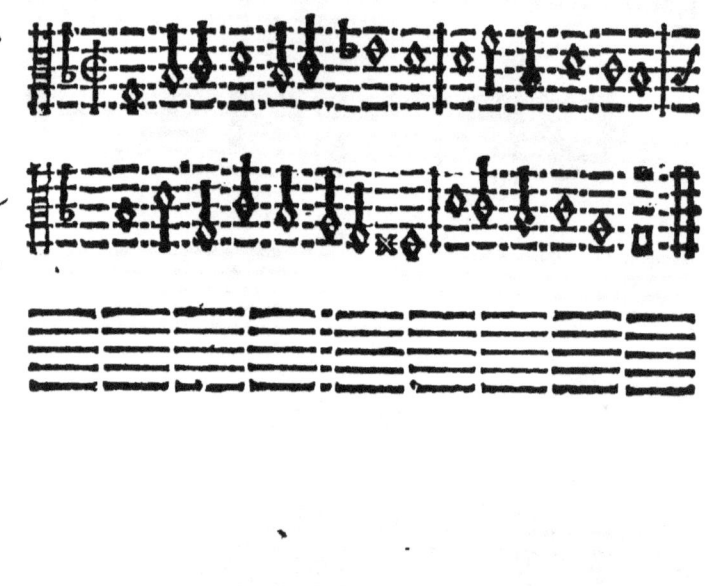

The

The Psalmes of David in Metre.

PSALM I. Metre 1.

BLessed, ô, blessed man is he
   that shuns the Sinners way:
The Counsel and the Company
   of such as go astray:
   That hath the scorners seat abhorr'd:
2 But placeth his delight
   Upon the law of God the Lord,
    and minds it day and night.

3 He's like a planted Tree whose root
   grows by the Rivers side;
That in his season brings forth fruit,
   whose leaf shall fresh abide.
And all he doth shall prosper well.
4 Th' ungodly are not so;
But are like chaff which winds dispell,
   and scatter to and fro.

5 Therefore th' ungodly shall not stand
   in day of judgment, clear:
Nor with the just at God's right hand
   Shall wicked men appear.
6 For lo, the way of men upright
   the Lord with favour knows,
Whereas the way shall perish quite
   wherein the sinner goes.

PSALM I. Metre 2.
Tune. *O Lord Consider, &c.*

THe man is blest that neither strayes
   by Counsels of ungodly men,
Nor standeth in the sinners wayes,
   nor sits in scorners seat with them.
2 But his delight continually
   is in the Law of God most high,
And in that Law of his delight
   he meditateth day and night.

3 He shall be like a planted tree
  set by the streaming Rivers side,
Which when his timely seasons be
  with plenteous fruit is still supply'd.
Whose leaf shall never fade nor fall,
and he shall prosper well in all:
4 Ungodly men are nothing so,
But are like Chaff when Whirlwinds blow.

5 Therefore shall not ungodly men
  in final day of Judgment stand,
Nor sinners have admission then,
  among the just at God's right hand.
6 For lo, the Lord with favour knows
the way wherein the righteous goes,
But paths of all impiety
  shall perish everlastingly.

PSALM. I. *Metre.* 3.
(*Give Laud,* &c.)

THrice blessed men are they
  that no bad Counsels hear;
Nor walk in Sinners way,
  nor sit in scorners Chair,
2   But with delight
Do mind the word of God the Lord,
    both day and night.

3 Such shall be like a tree
  by Rivers spreading root,
Which when his seasons be,
  brings forth his pleasant fruit;
    Whose leaf likewise
Is always seen most fresh and green,
    And never dies.

And whatsoever deed
  he puts his hand unto,
Shall prosper and succeed,
4 as shall no sinners do:
    For surely they
Shall be like Chaff which Winds blow off,
    and drive away.   5 There-

5 Therefore th' ungodly race
 in judgment shall not stand,
Nor sinners have a place
 with Saints at Christ's right hand.
6   For God well knows
The just mens path, but theirs in wrath
 He overthrows.

PSALM II. *Metre* 1.

Why do the Heathen rage and fret,
 and people plot vain things?
2 They rise, and are in Counsel set,
 both Governours and Kings.
God and his Christ oppose they do,
 and thus presume to say,
3 Come let us break their Bands in two,
 and cast their Cords away.

4 But God the Lord that dwells on high,
 and doth in Heaven abide,
Shall laugh at this Conspiracy,
 and their attempts deride.
5 Then also shall He speak to those
 in wrath of fullest measure;
And very sorely vex his foes,
 in his extream displeasure.

The Second part.

6 Yet have I set my King on high,
 according to my will,
To reign in *Sion* gloriously,
 upon my Holy Hill.
7 I'le publish the Decree, and say,
 the Lord hath said to me,
Thou art my Son: and lo this day
 I have begotten thee.
8 Ask me and I will give to thee
 the priviledge of thy Birth:
For thine the Heathen Lands shall be,
 and utmost parts on Earth.

9 Thine Iron Rod shall break them all,
  and Lord, thou shalt not spare,
To dash thy foes in pieces small,
  as Potters Vessels are.

The Third part.

10 Be wise now therefore, O ye Kings,
  Ye Judges of the Land,
Be well instructed in the things
  which ye should understand.
11 See that ye do your selves employ
  in God's true Service here,
Mix trembling always with your joy,
  and worship him in fear.
12 The Son of God embrace and kiss,
  lest ye provoke his wrath;
And so should take your way amiss,
  and perish from the path.
For if his anger ne're so small
  be kindled in his brest;
Then happy, happy are they all,
  that on their Saviour rest.

PSALM II. *Metre 2.*

(Tune, *Have Mercy*, &c.)

Why do the Heathen rage,
  and people plot in vain?
The Kings on Earth themselves ingage,
  with all their pompous Train;
The Rulers all accord,
  and both the Bench and Throne
Consult together against the Lord,
  and his Anointed One.

3, 4.

And thus they speak in spight,
  with most audacious words:
Break we their Bands asunder quite,
  and cast from us their Cords.
But He that sits in Heaven
  shall laugh while they combine,

The Lord, to whom th' affront is given,
  shall mock at their design.

5, 6.

Then shall He speak to them
  in anger unappeas'd:
And greatly shall He vex those men,
  when he is sore displeas'd.
Yet have I done my will,
  and set my King to reign
In *Sion* my most Holy Hill,
  in spite of their disdeign.

The Second part. 7, 8.

And now I will declare,
  what God hath said to me,
Concerning Christ, the Sovereign Heir,
  according to decree;
Thou art my Son, said He,
  and I the same disclose:
This Day I have begotten Thee,
  Thy Resurrection shows.

8.

Then ask it at my hands,
  I will the Work advance,
And give thee all the Heathen Lands,
  for thine Inheritance:
This privilledge of thy Birth
  I give to thee alone:
And utmost parts of all the Earth
  for thy Possession.

9.

Thou shalt thine Enemies smite,
  as with an Iron Rod:
And dash them into pieces quite,
  Like Potters shards, O God.

The Third part. 10, 11.

Now therefore, O be wise,
  Ye Kings of Mortal Birth:

Be learn'd in Heavenly Mysteries,
  Ye Judges of the Earth.
Serve ye the Lord with fear,
  according to his Law:
Rejoycing with an Heart sincere,
  and with a trembling awe.

12.

O kiss the Son, I say,
  lest he should angry be:
And so ye perish from the way,
  and no salvation see.
For if his angry wrath
  to kindle once begin,
Blessed are all that keep his path,
  and put their trust in him.

PSALM iij. *Metre* 1.

O Lord, how much do they increase,
  that rise to trouble me:
And they that do disturb my peace,
  how many, Lord, they be?
2 How many of my Soul have said
  he shall be undertrod?
There is for him no hope of aid,
  or help to come from God.
3 But thou, O Lord, art my defence,
  when I am hard bestead:
My Glory and my Confidence,
  and thou hold'st up my head.
4 My prayer to thee I did address,
  and cry'd to God most high:
And from his Hill of Holiness
  he heard me graciously.
5 I laid me down at rest secure,
  I slept and rose again,
Because I knew, and was full sure,
  the Lord did me sustain.
6 And though ten thousand of my foes
  were round about me laid,

I would not be afraid of those,
    nor any whit dismay'd.
7 O God my Saviour now arise,
    for thou hast own'd my Cause;
And smitten all mine Enemies
    upon the very Jaws.
Thou brok'st the Teeth of all the Train
    that wrought Ungodliness:
8 Salvation doth to God pertain,
    thou dost thy people bless.

PSALM iij. Metre 2.

Lord how their number multiplies,
    that vex and grieve me sore?
Yea they that do against me rise,
    wax hourly more and more.
Many there are, Lord, many a one,
    that of my Soul have said,
Behold his God from him is gone,
    he hath no hope of aid.

3, 4.

But, Lord, Thou art a Shield for me,
    Thou art my sure defence:
By thee my head upheld shall be
    with glorious confidence.
I cried to the Lord aloud,
    and found his favour free:
For from his Holy Hill he bow'd
    his gracious Ear to me.

5, 6.

I laid me down and sweetly slept,
    and safely wak'd again;
Because it was the Lord that kept,
    and did my Soul sustain.
Although ten thousand of my foes
    beset me round about,
I will not be afraid of those,
    nor of my safety doubt.

7

O Lord my God, awake, arise,
   defend my righteous Cause:
For thou hast smote mine Enemies
   upon the very Jaws.
Thou brok'st the Teeth of impious men,
   Salvation is of Thee:
Upon thy Chosen People then
   thy Blessing sure shall be.

PSALM iij. Metre 3.
(Ye Children, &c.)

Lord how the number multiplies
   Of my vexatious Enemies
     that fain would have me undertrod?
2 Many, O Lord, many are they,
   That of my Soul presume to say,
     there is no help for him in God.
3 But Lord thou art a Shield for me,
   Thou art my Glory, and shalt be
     the sure upholder of my Head:
4 Unto the Lord I sent my Cry,
   And from his Holy Hill on high,
     he heard me, and my prayer sped.
5 I laid me down and sweetly slept;
   I wak'd and was in safety kept;
     for God's Good Hand protected me.
6 I will not fear to take repose,
   Although ten thousand of my foes
     set round on every side should be.
7 Up Lord my God, and plead my Cause,
   Thou smot'st mine Enemies on the Jaws,
     Thou brok'st the Teeth of impious men.
8 Salvation is of God alone;
   Thy Blessing is upon thine own,
     and thou hast given it unto them.

PSALM IV. Metre 1.

Hear me, O God, my righteousness,
   when I to thee repair:

Thou haſt inlarg'd me from diſtreſs,
  in mercy hear my prayer.
2 O Sons of Men, how long will ye
  my dignity deſpiſe :
How long will ye love vanity,
  and follow after lies ?

3 But know that God hath ſet apart,
  for his own ſake alone,
The Man that's after his own Heart,
  to ſit upon the Throne.
And he will ſurely hear my prayer,
  when unto him I call :
4 Then ſtand in awe, and have a care
  not to offend at all.

In your own heart conſider it,
  upon your ſecret bed :
And quietly your ſelves ſubmit
  unto your lawful Head.
5 The Sacrifices offer ye
  of righteouſneſs alway :
And let the Lord Almighty be
  your only truſt and ſtay.

6 Many inquire for outward good,
  and Riches they embrace :
But we deſire of Thee, O God,
  the ſhining of thy face.
7 For thou haſt made this heart of mine,
  more joyful and more glad,
Than when they brought in Corn and Wine,
  and great increaſe was had.

8 In peace therefore I will lie down
  and take my reſt full well :
For thou, O Lord, and thou alone
  doſt make me ſafely dwell.

PSALM IV. *Metre 2.*

O God that art my righteouſneſs,
  hear when I call to thee :

For in the day of my distress
   thou hast inlarged me.
In mercy hear me now agen,
   and quell my foes disdain:
How long will ye, O Sons of Men,
   my Glory turn to shame?

3, 4.

How long will ye vain things affect,
   and follow after lies?
Know Godly Men are God's Select,
   and he will hear my Cries.
All sinful Courses set apart,
   and stand in awful dread:
In silence commune with your heart,
   upon your secret bed.

5, 6.

For Incense offer Innocence,
   and righteousness present:
And wholly put your Confidence
   in God Omnipotent.
What way they might themselves advance,
   great multitudes inquire:
But Lord thy shining Countenance
   is all that we desire.

7, 8.

For thou hast made my heart to feast
   with Sacred Comforts more,
Than Worldlings when they were increast
   with Corn and Wine full store.
I'le both lie down sweet rest to take,
   and also sleep secure:
For only thou, O Lord, dost make
   my dwelling safe and sure.

PSALM IV. *Metre* 3.
To the first New Tune.

Hear me O God my righteousness,
   Thou hast inlarg'd me from distress,

when

  When plung'd in care:
O shew to me thy mercy free,
  and hear my prayer.

How long will ye, O Sons of Men,
My Glorious Dignity contemn,
  And me despise?
How long will ye love Vanity,
  and follow Lies?

   3.
But know that God hath set apart
The Man that's after his own heart,
  His King to be:
The Lord will hear when I draw near
  with bended Knee.

   4.
Then stand in awe, and do not sin,
To Commune with your hearts begin,
  And silently
Examined, upon your bed
  in secrecy.

   5.
The Sacrifices offer ye
Of Righteousness and Puritie,
  And then be bold
To trust upon the Holy One
  as your strong hold.

   6.
But many men false wealth admire,
And all for worldly goods inquire:
  That's their design;
But Lord advance thy Countenance
  on us to shine.

   7.
Thou hast put gladness in my heart,
By Comforts which thou didst impart
  A great deal more,
Than in the time their Corn and Wine
  increast in store.

         I will.

8.
I will both lay me down in peace,
And sleep while all my sorrows cease;
    For thou alone
Dost make me dwell full safe and well,
    O Holy One!

PSALM V. *Metre* 1.

O Lord unto my words give ear,
    my meditation weigh:
2 My King, my God, my Crying hear,
    for I to thee will pray.
3 At morning thou shalt hear my Cry,
    at morning it shall be,
That I'le direct my prayer on high,
    and will look up to thee.

4 Because thou art a God most pure,
    whom sin cannot delight:
Nor any evil canst endure
    to harbour in thy sight.
5 Within the View of thy pure Eye
    the foolish shall not rest:
All workers of Iniquitie
    thy Nature doth detest.

6 All Lyers shall be overthrown,
    escape they never can:
God will abhor the bloody one,
    and the deceitful man.
7 But I will to thy house draw near,
    in thine abundant grace:
And I will worship in thy fear
    towards thy Holy Place.

The Second part.

8 Lord lead me in thy righteousness,
    because of all my foes:
And thy straight paths (lest I transgress)
    before my face disclose.
9 For in their mouth no truth appears,
    their heart with mischief throngs:

Their throats are open Sepulchers,
  they flatter with their tongues.
10 Destroy them Lord, destroy them all,
  let them be overthrown,
And into just destruction fall;
  by Counsels of their own.
And let them be cast out and quell'd
  for their excessive sin :
For they have wickedly rebell'd
  against the Lord therein.
11 But let, O Lord, all those rejoyce
  that put their trust in thee :
Let them with shouts lift up their Voice,
  and ever joyful be.
Let them likewise that love thy Name
  be joyful in thee still :
Because thy power which they proclaim
  defends them from all ill.
12 For to the righteous man, no doubt,
  thou wilt thy Blessing yield :
And ever compass him about
  with favour as a Shield.

PSALM V. *Metre* 2.

Our Father, &c.

Lord weigh my thoughts, my words attend,
  my King, my God, my Crying hear :
To thee my prayers and cries ascend,
  my voice i'th' morning thou shalt hear :
I'th' morning, Lord, I will direct
My prayer to thee, and will expect.

2.

For thou in sin hast no delight,
  no ill shall dwell with thee O Lord :
The fool abides not in thy sight,
  all wicked doers thou hast abhor'd :
Falshood, deceit, and cruelty,
Thou dost detest, and wilt destroy.

But

3.

But I in thine abundant grace
  thy House will visit in thy fear,
And worship in thy Holy Place,
  O teach me, Lord, thy Counsels there:
Make straight thy paths before mine Eyes,
Because of all mine Enemies.

4.

For in their mouth no truth they have;
  their inward parts all wickedness:
Their throat is like a gaping grave;
  foul flattery doth their tongue express:
Destroy them, Lord, destroy them all
By their own Counsels let them fall.

5.

O cast them out as men abhor'd
  for their transgressions multitude:
For they have still rebell'd, O Lord,
  against thee by offences lewd:
But let all those that trust in thee
Be joyful in a high degree.

6.

Yea let them ever shout for Joy
  in thy defence, which they implore;
Let them that love thee, O Most High,
  be joyful in thee evermore,
For thou wilt bless the Just, O Lord,
And make thy grace his shield and guard.

PSALM VI. *Metre* 1.

O Lord my God, rebuke me not
  when angry thou shalt be:
When thy displeasure waxeth hot,
  then do not chasten me.

2 O Lord have mercy on my Soul,
  so weak and sore perplext:
Lord, I beseech thee, make me whole,
  for all my bones are vext.

3 My Soul is also vexed sore,
   but Lord how long a space?
4 Return, O Lord, my Soul restore,
   and save me of thy grace,
5 For who can praise or think on thee,
   when dead in grave they lie?
6 And now my groaning wearieth me,
   so near to death am I.

All night I make my bed to swim,
   my Couch with tears o'reflows:
7 Mine Eyes, consum'd with grief, wax
   because of all my foes.
8 Ye workers of Iniquity
   go from me every one:
For God hath heard me graciously,
   when I did weep and moan.

9 The Supplications which I made
   the Lord did entertain:
And he that heard me when I pray'd
   will hear me yet again
10 Let all mine Enemies therefore
   be vext and sham'd thereby;
Let them return vext very sore,
   and shamed suddenly.

PSALM VI. *Metre 2.*
O Lord Consider, &c.

IN anger Lord rebuke me not,
   for I am very weak and low:
Nor scourge me when thy wrath is hot,
   but Lord, to me thy mercy show.
Lord heal me for my bones are vext,
   but thou, O Lord, how long a space?
My Soul is also sore perplext,
   return, and save me of thy grace.

4, 5, 6.

My Soul, O Lord, preserve and save,
   for none in death remembers thee:

Nor any thanks thee in the Grave,
  see how my groaning wearieth me.
All night I make my Bed to swim,
  wat'ring my Couch with weeping Eyes;
Mine eye with grief grows old and dim,
  because of all mine Enemies.

8, 9, 10.

Ye workers of iniquity,
  depart from me, depart ye all:
For loe the Lord hath heard my Cry,
  my weeping Voice, and Tears that fall.
The Lord will hear the prayer I frame,
  the Lord hath heard, and hath reliev'd:
Let all my foes return with shame,
  with sudden shame, sore vext and griev'd.

PSALM VII.

The First part.

O Lord my God, I do repose
  my Confidence in thee:
O save me from my furious foes,
  and now deliver me.
2 Lest like a Lion he should tear,
  and piece-meal rend my Soul:
While there is no deliverer
  his fury to controll.
3 O Lord my God, if I did this;
  if my hands be not free:
4 If I rewarded him amiss
  that was at peace with me;
(Yea, Lord, I have delivered,
  and let him safely go,
That causelesly hath injured,
  and us'd me as a foe,)
5 Then let the foe pursue my Soul,
  take it, and tread it down:
Tread down my Life with proud controul,
  and bury my Renown.

The Second part.

6 Rise Lord, in wrath thy self address,
    mine enemies rage withstand:
  Awake for me in righteousness,
    as thou didst give command.
7 So shall the Congregation great
    inclose thee generally:
  Return then to thy Judgment Seat,
    for their sakes sit on high.
8 The Lord shall judge the people, sure,
    judge me O Lord, likewise,
  According as my heart is pure,
    and upright in thine Eyes.
9 Let sinners ways be overthrown,
    but stablish righteous mens:
  For God that is a righteous one,
    doth try both Heart and Reins.
10 All the defence and help I have
    is of the Lord alone:
  Who always will be sure to save
    the upright-hearted one.

The Third part.

11 God judgeth even righteous men,
    but will the wicked slay:
  So much is God provok'd by them
    to anger every day.
12 Unless he speedily repent,
    his glittering Sword is whet:
  His angry bow the Lord hath bent,
    and hath it ready set.
13 He hath prepared deadly darts,
    determining to shoot
  sharp arrows at the viperous hearts
    of those that prosecute.
14 Behold he travelleth in birth
    with his iniquity;
  Conceiving mischief, and brings forth
    no better than a lie.

15 He made a Pit and digged it,
and mighty pains did take:
And now is fal'n into the Pit,
which he himself did make.
16 Upon his own head shall reboun'
his mischief spite and hate:
His violent dealing shall come down,
and light upon his pate.
17 Unto the Lord give thanks will I,
for all his righteous ways:
And to the Name of God most high
sing chearful Songs of praise.

PSALM VIII. *Metre* 1.

O Lord our Lord, how Excellent
is thy Name every where?
Behold thou hast thy Glory plac't
above the Starry Sphere.
2 Weak babes and sucklings thou ordaind'st
thy power and praise to show:
To still thereby the Enemy,
and the avengeful foe.
3 When I behold attentively
the Heavens which thou didst frame;
The Moon on high and Starry Skie,
which by thine Ordinance came.
4 What's Man or Man's posterity,
think I, what wond'rous Love
He should of thee remembred be,
or visited from above?
5 For thou hast made him little lower
than Angels in degree,
And did'st him Crown with great Renown,
and glorious Dignity.
6 Thou mad'st him have dominion o're
the Works which thou hast wrought:
And by thy care all Creatures are
to his subjection brought.

7 All Oxen, Sheep and Fowl, with these,
  and Cattle him obey:
8 All that the Field or Air can yield,
  and Fishes of the Sea.
  What ever is in the paths of Seas,
  or passeth through the same:
9 O Lord our Lord, all Lands record
  the Glory of thy Name.

PSALM VIII. Metre 2.

Give Laud, &c.

O Lord our Sovereign Lord,
  of how excelling worth
Thy Name must we Record
  in all the spacious Earth?
    Whose Glory bears
A Stamp Divine, with beams to shine
    above the Spheres.

2.

Out of the Infant mouth
  of babes and sucklings small,
Thou hast ordain'd thy Truth
  with strength to conquer all:
    To lay them low
That bear ill will, and for to still
    th' avengeful foe.

3.

Thy Heavens there on high,
  when, Lord, I think upon,

4.

The Moon and Starry Skie,
  the Works which thou hast done:
    Lord, what is Man,
Or what's his Seed, that thou shouldst heed
    so poor a span?

5.

Thou madest him to be
  of an inferior state

To Angels in degree,
  yet to participate:
    And did'st him Crown
With Glory great, to sit in seat
  of high Renown.

6.

Thou gav'st him absolute
  dominion over all:
And all things at his foot
  in bound obedience fall,
    To him they yield,
All Oxen, Sheep, and Beasts that keep
  i'th' open field.

7.

The Fowls of all the Air,
  and Fishes of the Seas:
Which have a thorow-fare
  to pass there as they please:
    O Lord our Lord,
Th' excelling fame of thy great Name
  all Lands Record!

PSALM VIII. *Metre 3.*
Ye Children, &c.

O Lord our Lord, of how great worth
  Is thy great Name in all the Earth,
who mak'st thy Glory pass the Skie?
From babes and sucklings mouths thou hast
Ordained strength thy foes to blast,
  and still th' avengeful Enemy.
When I have Heaven in my thought,
And see the Works thy finger wrought,
  the Moon and Stars ordain'd by thee;
Lord what is Man, or his frail Race,
That thou should'st such a shadow grace,
  with visits of thy favour free?

2.

For thou hast made him little less,
Than Angels in their blessedness;
  Glory and Grace compose his Crown:

Thou

Thou mad'st him have dominion o're
Thy handy-works both less and more,
  and at his feet must all sit down.
All Sheep and Oxen, Birds and beasts,
The Waters, Woods, and Fields increase,
  and all that through the Ocean glide:
O Lord our Lord, of how great fame
Is therefore thy Illustrious Name
  in all the Earth both far and wide?

PSALM IX.
The First part.

O Lord, I'le praise thy Holy Name
  with true and hearty Zeal:
Thy wond'rous works I will proclaim,
  and none of them conceal.
2 I will be glad, and much rejoyce
  in thee continually:
I will sing praise with chearful voice
  to thy Name, O most high.

3 When as my wicked Enemies
  are put to shameful flight;
Then they shall fall before thine eyes,
  and perish at thy sight.
4 For thou, O Lord, thou hast alone
  maintain'd my righteous cause:
Thou satest in thy righteous Throne
  to judge by righteous Laws.

5 Thou hast rebuk'd the Heathen men,
  the wicked are destroy'd:
Thou hast put out the name of them,
  and made it ever void.
6 O Enemy, all's accomplished,
  destructions now are done:
The Cities thou hast ruined,
  they and their memory's gone.

7 But God the true Eternal One,
  for ever shall abide:

He hath prepar'd his Princely Throne
just Judgment to decide.
8 And he will judge the world throughout
in justice faithfully:
And deal to all men round about
his Truth and Equity.
9 The Lord moreover will become
a refuge for th' opprest;
In times extreamly troublesome
he'l be a place of rest.
10 All they that know thy faithful Name,
will trust upon thy Grace;
For never did'st thou Lord disclaim
any that sought thy face.

The Second part.

11 Sing praises to the Holy One,
that doth in Sion dwell:
The glorious deeds that he hath done
among all people tell.
12 When he inquireth narrowly
for blood which they have spilt;
He calls to mind the poor man's Cry,
and their oppressors guilt.
13 Lord pity me, think on my grief
caus'd by mine Enemies hate:
Thou that dost raise me with relief
from deaths destructive gate.
14 That I in Sions daughters gates
may all thy praise record;
For thy Salvation consolates
my thankful heart, O Lord.
15 The Heathen sink into the pit,
which they themselves prepar'd;
And in the net that they did set
are their own feet insnar'd.
16 The Lord is known in these affairs,
by Judgments which are wrought;

Psalm ix.

When sinners hands do make the snares,
  wherewith themselves are caught.
17 The wicked shall be turn'd to Hell,
  people of every kind,
Whoever on the Earth do dwell,
  that have not God in mind.
18 For needy Souls may well be sure
  not still to be forgot:
Those Expectations of the poor
  for ever perish not.
19 Up Lord, and let not men have leave
  still to prevail by might:
But let the Heathen folk receive
  their judgment in thy sight.
20 And strike them Lord, with fear so far,
  that all the Nations then
May know themselves (who e're they are)
  to be but mortal men.

PSALM X.

Why dost thou, Lord, stand off so far,
  and seem'st thy self to hide;
And seest what troublous times here are,
  and what oppressing pride?
2 Wherewith the wicked hunt the poor,
  O let them be surpriz'd,
Caught in the snare they thought so sure,
  and which themselves devis'd.
3 For of his hearts ungodly lusts
  the wicked boasts, O Lord:
And he doth bless the covetous,
  that is of God abhor'd.
4 He seeks not after God a jot,
  such is his haughty pride:
In all his thoughts God cometh not,
  but is indeed deni'd.
5 He ever loves to tyrannize,
  Judgment he counts far off:

He puffs at all his Enemies
with a difdainful fcoff.
6 He faith in heart, I know that I
shall never be difplac't;
Nor of the leaft adverfity
at any time shall taft.

7 His mouth is full of blafphemy,
of fraud, deceit, and wrong;
Mifchievoufnefs and vanity
fit underneath his tongue.

8 In Villages he fits obfcure,
the Innocent to flay:
His eyes are bent againft the poor,
but in a private way.

9 He Lion-like lurks in his den
the poor to catch and get;
Waiting to take poor fimple men,
when drawn into his net.

10 He croucheth and doth lowly bend,
humbling himfelf withal;
That fo the poor man in the end
by his ftrong ones may fall.

11 He faith in heart God hath forgot,
he hides away his eyes;
And willingly beholds it not,
12 but O Lord God arife.
Forget not but thy hand forth-ftretch,
for poor men undertrod:
13 O wherefore fhould a wicked wretch
contemn Almighty God?

It fhall not be requir'd at all,
thus fpeaks he in his heart:
14 But of their mifchief, fpite and gall,
thou Lord a Witnefs art.
And what thou feeft shall furely be
by thy juft hand repay'd:
The poor commits himfelf to thee,
thou art the Orphans aid.

15 The arm of Tyrants merciless,
  Lord break in sunder quite;
Search out his secret wickedness,
  till all be come to light.
16 God reigneth an Eternal King,
  and he hath purged his Land
Of Heathen people, perishing
  by his revenging Hand.
17 Lord, the desire of humble men
  hath pierc'd thine easie Ear;
An Heart thou wilt prepare us then,
  and cause thine Ear to hear.
18 To judge the poor and fatherless,
  that are oppreſt full sore;
That Earthly men may not opprefs,
  nor vex them any more.

PSALM XI. Metre 1.

1 Put my Confidence in God,
  why therefore do ye say,
That as a Bird unto her hill
  my Soul should haſt away?
2 For lo the wicked bend their Bow,
  and fit their Shafts with art;
Upon their strings, to shoot unseen
  at men upright in heart.
3 If the foundations, verily,
  be ruin'd and deſtroy'd,
Alas, what can the righteous do
  the danger to avoid?
  The Lord is in his holy place,
    his Throne's in Heaven on high;
His Eyes behold the Sons of Men,
  and them his Eye-lids try.

By him the righteous man is try'd,
  the wicked man abhor'd:
And he that loveth Violence
  is hated of the Lord.

6 On sinners he shall rain down snares,
   and wrath must they drink up ;
 Brimstone and fire, and horrid storms
   the portion of their Cup.

7 For God that is a righteous one
   in Justice takes delight :
 And with a pleased countenance
   beholdeth the upright.

PSALM XI. *Metre* 2.
All People, &c.

IN God I put my Confidence,
   why do ye utter such a word?
 Why say ye to my Soul, flee hence
   unto your Mountain as a Bird?

2.
For lo! the wicked bend their Bows,
   they string their Arrows, and prepare
 In secret for to shoot at those,
   that upright-hearted persons are.

3, 4.
If the foundations be destroyed,
   what can the Just do any where?
 Heavens Holy Temple stands not void,
   for God is ever present there.

5.
The Lord within the Heavens high
   hath stablished his Royal Throne:
 His Eyes behold, his Eye-lids try
   the Sons of mortal men each one.

The Lord the Righteous throughly tries,
   but he the wicked greatly hates:
 And him that loveth Cruelties,
   his righteous Soul abominates.

6.
On sinners he shall rain down snares,
   Brimstone and fire must they drink up;
 An horrible Tempest he prepares
   to be the portion of their Cup.

For God that is a righteous One,
　doth righteousness as much affect:
The upright Man he looks upon
　with very singular respect.

PSALM XI. Metre 3.

The Mighty God, &c.

IN God the Lord I put my Confidence,
　What means that word unto my Soul, flee hence?
　　Flee to your den,　as Birds do to their Hill,
　　For wicked men　do bend their Bow to kill:
　Their Arrows keen　are quickly strung & darted
　To shoot unseen　and hit the upright-hearted.

2.

If faith decay,　　and the foundations too,
Where is the stay?　what can the righteous do?
　　The Holy One　is in his Temple great,
　　God hath his Throne in Heaven, there's his seat:
　His Eyes behold,　his Eye-lids try most truly
　Both Young and Old,　and search out all men
　　　　　　　　　　　　　　(throughly.

3.

The Lord doth try　the patience of the Just,
How stedfastly　　they can believe and trust:
　　But wicked men,　of sin that have no sense,
　　And any of them　that loveth violence,
　Such sinners sure　the Lord abominateth,
　His Soul most pure　such persons greatly hateth.

4.

Down doth he pour snares, fire & brimstone fierce:
An horrible show'r, which to the quick doth pierce,
　　This Cup to suit　with sinners he provides,
　　That persecute　him through his peoples sides:
　For God that is　most just, just men affecteth,
　And beams of his　sweet face on them reflecteth.

How long shall my exalted foe
  bear o're me such controul?

3 Behold and hear me, Lord my God,
  that am so sore opprest:
Lighten mine eyes left that I sleep,
  as one by death possest.

4 And lest my foes lift up their voice,
  and say we do prevail:
And they that trouble me rejoyce,
  when I begin to fail.

5 But from thy mercy and thy grace
  my hopes shall not depart:
Thy sweet relief and saving health
  shall greatly glad my heart.

6 And I will sing unto the Lord,
  because I find that he
Hath dealt, according to his word,
  most bounteously with me.

PSALM XIII. *Metre 2.*

How long wilt thou forget me, Lord,
  and from me hide thy face?
Shall I for ever seem abhor'd,
  and tast no more thy grace?
How long shall I sit musing so,
  with hearts continual grief?
How long shall my exalted foe
  be made the head and chief?

3, 4.

Consider, Lord my God, and hear,
  enlighten thou mine eyes;
And let thy succour soon appear,
  lest death my Soul surprize.
And lest mine enemies boast should be
  against me to prevail;
And they rejoyce that trouble me,
  when I begin to fail.

5, 6.

But I, O Lord, such hopes have had
  thy mercy still to find:

That thy Salvation makes me glad,
  and cheers my heart and mind.
And I will sing unto the Lord,
  because I prove and see,
How bounteously he doth afford
  his favour unto me.

PSALM XIII. *Metre* 3.

Have Mercy, &c.

How long, O Lord, of thee
    forgotten shall I be?
How long a space wilt hide thy face
  for evermore from me?

2.
How long shall I condole,
  take counsel in my Soul,
And daily bear such griefs and care,
  and enemies proud controul?

3.
Consider, hear my Cries,
  my God, clear thou mine eyes,
Lest sleep of death exhaust my breath
  amidst my miseries.

4.
And lest mine enemy say,
  Lo! I have got the day:
And glad they be that trouble me,
  when put beside my stay.

5.
But I thy mercy made
  the Rock whereon I stay'd:
My heart in me right glad shall be
  in thy Salvations aid.

6.
Unto the Lord will I
  sing praises cheerfully;
Because that he hath dealt with me
  exceeding bounteously.

PSALM XIV. Metre 1.

The fools affirm there is no God,
   for so in heart they say:
Vile deeds they do, and none doth good,
   so quite corrupt are they.
2 For lo the Lord from Heaven view'd
   the race of all mankind,
To see if any understood,
   or sought his God to find.
3 But they were all corrupt and naught,
   all turn'd aside and gone;
Not one that any good hath wrought,
   no verily not one.
4 Are wicked workers so misled,
   so blind and bruitish all,
That they should eat my folk like bread,
   on God they do not call?
5 But yet in all their jollity
   great fear upon them fell;
For in the sweet Society
   of good men God doth dwell.
6 Ye mock the wisdom of the poor,
   and would his Counsel shame;
Because he makes himself secure
   by faith in God's great Name.
7 But O that all which we hear tell
   the Lord would once fulfill;
With saving health to *Israel*
   from out of *Sion* hill.
When God his peoples bondage turns,
   that freedom once is had,
Then *Jacob* shall rejoyce that mourns,
   and *Israel* shall be glad.

PSALM XIV. Metre 2.
Give Laud, &c.

The fool hath said in heart
   there is no God at all:

Psalm xiv.

They are in every part
  corrupted by the fall :
    There's none doth good,
But they have wrought things vile and naught,
    and grace withstood.

The Lord did cast his eye
  from Heaven, his Holy Throne,
On man's Posterity,
  to see if any one
    He might discern,
That understood the things of God,
    or sought to learn.

3.
But all are gone aside,
  they do themselves defile ;
They all are wand'red wide,
  become exceeding vile :
    And there is none
Of all mankind to good inclin'd,
    no sure not one.

4.
Have wicked workers all
  no knowledge generally,
Who have not grace to call
  upon the Lord most high?
    But they are fed,
Devouring here my people dear,
    like unto bread.

5.
But yet they were in fear,
  and great the fear must be :
For God doth still appear
  in just mens progenie :
    And keepeth them
In every place, I mean the Race
    of righteous men.

6.
But ye have put to shame
  the Counsels of the poor,

Becaufe the Lord became
 his refuge fo fecure:
  O that there might
Come fuccour ftill from *Sion* hill
 to th' *Ifraelite.*

7.

When as the Lord brings back
 our hard Captivity;
And lets not *Ifrael* lack
 fo great a caufe of joy:
  Jacob, no doubt,
Shall then rejoyce with cheerful voice,
 and *Ifrael* fhout.

PSALM XV. *Metre* 1.

Lord, who fhall have a bleft abode
 within thy Tents of grace?
And who fhall dwell with thee, O God,
 in thy moft holy place?
2. The man that walketh uprightly;
 and worketh righteoufnefs,
And doth from hearts integrity
 the very truth exprefs.
3. That hurts his neighbour in no fort,
 nor flandereth with his tongue,
Nor taketh up a falfe report
 to do his neighbour wrong.
4. The man in whofe difcerning eyes
 vile perfons are abhor'd:
But them he highly magnifies
 that truly fear the Lord.
That keeps his Covenant faithfully,
 though he the lofs fuftain;
5. And puts not out to Ufury
 to get unlawful gain.
That will not for a world be brib'd
 to make the Innocent fall:
He that doth thefe things here prefcrib'd
 fhall not be moved at all.

PSALM XV. Metre 2.
All People, &c.

Lord who shall have a dwelling place
In Tabernacles of thy Grace?
Thy holy hill who shall possess?
sure he that worketh righteousness;

2, 3.
That walks upright, and speaks the truth
And this even from his heart he doth:
He that backbites not with his tongue,
nor doth his neighbour any wrong.

4, 5.
That takes not up a false report
To's neighbour's hurt in any sort:
Vile men are in his eyes abhor'd,
but honour'd they that fear the Lord.

5.
That changeth not what once he swears,
Though he the loss and damage bears:
That puts not out his Coyn, whereby
to get his wealth by Usury.

Nor takes reward to circumvent,
Or prejudice the Innocent:
He that doth these things is approv'd,
and never shall that man be mov'd.

PSALM XV. Metre 3.
Ye Children, &c.

Lord who shall have a dwelling place
Ith' Tabernacle of thy grace?
thy holy hill who shall possess?
The man that walketh uprightly;
And worketh no iniquity,
shall surely have that happiness.
The man that walks in God's true fear,
And speaks the truth with heart sincere
according to his just intent;
He that backbites not with his tongue,

Nor doth his neighbour any wrong,
  is such a man as here is meant.

2.

That takes not up an evil fame
Reproachful to his neighbour's name,
  nor useth an opprobrious word:
He that doth look with just disdain
Upon vile persons and profane,
  but honours them that fear the Lord.
That to his promise goes not cross,
Although engaged to his loss,
  nor puts out Coyn to Usury:
Nor takes reward against the Just;
He that doth thus may boldly trust
  not to be mov'd eternally.

PSALM XVI. *Metre* 1.

Lord save me for I trust in thee,
  sincerely from my heart,
Confessing thee my Lord to be,
  and so indeed thou art.
My goodness cannot have extent
3 to thee, but to th' upright:
The Saints on Earth, the excellent,
  in whom's all my delight.

4 But they shall sorrows multiply,
  and be in woful case,
That hasten to Idolatry,
  and other Gods embrace.
The blood of their Drink-offerings
  I'le not present, O Lord;
Nor move my lips to name the things
  so much to be abhor'd.

5 The Lord is mine Inheritance,
  and portion of my Cup:
Of mine allotted maintenance
  thou art the holder up.
6 The Lines are fall'n successively,
  and happily to me:

A good-

A goodly heritage have I,
  and pleasant for to see.

The Second part.

7 I bless the Lord, because that he
  did counsel me aright;
So that my reins instructed me
  in seasons of the night.
8 I still conceived the Lord to stand
  before me as my Guide:
Since he doth stand at my right hand
  I know I shall not slide.
9 Therefore my heart and tongue are glad,
  and both rejoyce in this,
The certain hope my flesh hath had
  of everlasting bliss.
10 Thou wilt not leave my Soul in Hell,
  nor wilt thou suffer me
Thy holy one belov'd so well
  Corruption for to see.
11 The path of Life thou W I L T shew M E,
  for thou hast all those Treasures:
Full joys at thy right hand there be,
  and everlasting pleasures.

PSALM XVI. *Metre* 2.

All People, &c.

O God the great and mighty one,
  be thou my sure and safe defence;
Because in thee and thee alone
  I put my trust and confidence.
O thou my Soul, thou didst report
  the Sovereign Lord thy Lord to be;
But Lord, my goodness in no sort
  can ever reach to profit thee.

3, 4.
But to the Saints that are on Earth,
  and to the truly excellent;

In whom I find abundant worth,
  in whom I place my great content.
They shall their sorrows multiply,
  that after other Gods do run:
Their Blood-drink-offerings I defie,
  their Idol-names I hate and shun.

5, 6.

The Lord is mine Inheritance,
  he is the portion of my Cup:
As for my lot, thou dost advance,
  and ever strongly bear it up.
The Lines are fallen unto me
  in places pleasant for abode;
Yea, and I have obtain'd of thee
  a goodly heritage, O God.

The Second part.

7 I bless the Lord, by whose good means
  I was advis'd and counsel'd right:
For by thy Counsel have my reins
  wisely instructed me by night.
8 I set the Lord still in mine eye,
  and boldly trust him over all:
At my right hand he is so nigh,
  that, doubtless, I shall never fall.
9 This therefore doth my heart refresh,
  and joys abundant fill my brest:
Glad is my glory, and my flesh
  in sure and certain hope shall rest.
10 For Lord, thou wilt not leave alone
  my precious Soul in Hell to be:
Nor wilt permit thy holy one
  corruption in the Grave to see.
11 Thou wilt, O Lord, to me declare
  the blessed path of Life and Light:
For in thy presence Joys there are,
  and of a fulness infinite.
And there, O Lord, at thy right hand
  are such delights as never die;

And

And pleasures at thy full Command,
    that last to all Eternity.

PSALM XVII. Metre 1.

Lord hear the right attend my Cry,
    unto my prayer give heed,
That doth not in hypocrisie
    from feigned lips proceed.
2 And let my sentence uncontroll'd
    proceed with power from thee:
And let thy righteous eyes behold
    the things that equal be.
3 My heart thou hast examined,
    by night thou didst enquire:
Thou hast me prov'd and visited,
    and try'd me as by fire.
Yet by thy searching thou shalt find
    in me no wickedness:
For I am purposed in my mind
    my mouth shall not transgress.
4 Concerning works of men profane,
    thy lips did guide me so,
That from the paths I did refrain,
    wherein Destroyers go.
5 Uphold my goings, Lord my guide,
    in all thy paths Divine;
So that my foot steps may not slide
    out of those ways of thine.
6 I have with comfort call'd on thee,
    for thou O God wilt hear:
Incline thy self to answer me,
    and to my speech give ear.
7 Thy wonderful kind love disclose,
    O thou whose strong right arm
Saves all believers from their foes,
    that rise to do them harm,

Psalm xvij.

The Second part.

8 Preserve me, Lord, from hurtful things,
   as th' apple of thine eye;
And under covert of thy wings
   defend me secretly.

9 From wicked men that tyrannize,
   let thy hand help me out,
And from my deadly Enemies
   that compass me about.

10 In their own fat they are inclos'd,
   and bear themselves so high,
That with their mouth they are dispos'd
   to speak presumptuously.

11 They have encompassed us round
   in our own foot-steps now:
And down unto the very ground
   they bend their frowning brow.

12 Like th' greedy Lion that doth long
   to take his prey in chace:
And as it were a Lion young,
   that lurks in secret place.

13 Arise and disappoint him then,
   and cast him down, O Lord,

14 Defend my Soul from wicked men,
   which are thy sharp'ned Sword.

From worldly men thy help I crave,
   from men which are thy hand;
Which in this life their portion have,
   and do not see beyond.
Thy hidden stores their bellies fill,
   with many Children blest,
They spend their substance at their will,
   and leave their Babes the rest.

15 But I in righteousness abide,
   beholding thy sweet face;
And waking shall be satisfy'd
   with th' Image of thy grace.

PSALM XVII. *Metre* 2.

All People, &c.

Lord hear the right, attend my Cry
And prayers put forth unfeignedly:
My sentence let come forth from thee,
And let thine eyes things equal see.

3.
For thou hast prov'd my heart upright,
Thou visitedst me in the night:
Thou try'dst me, and shalt nothing find,
But blamelesness of heart and mind.

4, 5.
As for the works of bloody men,
Thy Counsels kept me safe from them:
Hold up my goings in thy way,
So that my steps may never stray.

6.
I call'd on thee whose paths I trod,
For thou wilt hear me, O my God:
Thy gracious goodness I beseech
To bow thine ear and hear my speech.

The Second part.

7.
Shew me thy marvellous kind love,
O thou that sav'st us from above:
Thou sav'st believers from surprize
Of those that do against them rise.

8, 9.
Keep me as th' apple of the eye,
And make thy wings my Canopie,
From deadly foes that do oppress,
And circumventing wickedness.

10, 11.
They are inclos'd in their own fat,
And proudly speak they care not what:
In our own paths they hem us round,
Their low'ring looks bow to the ground.

Like

Pſalm xvij.

12, 13.

Like Lions greedy of their prey,
Or Lions whelp in ſecret way :
   O Lord ariſe, defeat my foe,
   His enterpriſes overthrow.

The Third part.

14.

Save me from men that are thy Sword,
From men that are thy hand O Lord ;
   From wicked worldlings (men of ſtrife
   Which have their portion in this life.

Whoſe bellies thy hid treaſures fill,
They ſpend their ſubſtance at their will,
   And leave unto their Babes the reſt,
   With many Children being bleſt.

15.

But I ſhall have a near acceſs
To view thy face in righteouſneſs :
   And waking ſhall thy viſage ſee,
   And therewith ſatisfy'd ſhall be.

PSALM. XVIII.

O Lord my ſtrength I will love thee,
2   the Lord's my rock and fort :
My ſafe Deliverer is he,
   my God and my ſupport.
My ſtrength and buckler moſt ſecure,
   in whom my truſt ſhall be ;
The horn of my ſalvation ſure,
   and my high Tower is he.

3 Upon the Lord's Name I will call,
   who is moſt worthy praiſe :
So ſhall I ſcape mine enemies all
   with ſafety all my days.
4 The pangs of death did me incloſe,
   whereby I was diſmay'd :
The floods of wicked men aroſe,
   and made me much afraid.

Psalm xviij.

5 The pangs of Hell, which dreadful be,
  did compaſs me about :
The ſnares of death prevented me,
  and made me to cry out.
6 Then did I call in my diſtreſs
  upon the Lord moſt high :
And to my Ged with earneſtneſs
  I did ſend out my cry.

And from his Temple graciouſly
  the Lord my voice did hear :
Before him alſo came my Cry,
  yea even to his ear.

The Second part.

7, 8.
Then trembled all the Earth for fear,
  the hills. foundations ſhook :
And very greatly mov'd they were
  at his fierce angry look.
Out of his noſtrils went a ſmoak,
  and from his mouth there came
Devouring fire, which did provoke
  the ſulphurous Coals to flame.

9 Th' Almighty Lord the Heavens bow'd,
  and downward did deſcend :
Beneath his feet a ſable Cloud
  of Darkneſs did extend.
10 A Cherub-Chariot did him bear,
  whoſe plumes he made his ſail :
The winds his winged Courſers were,
  and darkneſs was his vail.
11 Dark his Pavilion, dark the Skie,
  dark Waters, dusky Clouds
Compoſe an airy Canopie,
  wherein himſelf he ſhrouds.
12 A brightneſs did before him flame,
  which did thick Clouds diſpell :
Then down the battering Hailſtones came,
  and Coals of fire there fell.

13 The Lord from Heaven in Thunder spoke,
   the Voice of God most high
 Did make the stormy Hailstones smoke,
   and Coals of fire to fly.
14 And he did make his arrows spread,
   and put his foes to flight:
 He shot out Lightnings to their dread,
   discomfiting them quite.
15 Then were the Water-channels seen,
   and Earth's foundations vast,
 Disclos'd at thy rebuke so keen,
   and at thy nostrils blast.

The Third part.

16 The Lord did send from Heaven high,
   he took and drew me out
 From waters of adversity
   that compass me about.
17 He sav'd me from my potent foe,
   and safely set me free
 From such as sought my overthrow,
   and were too strong for me.
18 They did prevent me craftily
   in that most dangerous day,
 That threatned my calamity,
   but God was then my stay.
19 He brought me to a spacious place,
   by his great power and might;
 And sav'd me freely of his grace,
   for I was his delight:
20 According to mine innocence
   was my reward made sure:
 The Lord did give me recompence,
   because my hands were pure.
21 For in the ways of God have I
   continually trod;
 And have not ever wickedly
   departed from my God.

Psalm xviij.

22 For unto all his Statutes still
  I had a great respect;
And no part of his holy Will
  did I at all reject.
23 Yea I was also most upright
  before the Lord most high;
And kept my self as in his sight
  from mine iniquity.
24 Therefore the Lord rewarded me,
  as I had done aright;
And as my hands were clean and free
  from sin in his eye-sight.

The Fourth part.

25 The merciful thou wilt requite
  with mercy in their kind:
And they that are themselves upright
  the like of thee shall find.
26 Unto the pure thy purity
  thou wilt O Lord declare:
And thou wilt deal as frowardly
  with them that froward are.
27 For Lord thou wilt those people save,
  whom sharp afflictions try'd:
But wilt bring down all those that have
  the lofty looks of pride.
28 For thou wilt make my Candle burn,
  and shine exceeding bright:
The Lord my God will surely turn
  my darkness into light.
29 For I ran through a Troop by thee,
  and safely scap'd them all;
And by my God assisting me
  have I leapt o're a wall.

The Fifth part.

30 As for the Lord his way is pure,
  the Word of God is try'd:

He is their buckler safe and sure
  that do in him confide.
31 For who except the Lord alone
  a God esteem'd may be;
And who a mighty Rock but one
  and our Almighty He.

32 'Tis God that by his power and might
  strongly girds up my loyns;
And makes me take my way aright
  to perfect my designs.

33 He makes my feet to be as swift
  as are the Hinds in pace:
And I must count it as his gift,
  that gains me each high place.

34 He taught my hands all warlike skill,
  my fingers how to fight;
So that a bow, a bow of steel
  is broken by my might.

35 Thou gav'st me thy salvation's shield
  to arm me most compleat;
And thy right hand hath me upheld,
  thy favour made me great.

36 Thou hast inlarg'd with liberty
  my steps to be so wide,
That both my feet stood stedfastly,
  and did not slip aside.

37 I overtook my foes that fled,
  for I pursu'd apace:
Nor till they were extinguished
  did I forsake the chase.

38 Mine enemies I did so greet
  with blows not dealt in vain,
That down they fell beneath my feet,
  and could not rise again.

The Sixth part.

39 For thou hast girt me powerfully
  to battle with my foes;

And

Pſalm xviij.

And haſt ſubdu'd them under me,
   that up againſt me roſe.
40 Mine enemies necks into my hand
   were given me by thee,
That I might root out of the Land
   all them that hated me.
41 They cry'd and called earneſtly,
   but there was none to ſave;
Yea even to the Lord moſt high,
   but he no anſwer gave.
42 Then like the duſt that's blown about,
   when boiſt'rous winds do meet,
I beat my foes, and caſt them out
   as dirt into the ſtreet.
43 Thou ſav'dſt me from ſeditious hands
   the Heathens Head to be:
I ſhall be ſerv'd by forreign Lands,
   and folk unknown to me.
44 As ſoon as they of me do hear,
   forthwith they ſhall obey:
The ſtrangers ſhall ſubmit with fear,
   and yield themſelves ſtreight-way.
45 The ſtrangers till they do ſubmit
   ſhall ſoon fall off and fade:
Their ſecret places they ſhall quit,
   they ſhall be ſo afraid.

The Seventh part.

46 O bleſſed be my Rock of power,
   that ever doth abide;
And let the Lord my Saviour
   be highly magnifi'd.
47 'Tis God that hath avenged me,
   my people he ſubjects;
My Saviour from my foes is he,
   my perſon he protects.
48 Yea thou haſt ſet me o're them all
   that did my hurt conſpire;

And

Pſalm xviij.

And ſav'd me from the rage of *Saul*,
  whom fury ſet on fire.
49 Therefore will I give thanks to thee
  in heathen Lands O Lord:
In Songs of praiſe with melody
  will I thy Name record.

50 Deliverance great he gives indeed,
  and mercy keeps in ſtore,
For *David* and his ſacred ſeed,
  and that for evermore.

PSALM XIX. *Metre 1.*

THe Heavens give to underſtand
  the Glory of the Lord:
The operations of his hand
  the Firmaments record.
2 Day unto Day hath made it known,
  and Night to Night declar'd;
3 And Speech and Language there is none
  where their Voice is not heard.
4 Their Line is gone throughout the Earth,
  the like their words have done:
And there's his Royal Tent ſet forth
  to hold the ſhining Sun.
5 Which as a Bridegroom bravely clad,
  doth leave his lodging place;
And Gyant-like with geſture glad
  ſets out to run a race.

6 He reacheth Heaven's vaſt Extreams,
  making his Courſe compleat;
And nothing can by any means
  be hidden from his heat.

The Second part.

7 The Law of God is very pure,
  the Soul it rectifies:
His Teſtimonies are moſt ſure,
  making the ſimple wiſe.

8 The

8 The Statutes of the Lord are right,
   and confolate the mind :
His precepts pure affording light
   to eyes by nature blind.
9 The fear of God is fpotlefs too,
   and doth endure for ever :
The Judgments of the Lord are true,
   and righteous altogether.
10 Far more than many treafur'd Sums
   of Gold to be embrac'd :
Far fweeter than the Honey-combs,
   or Honey to the taft.
11 Thy Servant is fore-warn'd thereby
   thy Precepts to regard ;
And he that keeps them carefully
   fhall have a great reward.

The Third part.

12 But who can all his errors fee,
   and what lies hid within ?
Lord cleanfe me and deliver me
   from all my fecret fin.
13 Thy Servant alfo Lord reftrain
   from each prefumptuous crime :
And let none fuch have power to reign
   in me at any time.

And then fhall I be moft upright,
   being reftrain'd by thee ;
I fhall be blamelefs in thy fight,
   and great tranfgreffions flee.
14 O let my mouth, O let my heart
   in all I think or fay,
Be pleafing to thee, Lord, that art
   my Saviour ftrength and ftay.

PSALM XIX. *Metre 2.*

The Mighty God, &c.

1 THe Heavens declare the glory of God most wise,
His handy-work the Firmament descries:
2 Day utters speech to Day, and Night to Night
shew forth the knowledge of his power & might:
3 There is no speech or language, tongue or nation,
But hears their voice and makes interpretation.

2.

4 Their Line is gone quite throughout the Earth,
Their words to th' end of all the world go forth:
In them the Lord this mighty work hath done
to set a Tabernacle for the Sun.
5 Which as a Bridegroom from his chamber coming
Rejoyceth as a strong man to be running.

3.

6 His going forth is from the Heavens end,
His Circuit all the Skie doth comprehend,
And there is nothing be it small or great,
That can be hidden from its burning heat:
So vast a Volume is the Book of Nature,
Much more the Scripture shewing the Creator.

The Second part. 4, 5.

7 The Law of God hath power to controul,
Instruct, admonish, and convert the Soul:
The Testimony of the Lord is sure,
And wisdom to the simple doth procure:
8 His Statutes right and heart-exhilarating,
His Precepts pure and eye-illuminating.

6.

9 God's fear can cleanse the Soul, & keep it bright,
His Judgments they are true and wholly right:
10 Sweeter than Honey or the Honey-comb,
Richer than Gold which fire cannot consume:
11 Moreover by them is thy servant warned,
And great reward have these things if performed.

Psalm xix.

The Third part. 7.

12 But who can see the error of his thoughts?
13 O cleanse thou me from all my secret fau'ts;
 Thy Servant from presumptuous sins restrain,
 And let them have no power in me to reign;
 And so shall I be free from sins oppression,
 And ever blameless from the great transgression.

8.

14 Lord let the words which from my mouth pro-
 And meditations which my heart doth heed,(ceed,
 The meditations of my heart, I say,
 Let them be pleasing to thee night and day:
 Let them be now and always so esteemed,
 O Lord my strength who hast my Soul redeemed.

PSALM XX. *Metre* 1.

The Lord now hear thee graciously
 in this distressful day:
The Name of *Jacob*'s mighty God
 be thy defence and stay.
2 And from the Sanctuary send
 assistance in thy need:
And out of *Sion* strengthen thee,
 and make thee strong indeed.

3 Remember all the Offerings
 which thou hast brought entire;
And now accept the Sacrifice,
 which thou hast made by fire.
4 Thy hearts desire he grant to thee,
 and all thy Counsels bless;
And make them be accomplished
 with sutable success.

The Second part.

5 We will rejoyce in thy defence,
 O God our health and stay:
And in the Name of our great God
 our banners we display.

Pſalm xx.

The Lord fulfill all thy deſire,
and grant what thou doſt crave:
6 And now I know that God moſt high
doth his Anointed ſave.

And he will hear him gracioufly
from his moſt Holy Heaven;
With ſaving ſtrength of his right hand,
which ſhall to him be given.
7 Some truſt in Charets, ſome in Horſe,
but we will think upon
The Name of thee the Lord our God,
and truſt to that alone.

8 For we do riſe and ſtand upright,
but they bow down and fall:
9 Save Lord, and let our heavenly King
now hear us when we call.

PSALM XX. *Metre 2.*
Give Laud, &c.

1 Lord hear thee in the day
    of danger and diſtreſs:
Great *Jacob's* God, we pray
defend and give ſucceſs;
2   Aſſiſt thee ſtill
With powerful grace from's holy place
in *Sion* hill.

2.

3 Thine Offerings all likewiſe
let in his mind be kept,
And thy Burnt-ſacrifice
he gracioufly accept:
4   Grant thee ſucceſs
To thine own will, and ſo fulfill
all thy requeſts.

3.

5 We will our joy proclaim
in thy ſweet ſaving aid,

And in our God's great Name
  our banners are display'd:
    The Lord our shield
Grant thy requests, whatever rests
  to be fulfill'd.

The Second part.

6 Now know I that the Lord
  saves his Anointed one,
And hears him with regard
  from Heaven his holy Throne:
    And will command
For him that pray'd the saving aid
  of his right hand.

5.

7 In Charets some repose,
  and some put trust in Horse;
But far above all those,
  or any outward force,
    We will record,
And still proclaim this mighty Name
  OUR GOD THE LORD.

6.

8 They are brought down, and bow,
  yea they are fallen quite:
But we are risen now,
  and also stand upright:
    Lord save us all,
Great King give ear our prayers to hear
  now when we call.

PSALM XXI. *Metre* 1.

THe King rejoyceth to record
  the Comforts of thy might;
And in thy saving health, O Lord,
  how much shall he delight?
2 For what his heart desir'd to have
  thou grantedst every thing;

    And what his lips of thee did crave
      was not deny'd the King.

3 With thy good blessings manifold
    thou hast him early sped;
And set a Crown of perfect Gold
    upon his Royal Head.

4 And when he asked Life of thee
    thereof thou mad'st him sure;
And gav'st it to Eternity
    for ever to indure.

5 His glory is exceeding great
    in thy Salvation's aid:
Honour and Majesty compleat
    thou hast upon him laid.

6 Thy blessings ever-flowing streams
    to him thou didst impart;
Thy Countenance with chearful beams,
    doth greatly glad his heart.

7 Because the King unfeignedly
    doth put his trust in thee:
And through thy mercy, O Most High,
    remov'd he shall not be.

8 But thine Almighty hand, O Lord,
    shall find out all thy foes;
And all that have thy Name abhor'd
    thy right hand shall disclose.

9 And make them like a fiery hearth
    in thy most angry hour:
The Lord shall swallow them in wrath,
    and fire shall them devour.

10 Their fruit shalt thou abolish then,
    destroying their increase;
And from among the Sons of Men
    shalt cause their seed to cease.

11 Against thee they intended ill,
    and mischief they did plot;
which they endeavoured to fulfill,
    but speed it they could not.

12 For these things thou shalt make them fly,
   turning their backs in chace;
Charging thy bow-strings readily
   against thine enemies face.

13 In thy peculiar strength, O Lord,
   thy matchless glory raise:
So shall our chearful Songs record
   thy powers deserved praise.

PSALM XXI. *Metre 2.*

Now Israel may say.

THe King shall joy in thy great strength, O Lord,
   and in thy saving health lift up his voice,
and how exceedingly shall he rejoyce?
His hearts desire thou didst to him afford,
And not hold from him what his lips implor'd.

2.

For thou preventest him as heretofore
   with blessings of thy goodness largely spread,
   and set'st a Crown of pure gold on his head:
He askt thee Life, thou gav'st it in great store,
Even length of days to live for evermore.

3.

He greatly glories in thy saving aid,
   Honour and Majesty do him invest;
   for thou hast made him to be ever blest;
Exceeding glad thou also hast him made
With thy sweet Countenance on him display'd.

4.

For, Lord, in thee the King doth still repose,
   and through the mercy of the Lord most high
   he shall not be remov'd undoubtedly;
Thy hand shall find out all thy bitter foes,
Thy right hand all thy haters shall disclose:

5.

And thou shalt make them as a fiery flame
   of some hot Oven when thy wrath shall fall;
   the Lord shall swallow and consume them all,

Their whole increase, their off-spring, & their name
shall feel thy wrath, and perish in the same.

6.

For they intended evil against thee,
   they had imagin'd a mischievous plot,
   but speed it and perform it they could not:
And therefore quite dispersed they shall be,
For thou shalt make them turn their back and flee.

7.

When thou shalt fit thine arrows for the flight,
   when thou shalt make them ready on the strings
   against the face of them, O King of Kings;
Be thou exalted, Lord, in thine own might,
So shall we sing, and praise thy power aright.

PSALM XXII.

The First part.

MY God my God, wherefore hast thou
    forsook me, O wherefore,
And art so far from helping now,
    when I so cry and roar?
2 My God I cry in time of day,
    yet am not heard of thee,
And all the night, O Lord, I pray,
    and silent cannot be.
3 But Lord thou art the Holy One,
    and in that place dost dwell,
Where always thou inhabitest,
    the praise of Israel.
4 Our fathers in the time forepast
    did put their trust in thee:
They trusted, and their faith held fast,
    and thou didst set them free.
5 They were delivered evermore
    by calling on thy Name:
    and for the faith they had in thee,
    they were not put to shame.

Pſalm xxij.

6 But I, alas, am not a man,
    a deſpicable worm,
  A meer reproach of men I am,
    whom all the people ſcorn.
7 All they that ſee me laugh at me,
    and in a ſcornful way
  Shoot out the lip, and ſhake their head,
    and thus preſume to ſay,
8 He truſted that the Lord would be
    his Saviour by his might:
  Let him deliver and ſet him free
    if he in him delight.
9 But Lord thou know'ſt me from the W
    and thou didſt take me thence,
  When I was on my mothers breaſt
    thou waſt my Confidence.
10 And I was caſt upon thy care
    from my birth-day till now:
  And from the Womb that did me bear
    my God and guide art thou.

The Second part.

11 O Lord depart not now from me
    in this my preſent grief;
  Since I have none my help to be,
    none elſe to ſend relief.
12 For many Bulls have compaſſed,
    and all beſet me round;
  The ſtrongeſt Bulls that have been fed
    on *Baſhan*'s fat'ning ground.
13 They gape upon me greedily
    to kill me if they may,
  Much like a Lion ravening,
    and roaring for his prey.
14 Like water I am pou'red out,
    my joynts aſunder part:
  As wax with fire runs all about,
    ſo ſorrow melts my heart.

D 5

15 My strength is like a potsherd dry'd;
   my tongue cleaves to my jaws:
 I am brought down to dust of death,
   and thy hand is the cause.
16 And many dogs do compass me,
   the wicked joyntly meet,
 They compass me with treachery,
   they pierc'd my hands and feet.
17 Yea I may reckon every bone,
   on me they gaze and stare:
18 Upon my Vesture Lots are thrown,
   and they my Garments share.
19 Therefore I pray thee be not far
   from me in my great need:
 But rather, since thou art my strength,
   to help me, Lord, make speed.
20 And save me from the cruel sword,
   by thine Almighty Power,
 Preserve my dear and darling Soul
   from dogs that would devour.
21 And save me from the Lyons mouth,
   as thou hast answered me,
 When from the horns of Unicorns
   I made my prayer to thee.

The Third part.

22 I will declare thy Name, O Lord,
   unto my Brethren dear:
 Amidst the Church I will record
   thy praise that they may hear.
23 O ye his Saints that fear the Lord
   set forth his praise and fame,
 Let Israel's and Jacob's seed
   for ever praise his Name.
24 For he despis'd no poor man's Case,
   nor set his cause aside;
 Nor from him ever hid his face,
   but heard him when he cry'd.

25 There

Pſalm xxij.

25 Therefore in Congregations great
my praiſe ſhall be of thee:
And I will pay my vows, O Lord,
where all thy Saints ſhall ſee.

The Fourth part.

26 The meek ſhall eat and be ſuffic'd;
and thoſe that do endeavour
To know the Lord, ſhall praiſe his Name,
your hearts ſhall live for ever.
27 And all the ends of all the Earth
ſhall readily record;
And call to mind his works ſet forth,
and turn unto the Lord.

The kindreds of the Nations all
ſhall worſhip in his ſight:
28 For he muſt govern great and ſmall,
all Nations are his right.
29 All fat ones of the Earth ſhall eat,
and worſhip the moſt high:
They that go down to duſt ſhall bow
before him reverently.

And there is no man rich or poor,
however he may ſtrive,
Can by himſelf, himſelf ſecure,
and keep his Soul alive.
30 A ſeed of Saints ſhall ſerve the Lord,
accounted and foreknown;
A Generation of the Lord's
which he himſelf doth own.
31 They ſhall come forth and there declare
his righteouſneſs to thoſe
That born in after-ages are,
that God did thus diſpoſe.

PSALM XXIII. *Metre I.*

MY ſhepherd is the Lord moſt high,
I ſhall be well ſupply'd;

Psalme xxiij.

2 In pastures green he makes me lie,
   by silent waters side.
3 He doth restore my Soul that strayes,
   and then he leads me on
To walk in his most righteous ways,
   for his Names sake alone.

4 Yea though through deaths dark Vale I go,
   yet will I fear no ill;
Thy rod and staff support me so,
   and thou art with me still.
5 My Table thou hast furnished
   in presence of my foe,
With Oyl thou dost anoint my head,
   my cup doth overflow.

6 Surely thy goodness and thy grace
   shall always follow me,
And my perpetual dwelling place
   thy holy house shall be.

PSALM XXIII. *Metre 2. Imitatio Herberti.*

Have Mercy, &c.

THe Lord my shepherd is,
   and he that doth me feed:
Since he is mine, and I am his,
   what comfort can I need?

2.
He makes me to lie down
   upon the flowry grass:
Then to the streams he leads me on,
   where waters gently pass.

3.
And when I go astray
   he doth my Soul reclaim:
Conducting me in his right way,
   for his most holy Name.

4.
Yea though the paths I trod
   through Death's dark Vale should be,

I would

I would not fear, for there's my God,
　a staff of strength to me.
5.
And in mine enemies sight
　thou mak'st me sit and dine:
Anoint'st my head in foes despite,
　and fill'st my Cup with Wine.
6.
Surely thy grace and love
　shall measure out my days:
And from thy house I'le not remove,
　nor there from thee my praise.

PSALM XXIII. *Metre* 3.
The first New Tune.

The Lord's my shepherd to provide,
　I shall be sure to be supply'd,
　　And by this means
In pastures green I couch between
　the silent streams.

2.
He doth restore my Soul that strayes;
He leads me in those righteous wayes
　　which I should take;
And therein he still guideth me
　for his Name sake.

3.
Yea though I walk through death's dark Vale,
No evil will I fear at all:
　　For there thou art
With me, O God, thy staff, thy rod
　uphold my heart.

4.
Thou spread'st my Table in despite
Of envious foes, and in their sight
　　Anoint'st my head,
And filleft up my bounteous Cup
　until it shed.

Thy

5.
Thy goodness and thy mercy sure
Shall follow me whilst I indure:
   And I therefore
Will have abode i'th' house of God
   for evermore.

PSALM XXIV. *Metre* I.

THe Earth is God's, the people his,
   the World and all her goods:
2 He founded it upon the Seas,
   and fixt it on the floods.
3 Who shall ascend God's sacred Hill?
   and who may make account
To stand and to continue still
   within his holy Mount?
4 Whose hands and heart are free from stain
   of foul Impurity:
Whose Soul affects not Idols vain,
   nor swears deceitfully.
5 He shall receive the blessedness,
   which is through Christ convey'd:
And justifying righteousness
   from God his saving aid.
6 For such do seek the Lord indeed,
   this is the godly race:
O *Jacob* this is sure the seed
   of them that seek thy face.

The Second part.

7 Ye everlasting gates make room,
   ye doors lift up your head:
Then shall the King of Glory come
   within your Courts to tread.
8 Who is this great and glorious King;
   his Royal Name record:
The strong and ever-conquering
   Almighty Glorious Lord.

9 Ye everlasting gates make room,
  ye doors lift up your head:
 Then shall the King of Glory come
  within your Courts to tread.
10 Who may this King of Glory be?
  declare that Name of his,
 The Lord of Hosts, and none but he
  the King of Glory is.

PSALM XXIV. Metre 2.

O Lord Consider, &c.

THe Earth is God's, and wholly his,
  the World so wide is all his own:
And whatsoever therein is
  belongs to him, to him alone.
For he as he himself did please
Hath founded it upon the Seas:
  And firmly he hath stablisht it,
  upon the watry floods to sit.

3, 4.

Who shall ascend the Hill of God,
  that holy Hill of Sanctity?
And who shall have his blest abode
  within his holy place on high.
That grace to him will God impart,
That's clean of hand, and pure of heart,
  That lifts not up to vanity
  his Soul, nor swears deceitfully.

5, 6.

He shall receive what shall him bless,
  and all that blessing he shall have,
That rich reward of righteousness
  from God the Lord who doth him save.
This is the Generation pure
Of them that seek him to be sure:
  O *Jacob*'s God, this is the race
  of them that truly seek thy face.

Pſalm xxiv.

The Second part. 7, 8.

Ye everlaſting doors and gates
  lift up your heads and hearts for him:
And then the Prince of Potentates
  and King of Glory ſhall come in.
Who is this King of Glory bright?
The Lord moſt ſtrong and full of might:
  The mighty and victorious Lord
  in War and tryal of the Sword.

9, 10.

Ye everlaſting doors and gates
  lift up your heads and hearts for him:
And then the Prince of Potentates,
  and King of Glory ſhall come in.
Who is this King of Glory bright?
The Lord of Hoſts of Sovereign might:
  The Lord of Hoſts, and none but he
  the King of Glory ſtil'd may be.

PSALM XXV. Metre 1.

Have Mercy, &c.

Lord I lift up my Soul
  to thy moſt holy Name:
2 My God, I put my truſt in thee,
  O put me not to ſhame.
Let not my foes rejoyce,
  nor triumph over me:
3 Yea let not any be aſham'd
  that duly wait on thee.

Let them be all aſham'd
  which cauſeleſly tranſgreſs:
4 Shew me thy ways, Lord teach thou me
  thy paths of righteouſneſs.
5 Lord lead me in thy truth,
  and teach me in thy way:
Thou art my God and Saviour,
  on thee I wait all day.

Psalm xxv.

6 Remember, O good Lord,
   thy mercies manifold ;
And tender loving-kindnesses
   which ever were of old.
7 My youthful sins and faults
   O keep not on record :
In mercy, for thy goodness sake,
   remember me, O Lord.
8 The Lord is good and just,
   and therefore takes delight
To teach poor sinners in his way,
   that they may walk aright.
9 The meek ones God will guide
   in judgment not to swerve :
The meek and humble he will teach
   his ways how to observe.
10 For all the ways of God
   are truth and mercy still
To them that keep his Covenant
   and do obey his Will.

The Second part.

11 And now for thy Name sake,
   O Lord I thee intreat
To pardon my iniquity,
   for it is very great.
12 Whoever fears the Lord,
   the Lord will let him know
The perfect path of righteousness
   wherein he ought to go.
13 In goodness evermore
   his Soul shall sweetly rest :
And by his good and godly seed
   the Earth shall be possest.
14 The secret of the Lord
   shall all that fear him know,
His Counsel and his Covenant
   he to his Saints will show:

15 Mine eyes continually
   upon the Lord are staid,
To pluck my feet out of the net
   which for my Soul is laid.
16 Turn to me, Lord, in love,
   and pity my distress;
For I am very desolate,
   and left quite comfortless.
17 The troubles of my heart
   do every day increase:
O bring me out of misery,
   and let my sorrows cease.
18 See mine affliction Lord,
   my anguish and my pain;
And take my sins so clean away,
   that none of them remain.
19 Consider, Lord, my foes,
   for many such there be,
Which bear a hate inveterate,
   and cruel unto me.
20 O keep my harmless Soul,
   and Lord deliver me:
And let me never be asham'd,
   because I trust in thee.
21 Let mine integrity
   and uprightness defend
And keep me safe, because, O Lord,
   on thee I do depend.
22 And now, O Lord, redeem,
   and bring thine Israel out
Of all the straits and miseries
   that compass him about.

PSALM XXV. *Metre* 2.
To the Tune of the Tenth Commandment.

TO THEE, LORD, I lift up my Soul,
   O Lord my God I trust in thee:

O let

Pſalm xxv.

O let no ſhame my truſt controll,
   nor enemies triumph over me.
3, 4.
Yea, ſhame thou none that wait on thee,
   ſhame ſuch as cauſeleſly tranſgreſs:
Declare thy ways, O Lord, to me,
   teach me thy paths of righteouſneſs.
5.
O lead me, Lord, as I have pray'd,
   teach me thy truth and holy way:
For thou art God my ſaving aid,
   on thee do I wait all the day.

Remember thou, O gracious Lord,
   thy tender mercies manifold;
Thy loving-kindneſſes afford,
   for they have ever been of old.

The Second part. 7.

Remember not my ſins of youth,
   nor my tranſgreſſions once record:
Think on me in thy grace and truth,
   and for thy goodneſs ſake, O Lord.
8, 9.
Good and upright is our Lord God,
   therefore his way he'l ſinners ſhow;
The meek in judgment he will guide,
   the meek he'l teach his way to know.
10.
For all the paths of God moſt high
   are grace and truth which they receive,
Which keep his Covenant faithfully,
   and to his Teſtimonies cleave.
11.
For thy Names ſake, Lord, hear my Cries,
   which beg it at thy Mercy Seat,
To pardon my iniquities,
   for I acknowledge them full great.

Psalm xxv.

The Third part. 12, 13.

What man is he that fears the Lord
  him shall he teach what way to choose?
His Soul shall be with goodness stor'd,
  his seed shall have the Earth to use.

14.

The secret of the Lord's with those
  that have his Name in awful fear:
And unto them he will disclose
  his Covenant, and make it clear.

15, 16.

Mine eyes are ever towards the Lord,
  to pluck my feet out of the snare:
Turn thou to me, thy grace afford,
  for I am desolate and in care.

17, 18.

Enlarg'd my hearts afflictions be,
  O bring me out of all distress:
My pain and my affliction see,
  and pardon all my sinfulness.

The Fourth part. 19.

Consider thou my Enemies,
  because they very many are,
In whom a cruel hatred lies,
  which unto me they causeless bear.

20.

O let my Soul be safe sustain'd,
  and, Lord, do thou deliver me:
And let me never be asham'd,
  for I do put my trust in thee.

21.

O Lord, let that Integrity
  and uprightness which is in me,
Preserve me safe continually,
  for I do always wait on thee.

22.

Redeem O God thy Church abroad,
  to *Israel* thy Redemption send;

And bring all his Adversities
unto a very happy end.

PSALM XXVI. Metre 1.

Judge me, O Lord, for I am just,
and blameless I abide :
In thee likewise I put my trust,
therefore I shall not slide.

2 Prove me, my God, I thee desire,
and search me thoroughly :
Try me with thy refining fire ;
my heart and reins, O try.

3 Thy loving kindness, Lord my God,
before my face I lay :
And in thy paths of truth have trod,
and kept that holy way.

4 I do not hold society
with men whose deeds are vile :
I will not come in company
with them that practise guile.

5 The congregation of the lewd
I do detest and hate :
And with the wicked multitude
will not associate.

6 In innocency I will wash,
and purifie my hands :
Then will I hasten to the place
where thy pure Altar stands ;

7 That I may publish and proclaim,
with voice of joy and praise :
And tell of thy most worthy fame,
in all thy works and ways.

8 The habitation of thy house,
Lord, I have loved well :
And that same place so glorious,
where thy renown doth dwell.

9 O gather not my Soul with them
in sin that take their fill :

Nor yet my life among those men
 that seek much blood to spill.
10 Within whose hands mischievousness,
 and wickedness abides:
And their right hand is fill'd no less
 with Soul-corrupting bribes.

11 But as for me walk on I will
 in mine integrity:
Redeem me, and be merciful
 unto me, O most high.
12 My foot stands in an even place,
 thy Name I will record,
And shew before the Churches face,
 the praises of the Lord.

PSALM XXVI. *Metre 2.*
Ye Children, &c.

MY righteous Judgment, Lord, decide,
  For I in uprightness abide,
 I trust in God, and shall not slide.
2 Examine me, O Lord most high,
 And prove my Souls integrity,
  my heart and reins, O search and try.
3 For thy kind love is night and day
 Before mine eyes without decay,
  and I have walk'd in thy true way.
4 I have not sat with persons vain,
 The gross dissemblers I disdain,
  and joyn not with the men profane.
5 I hate th' Assemblies of the lewd,
 Nor have I followed or pursu'd
  with the ungodly multitude.
6 I'le wash my hands in innocence,
 And compass then, with confidence
  thine Altar with pure Conscience;
7 That I may publish and declare
 With thankfulness what THY Works are,
  and tell of all thy Wonders RARE.

8 Lord

8 Lord I have lov'd paſt all things elſe
   Thy dwelling houſe, which moſt excells,
      even THAT place where thine honour dwells.
9 My Soul with ſinners gather not,
   Nor yet my Life to ſhare a Lot
      with men whom bloody crimes do blot.
10 Within whoſe hands are miſchiefs great,
   and their right hand it is compleat
      with bribery and baſe deceit.
11 But as for me reſolv'd am I
   To walk in mine integrity,
      redeem me of thy clemency.
12 My foot ſtands in an even place,
   And I before the peoples face
      will bleſs the Lord that ſhews us grace.

PSALM XXVII.

THe Lord's my ſaving health and light,
   why ſhould I be diſmaid?
He is my life, my ſtrength and might,
   why ſhould I be afraid?
2 When as the ſons of wickedneſs,
   my foes and enemies all
Came on me, to eat up my fleſh,
   they ſtumbled and did fall.
3 Though hoſts againſt me pitch their tent,
   my heart ſhall fear no foes:
But in this caſe be confident,
   though wars againſt me roſe.
4 One thing I have deſir'd of God,
   which I will ſeek for ſtill:
That I may have a bleſt abode
   in *Sions* ſacred hill.

That I may there ſpend all my days,
   beholding God's ſweet face:
Inquiring after bleſſed ways
   within his holy place.
5 For he ſhall in the evil hour,
   me in's pavilion hide:

    And make his secret tent my tow'r,
      where I shall safe abide.

6 And now behold, my head shall be
    exalted and renown'd
Above my foes that compass me,
    in all the circuits round.
Therefore will I bring to his tent
    the sacrifice of joy :
And songs of praise will I present
    unto the Lord most high.

7 Hear me, O Lord, when as I cry
    with earnest voice to thee :
Have mercy on me, O most high,
    and kindly answer me.

8 When as thou said'st, my face seek ye :
    instructed by thy grace,
My heart made answer unto thee,
    Lord, I will seek thy face.

9 Hide not thy face, O Lord, I pray,
    hide not thy face from me :
In anger do not put away
    thy servant, Lord, from thee.

Thou wast my helper heretofore,
    O do not leave me quite :
Forsake me not for evermore,
    O God my saving might.

10 When parents cast their care aside,
    and leave me desolate ;
Then will the Lord for me provide
    in my forlorn estate.

11 Teach me, O Lord, thy way to know,
    and graciously dispose,
That in a plain path I may go,
    because of all my foes.

12 Give me not over to my foes,
    for most maliciously
False witness are against me rose,
    that breath out cruelty.

13 And surely I had fainted quite,
   but that I hop't to see
Thy goodness in the land of light
   dispensed unto me.
14 Wait on the Lord continually,
   he is thy strength and stay:
Thy heart with faith to fortifie,
   wait on the Lord, I say.

PSALM XXVIII. Metre 1.

TO thee I cry, O Lord, my rock,
   thine answer let me have:
Lest by thy silence I be like
   to dead men in their grave.
2 O hear the voice of my request,
   now that to thee I cry;
When towards thy holy Oracle
   I lift my hands on high.

3 O draw me not with wicked men
   to act the sinners part
That speak unto their neighbours peace,
   while mischief fills their heart.
4 Give them according to their deeds,
   and mischief of their hearts:
O recompence their handy-works,
   and render their deserts.

5 Since they regarded not God's works,
   nor what his hands have wrought;
He shall not build, but break them down,
   and bring them all to nought.
6 Blessed for ever be the Lord,
   because that he hath heard
My voice and supplications,
   which I to him preferr'd.

7 The Lord's my strength and fortitude,
   my safest shield is he:
My heart reposed trust in him,
   and he hath holpen me.

7 God's voice divides the flames of fire,
  it makes the desart shake :
8 It shakes the wilderness entire,
  it makes all *Kadesh* quake.
9 It makes the Hinds to calve for fear,
  it makes the forrest bare :
  And in his Temple, all men there
  his glory do declare.
10 The Lord sits King on floods that swell,
  his Kingdom shall not cease :
11 He will give strength to *Israel*,
  and bless his Church with peace.

PSALM XXIX. *Metre* 2.
Ye Children, &c.

1 Give to the Lord ye mighty ones,
  Give to the Lord your Crowns and Thrones :
   his strength and glory to confess.
2 Ascribe due glory to his Name,
  Worship the Lord, his praise proclaim
   in beauty of his holiness.
3 Heark, you may hear his ratling cloud,
  The God of glory thunders loud,
   this is the voice of God most high.
  The Lord on many waters is,
4 And that loud sounding voice of his,
   is full of power and majesty.

  Heark how his voice with terror speaks :
5 The Lord the lofty cedars breaks,
   the cedars of Mount *Lebanon*,
6 Like wanton Calves he makes them skip,
  Like a young Unicorn they trip,
   Mount *Lebanon*, and *Syrion*.
7 The flames of lightning they divide,
  The fire doth flash on every side,
   his thund'ring voice effects no less.
8 The thund'ring voice of God doth make
  The mighty desarts move and quake,
   it shakes all *Paran* wilderness.

9 The

9 The voice of God (so very strong)
 Doth cause the Hinds to cast their young,
  and the bare forrests to appear:
 While his renown by every tongue,
 Is through his holy Temple sung,
  and these works celebrated there.
10 For God sits King upon the flood,
 Yea, from the first his Kingdom stood,
  and it shall never, never cease.
11 The Lord that is our strength and tower,
 Will give his people ample power,
  the Lord will bless his Church with peace.

PSALM XXX. *Metre* 1.

1 Will extoll thee, O most high,
 for I am rais'd by thee:
Thou hast not made mine enemy
 to triumph over me.
2 O Lord my God, to thee I cry'd
 for succour and relief:
And graciously thou didst provide
 to heal me of my grief.
3 Thou brought'st my Soul up from the pit,
 thou kept'st me, Lord, alive
From them that are gone down to it,
 while safely I survive.
4 Sing to the Lord ye Saints of his,
 and thanks to him confess,
Upon the due remembrances
 of his pure holiness.
5 His wrath is in a moment past,
 life from his favour springs:
Though weeping for a night may last,
 the morning comfort brings.
6 And I in my prosperity,
 did confidently say,
Surely I shall live happily,
 and see no evil day.

7 So very strongly by thy grace
   my mountain, Lord, was laid:
Then didst thou hide away thy face,
   and I was sore dismay'd.
8 Then in my tribulation,
   to thee, Lord, did I cry:
And made my supplication
   unto the Lord most high.
9 What gain is in my blood, said I,
   when I to grave go down?
Can dust thy praises testifie,
   can dust thy truth renown?

10 Lord, I beseech thee, hear me now
   in that which I have pray'd:
Have mercy on me, and be thou
   my all-sufficient aid.
11 To joyful dancing thou hast turn'd
   my sorrows doleful noise;
My sackcloth loos'd wherein I mourn'd,
   and girt me round with joys.
12 To th' end my tongue may sing thy praise,
   and never silent be:
O Lord my God, through all my days
   I will give thanks to thee.

PSALM XXX. Metre 2.
Ye Children, &c.

THy Name, Lord, I will magnifie,
   For thou hast lifted me on high,
     that I might not be undertrod:
Nor th' enemy triumph over me:
2 For I, O Lord, have cry'd to thee,
   and thou hast heal'd me, O my God.
3 O Lord thou didst my Soul revive,
From gaping grave me kept alive,
     that I to th' pit should not go down.
4 Sing to the Lord ye Saints of his,
Proclaim with due remembrances,
     his holiness and his renown.

5 For lo his anger soon is past,
  And doth but for a moment last ;
    but in his favour life is had:
  Weeping may for a night endure,
  But in the morning comes a cure,
    and joyful tidings make us glad.
6 And in my full prosperity
  I never shall be mov'd, said I,
7   thy favour laid my hill so strong:
  Then didst thou hide thy face from me,
8 And I was griev'd and cry'd to thee,
    and into suits I turn'd my song.
9 What profit's in my blood, said I,
  When I go down to dust and die,
    shall dust thy praise and truth declare?
10 Hear me O hear me, Lord, I said,
  Help me and be my pow'rful aid,
    according to mine earnest prayer.
11 Then turn'd my grief to joyfulness,
  Thou took'st from me my mourning dress,
    and girdedst me with glad array :
12 To th' end my tongue may sing thy praise,
  And not be silent all my days,
    I'le give my God great thanks alway.

PSALM. XXXI.

IN thee, O Lord, I put my trust,
  O put me not to shame :
Deliver me as thou art just,
  even for thy righteous Name.
2 Bow down thine ear and hear me now,
  deliver me with speed :
My castle, and strong rock art thou,
  to save me at my need.
3 For, Lord, thou art my fort and tower,
  which I for safety take :
Then lead and guide me by thy power,
  O God, for thy names sake.

E 4   4. Pull

4 Pull me out of the net which they
 for me have closely laid:
Because thou art my strength and stay,
 to whom I fly for aid.
5 The spirit which thou gav'st to me,
 I to thy hands commit:
For thou, Lord God of truth, art he
 that hast redeemed it.
6 All such as set their heart on lies,
 I utterly abhor'd:
Detesting all such vanities,
 I trusted in the Lord.
7 Thy mercies great do make me glad,
 my joys do overflow:
For thou hast weigh'd what cares I had,
 and known my Soul in woe.
8 Thou hast not, Lord, deliver'd me
 into mine enemies hand:
But in a place of liberty
 hast made my feet to stand.

The Second part.

9 Lord, pity me, do thou condol,
 for I am in distress:
Mine eye, my belly, and my soul
 consume with heaviness.
10 My life is spent with misery,
 my years with sighs decay:
Strength fails me through iniquity,
 my bones consume away.
11 I was a scorn to all my foes,
 chiefly to neighbours nigh;
A fear to friends, for even those
 see me without and fly.
12 Like to a dead man out of mind,
 so am I quite forgot;
And disregarded of mankind,
 like to a broken pot.

13 For

Psalm xxxj.

13 For many slanders have I heard,
  and fear on all sides lay:
 While they devised and conspir'd
  to take my life away.
14 But yet I trusted to thy power:
  O Lord, my God, said I,
 Thou art my God and Saviour,
  on whom I do rely.

15 My times are all at thy dispose;
  do thou then set me free
 From bloody hands of all my foes,
  with spite pursuing me.
16 Upon thy faithful servant make
  thy gracious face to shine:
 And save me for thy mercies sake,
  for I am one of thine.

17 Lord, let me not ashamed be,
  for I thy succour crave:
 Let wicked men be sham'd by thee,
  and silenc'd in the grave.
18 Let lying lips in silence die,
  which speak the worst they can,
 Most proudly and contemptuously
  against the righteous man.

19 O Lord, how great felicity
  hast thou laid up for them
 That fear thy name and trust in thee,
  before the sons of men!
20 Thou hid'st them with a careful eye,
  from proud mens cruel wrongs;
 Kept in thy secret canopy
  from all the strife of tongues.

21 O blessed be the Lord above,
  that succour'd me so far:
 And shew'd me such exceeding love,
  in a strong town of war.

22 I said in haste, I am remov'd,
   and cut off from thine eyes:
Yet was I so of thee belov'd,
   thou heard'st my doleful cries.

23 O love the Lord, all ye his Saints,
   for he the faithful guards:
And the proud man with punishments
   he plenteously rewards.

24 Be strong, and God shall stay your heart;
   be confident ye just;
And surely God shall take your part,
   since ye on him do trust.

PSALM XXXII. *Metre* 1.

Blessed, O blessed man is he,
   whose sin God passeth by:
And whose transgressions cover'd be
   from God's avenging eye.

2 Blessed is he to whom the Lord
   imputeth not his sin:
Whose heart hath all deceit abhor'd,
   and guile's not found therein.

3 For while I no confession made,
   but silent kept my tongue,
My bones (as if with age) decay'd
   with roaring all day long.

4 Thy hand on me was burdensome
   the day and night throughout:
So that my moisture did become
   like Summers parching drought.

5 Then I confest my sin to thee,
   and all my faults reveal'd:
My trespass and iniquity
   no longer I conceal'd.
I said, I will to God confess
   what all my sins have bin:
Then thou forgav'st the wickedness,
   and guilt of all my sin.

6. Hence

6 Hence all good men shall pray to thee,
  what time thou may'st be found:
Sure when great floods of water be,
  they shall not him surround.
7 O God, thou art my hiding place,
  from straits thou set'st me free:
And with sweet songs of saving grace
  thou dost encompass me.
8 I will instruct thee, saith my God,
  and teach thee in the way:
My watchful eye shall be thy guide,
  lest thou should'st go astray.
9 Be not so rude and ignorant
  as is the horse and mule:
Whose mouth if bit and bridle want,
  from harm thou canst not rule.
10 For certainly to men unjust,
  shall miseries abound:
But him that in the Lord doth trust,
  shall mercy compass round.
11 O all ye righteous men rejoyce,
  and in the Lord delight:
With joyful shouts lift up your voice,
  all ye whose hearts are right.

PSALM XXXII. *Metre* 2.
All People, &c.
or, *O Lord Consider,* &c.

The man is blest whose pardon's seal'd,
  And all his trespass hid and heal'd:
To whom the Lord imputes no sin,
  Whose spirit hides no guile therein:
For while I no confession made,
My strength with daily grief decay'd,
  thine anger burn'd the day throughout,
  my moisture turn'd to Summers drought.
Then I confest my wickedness,
I said I will my sins confess,

and

and thou forgav'ſt immediately
my guilt and great INIQUITY.
For this cauſe all the godly race
Shall ſeek thee in a time of grace,
   that when great floods of waters roul,
   no danger may come nigh thy Soul.

The Second part.

An hiding place I have of thee,
Songs of deliverance compaſs me:
   I tell and teach the faithful ſo,
   mine eye ſhall guide them how to go.
O be not like the horſe and mule,
Whom underſtanding doth not rule;
   whoſe ſtubborn mouth we muſt reſtrain
   from violence with bit and rain.

The wicked ſhall be curbed ſo,
And be reſerv'd to many a woe;
   but them that in the Lord confide,
   ſhall mercy cloſe on every ſide.
Be joyful therefore in the Lord
Ye righteous men with one accord,
   and ſhout for joy with great delight
   all ye that are in heart upright.

PSALM XXXIII. *Metre* 1.

YE righteous in the Lord rejoyce,
   for praiſe becomes the Saints:
2 Praiſe God with pſaltery, harp, and voice,
   and ten-ſtring'd inſtruments.
3 Sing to the Lord aloud with praiſe,
   with skilful ſongs and new:
4 For lo his word, his works, and ways
   are faithful, juſt, and true.
5 Juſtice and judgment he doth love,
   even this moſt righteous Lord:
And with his goodneſs from above
   the Earth is richly ſtor'd.

Psalm xxxiij.

6 The word of his eternal truth
   compos'd the spangled skie :
And by the breathing of his mouth
   the hosts of Heaven on high.

7 The waters of the Sea he keeps
   confin'd within the shore :
He layeth up the liquid deeps,
   as in a house of store.

8 Let all the Earth submit with fear
   to this Almighty Lord :
And all the Nations every where,
   let tremble at his word.

9 For he but spake, and it was done,
   and when his word was past,
His Ordinances thus begun,
   for evermore stood fast.

10 The counsel of the nations rude
    the Lord doth bring to nought :
He doth defeat the multitude,
    of their device and thought.

11 But God's own counsels do remain,
    They stand for ever sure :
The thoughts which his heart doth retain
    from age to age endure.

The Second part.

12 That nation's blest whose God's the Lord,
    foreknown in his decree ;
And chosen of his own accord,
    his heritage to be.

13 The Lord from Heaven cast his eye
    on men of mortal birth ;

14 Beholding from his seat on high
    all dwellers on the Earth.

15 Alike he frames and fashioneth
    the hearts of great and small ;
Their works he well considereth,
    and judgeth of them all.

16 No numerous host can save a King;
　it is not strength that can
Deliverance from danger bring
　unto a mighty man.
17 A horse is vain, and never can
　give safety in the fight:
Nor shall deliver any man.
　by his great strength and might.
18 But lo, the Lord doth set his eye
　with favour on the just,
And those that fear him faithfully,
　and in his mercy trust:
19 To save their precious Souls alive
　from death's destructive power:
And store of wholesome food to give,
　when famine would devour.
20 Our Soul doth wait with patience
　for God the holy one:
He is our help and our defence,
　he is our shield alone.
21 For lo, our heart in him shall joy,
　because we can proclaim,
That we have trusted stedfastly
　in his most holy Name.
22 Lord, let thy mercy and thy grace
　upon us ever be:
Accordingly as we do place
　our confidence in thee.

PSALM XXXIII. *Metre 2.*

Our Father, &c.

Rejoyce ye just in God most high,
　for praise is comely for th' upright;
With Harp, and Song, and Psaltery,
　and ten-string'd Lute his praise recite.
Sing to him a new Song of Joys,
Play skilfully with loudest noise.

For

For lo! the Word of God is right,
    and all his Works are done in truth,
In righteousness he takes delight,
    and just he is in all he doth.
And with the goodness of the Lord
The spacious Earth is richly stor'd.

And by the Word of God supream
    the Heavens were made from North to South,
And all the glorious Hosts of them
    by the free breathing of his Mouth:
He heaps up waters on the Seas,
And lays the deeps in store houses.

The Second part.

Let all the Earth still fear the Lord,
    and all that dwell from Sun to Sun.
Have him in awe and great regard,
    for he but spake, and it was done:
The Word from him no sooner past,
But all at his Command stood fast.

The Lord doth blast and bring to nought
    the Counsels which the Heathens take;
The peoples fond device and thought
    of none effect the Lord doth make.
But his own Counsels never fall,
His thoughts endure to ages all.

The Third part.

That Nation's blest whose God's the Lord,
    that people whom he doth advance,
And chooseth of his own accord
    to be his own Inheritance:
The Lord from his Cœlestial Throne
Beholds the Sons of Men each one.

He from his holy dwelling place
    looks down and doth exactly know,
Beholding all of humane race,
    who ever dwell on Earth below;

Their hearts alike he fashioneth,
And all their works considereth.

No King is sav'd by a numerous host,
   nor mighty man by strength of limb;
An horse is vain whereof to boast,
   and no man's safety lies in him:
By his great strength he never can,
Deliver any Mortal Man.

The Fourth part.

Behold the Eye that best can guard,
   the watchful Eye of God above
Is fixt on them that fear the Lord,
   and them that trust in his free love:
Their Souls from death for to reprieve,
And them in famine to relieve.

Our Soul waits for the Lord our God,
   he is our help, he is our shield;
For in him shall our hearts be glad,
   since on his holy Name we build:
Lord let thy mercy on us be,
According as we trust in thee.

PSALM XXXIV.

AT all times I will magnifie,
   and bless the living Lord:
My thankful mouth continually
   his praises shall record.
2 My Soul shall boast in God's great Name,
   with glad and glorying voice:
The humble men shall hear the same,
   and mightily rejoyce.
3 O magnifie the Lord with me,
   and let us all endeavour
Him to exalt in high degree,
   and praise his Name together.
4 I sought the Lord with fervent cries,
   and he my voice did hear:

Psalm xxxiv.

The Lord deliver'd me likewise
  from all my painful fear.
5 The Saints lookt up to him on high,
  from whom their comforts came;
And were enlightened gloriously,
  their faces took no shame.
6 This poor man cry'd, the Saints shall say,
  the Lord did hear his call:
And all his troubles took away,
  and helpt him out of all.
7 The Angel of the Lord most high
  encampeth every where;
Delivering them continually
  that walk in God's true fear.
8 O taste, ye Saints, and tasting see
  that God's a gracious one:
O happy, happy man is he,
  that trusts in him alone.
9 O fear the Lord, ye Saints of his,
  fear him with one accord;
For never any want there is
  to them that fear the Lord.
10 Young Lions lack, and shall endure
  sharp hunger's mortal sting:
But they that fear the Lord are sure
  to want for no good thing.

The Second part.

11 Come, Children, with alacrity,
  unto my words give ear:
And I will teach you perfectly
  the Lord's true filial fear.
12 What man unto long life aspires,
  and loveth many days;
To see the good that he desires,
  let him observe these ways.
13 All evil must thy tongue exclude,
  thy lips must guile eschew:

14 Depart from evil, and do good,
    seek peace, and peace pursue.
15 For on the righteous every where
    the Lord doth set his eye:
And opens his attentive ear
    to their unceffant cry.
16 The Lord hath set his countenance
    against the wicked race:
To cut off their rememberance
    on earth from every place.
17 The righteous cry, the Lord doth hear,
    and ends their troubles quite.
18 To broken hearts the Lord is near,
    and saves the Soul contrite.
19 Full many are the miseries
    of just and righteous men;
But out of all adversities
    the Lord delivereth them.
20 And by especial providence
    he keepeth every bone:
That none by any violence
    is broken, no not one.
21 But evil shall the wicked slay,
    and whosoever hate
The righteous for their righteous way,
    shall soon be desolate.
22 The Lord doth graciously redeem
    his servants Souls each one;
And none do put their trust in him
    that shall be overthrown.

PSALM XXXV.

Lord, plead my righteous cause with those
    that are with me at strife:
O fight against my mortal foes,
    that fight against my life.
2 Lay hold, O Lord, upon the lance,
    the buckler, and the shield:

Stand up for my deliverance,
and for me fight the field.

3 Draw out the sword, and stop the way
of those that follow me:
And to my Soul in mercy say,
thy Saviour I will be.

4 Confound them with rebuke and blame,
that seek my Soul to kill:
Let them turn back and fly with shame,
that think to work me ill.

5 As chaff doth fly before the wind,
so let them fly apace:
And let God's Angel come behind,
to prosecute the chase.

6 Set them in dark and slippery way,
that they may surely fall:
And let God's Angel make no stay,
but persecute them all.

7 For causelesly within a pit
a net for me they hid;
Even for my Soul they digged it,
and this they causeless did.

8 Let him be ruin'd unawares,
and taken in the net:
Yea taken in those very snares
which his own hand hath set.

9 And then my Soul shall joy in thee,
thy help, O Lord, to find:
And thy salvation then shall be
as musick to my mind.

10 And all my bones shall thus confess,
Lord, who is like to thee,
That sav'st the poor man from distress,
when foes too powerful be?

Yea, thou delivereft by thy power
the poor and needy man
From him that seeketh to devour
and spoil him if he can.

The Second part.

11 False witness did against me rise
   with evidence untrue;
And charg'd me with iniquities,
   whereof I nothing knew.
12 For good they did reward me ill,
   to th' spoiling of my Soul:
But as for me I used still
   their sorrows to condole.
13 I put on sackcloth for these men,
   my Soul did fast and mourn:
And into mine own bosome then
   my prayer did return.
14 I for my foe did make my moan,
   as for my friend or brother:
I bow'd down heavily as one
   that mourneth for his mother.
15 But they rejoyced in my woe,
   vile abjects met to plot:
They gather'd when I did not know,
   they tore me ceasing not.
16 With mocking hypocrites at feasts,
   they gnasht their teeth at me.
17 O Lord, how long shall these vile beasts
   both seen and suffered be?
Rescue my Soul in this sad state,
   from their destructive paws:
And bring my darling desolate
   safe from the Lions jaws.
18 And then will I give thanks to thee
   in great Assemblies, Lord:
And in the thickest throngs that be,
   will I thy praise record.

The Third part.

19 Let not my wrongful enemies
   lift up their horn on high:

Psalm xxxv.

Nor let them wink with scornful eyes,
  that hate me causelesly.
20 For not a word of peace they say,
  but take deceits in hand,
Contriving how they may betray
  men quiet in the land.

21 Yea and their mouths are opened wide
  against me spitefully:
Aha, aha, mine enemies cry'd,
  we saw it with our eye.
22 O Lord, thou canst not choose but see,
  O do not hold thy tongue:
O Saviour, be not far from me,
  Lord, be not absent long.
23 Stir up thy self, and undertake
  my judgment to decide:
My God my Lord, even now awake,
  and let my cause be try'd
24 According to thy equity,
  judge me, O Lord, my God:
Let them not triumph over me,
  while I am undertrod.
25 Nor suffer them in heart to say,
  ah! we would have it thus:
Nor let them say, he's made a prey,
  and swallow'd up by us.
26 Let bashful shame upon them fall,
  and let confusion sad
Be brought at once upon them all
  that at my hurt are glad.

Let them be cloath'd with infamy,
  let shame confound their face,
That do so proudly magnifie
  themselves in my disgrace.
27 But let them shout and triumph still,
  with gladness and applause,
That favour me, and bear good will
  unto my righteous cause.

Yea

  Yea let them say continually,
   extoll'd be God above,
  His servants true prosperity
   that doth so truly love.
28 And I most gladly will express
   thy praise with grateful tongue:
  And celebrate thy righteousness
   with praises all day long.

PSALM XXXVI. *Metre* 1.

THe wicked man's iniquities
   say thus within my heart,
  God's fear is not before his eyes,
   that acts the sinners part.
2 For in his own deluded eye
   self-flattery doth abound,
  Until that his iniquity
   an hateful thing be found.
3 His words are full of wickedness,
   and framed to deceive;
  But wisdom, truth, and righteousness
   he doth forsake and leave.
4 He plotteth on his bed by night,
   his mischiefs to fulfill:
  He sets himself in ways not right,
   and he abhors no ill.
5 O Lord, thy mercy doth ascend
   above the Heavens high:
  So doth thy faithfulness extend
   unto the Starry Skie.
6 Thy truth may with great hills compare,
   thy judgments are most deep:
  And, Lord, thy providential care
   both man and beast doth keep.
7 How excellent, Lord, is that grace,
   and love that from thee springs!
  Therefore the Sons of Men do place
   their trust in thy spread wings.

Psalm xxxvj.

8 With fatness of thine house on high
   thou shalt thy Saints suffice;
And make them drink abundantly
   the river of thy joys.

9 Because the spring of life most pure
   doth ever flow from thee:
And in thy light we shall be sure
   eternal light to see.

10 O then continue thy sweet grace
   to them that have thee known;
And let thy righteousness embrace
   the upright-hearted one.

11 But let not, Lord, the foot of pride
   against thy servant stand;
Nor let me ever fall or slide
   by any wicked hand.

12 Lo, there the wicked workers fall,
   they fall before our eyes:
They are cast down, and never shall
   be able more to rise.

PSALM XXXVI. *Metre 2.*

Have Mercy, &c.

Transgressions of the lewd
   have whispered to my heart;
And plainly shew'd he fears not God,
   but sets that care apart.

In his own blinded eyes
   self-flattery bears the sway,
Until the sin he liveth in
   be found an hateful way.

The words of his foul mouth
   are wickedness and guile:
Good things to do and wisdom too
   he leaves for things most vile.

He studieth on his bed
   foul mischiefs to fulfill;

He doth delight in ways not right,
 and he abhors no ill.

But yet thy mercy, Lord,
 is in the Heavens high:
Thy truth no less and faithfulness
 doth reach the cloudy Skie.

Thy justice, Lord, is like
 the Mountains of the East;
Thy judgments found like deeps profound,
 thou savest man and beast.

The Second part.

Thy love and kindness, Lord,
 how precious are those things?
Therefore the Sons of mortal ones
 trust in thy shady wings.

The fatness of thy house
 shall fill their appetites,
And thou shalt make them drink
 thy River of delights.

For, Lord, the Well of Life
 doth ever flow from thee;
And in thy light and presence bright,
 all comforts shall we see.

Thy loving kindness, Lord,
 always do thou impart,
And still express thy righteousness
 to men of upright heart.

Let not the foot of pride
 against me come, I pray,
Nor hand of those my wicked foes
 remove me from my stay.

But all those wicked doers
 destruction shall surprize:
Lo! there they fall, and never shall
 be able more to rise.

PSALM XXXVII.

FRet not thy self, nor be incens'd,
   for such as will transgress:
Nor be thou envious against
   the sons of wickedness.
2 For they shall soon be cut away,
   like to the tender grass:
And like green herbs they shall decay,
   and wither as they pass.
3 Trust in the Lord, and put thy hand
   to actions that be good:
So shalt thou dwell within the land,
   and be assur'd of food.
4 Also delight thy self in God,
   and he shall let thee have
Thy hearts desire accomplished,
   what ever thou dost crave.
5 Commit thy way unto the Lord,
   trust also in his Name:
And then, according to his word,
   he will effect the same.
6 And he shall publish and display
   thy justice as the light:
And make thy judgment as noon-day,
   to shine exceeding bright.
7 Rest on the Lord, with patience stay,
   fret not thy self a jot
For him that prospers in his way,
   and speeds his wicked plot.
8 Let not rash anger in thee rise,
   all wrath forsake and shun:
Fret not thy self in any wise
   that evil should be done.
9 For evil-doers shall be destroy'd
   by God's revenging hand:
But they that daily wait on
   they shall possess the land

10 For lo, within a little space
   the wicked shall be gone :
Yea, and thou shalt not find his place,
   though pondering thereupon.
11 But meek men shall possess the Earth,
   with all her rich increase ;
And shall delight themselves in mirth,
   and most abundant peace.

12 The wicked plots against th'upright,
   devising what he can ;
And grates his teeth for very spite,
   against the righteous man.
13 The Lord shall laugh at his lewd way,
   beholding from on high,
How unawares his fatal day
   doth hasten and draw nigh.
14 The wicked men their sword have drawn,
   prepar'd their bow and quiver,
The poor and needy to cast down,
   and slay the upright liver.
15 Their sword shall enter at their heart,
   and pierce themselves quite through :
And e're they can discharge their dart,
   their bows shall break in two.

The Second part.

16 A little that the just enjoys,
   is better far to them
Than all the wealthy treasuries
   of many wicked men.
17 For God will surely break the arm
   of sinners by his might :
But he will still uphold from harm,
   and stablish the upright.
18 God knows the days of upright men,
   and he reserves in store,
  A rich inheritance for them,
   which lasts for evermore.

Psalm xxxvij.

19 They shall not be asham'd at all,
   when evil doth betide:
But in the day of famine shall
   be sweetly satisfi'd.

20 But wicked men shall perish soon,
   and such as God provoke:
As fat of lambs they shall consume,
   and vanish into smoak.

21 The wicked man a borrowing goes,
   but cares not to repay:
Whereas the righteous mercy shews,
   and freely gives away.

The Third part.

22 By such as God pronounceth blest,
   the Earth shall be enjoy'd;
And such as he hath curst, supprest,
   cut off, and quite destroy'd.

23 A good man's steps the Lord doth bless,
   and orders them aright:
And in his way of godliness
   he greatly doth delight.

24 And though he fall, he falls not quite,
   but shall be made to stand;
For God upholds him by the might
   of his most mighty hand.

25 I have been young, and now am old,
   yet, to my hoary head,
The just, nor his, did I behold,
   cast off, to beg their bread.

26 Still he is merciful and kind,
   and out of kindness lends:
A blessing (too) he leaves behind,
   which to his seed descends.

27 Depart from evil and do well;
   lay up good works in store:
And then thou shalt be sure to dwell
   in peace for evermore.

28 For God loves judgment, and will not
   forsake his Saints at need :
  For ever he preserves their lot,
   but slays the sinners seed.
29 To all the earth the just are heirs,
   it is their heritage,
  To dwell therein both they and theirs,
   even from age to age.
30 The mouth of righteous men hath force
   deep wisdom to express :
  Of judgment doth his tongue discourse,
   and talk of righteousness.
31 The Law which his great God did make,
   doth in his heart abide;
  And of the steps that he doth take,
   not one shall ever slide.
32 The wicked watcheth narrowly,
   to catch the righteous man;
  And seeketh opportunity
   to kill him if he can.
33 But God will never let him fall
   into his wicked hands :
  Nor let him be condemn'd at all,
   when he in judgment stands.

The Fourth part.

34 Wait on the Lord and keep his path,
   he shall exalt thee then
  To dwell on earth, and see his wrath
   upon ungodly men.
35 The wicked in great power and pride,
   with terror I have seen,
  Spreading himself on every side,
   like to a lawrel green.
36 Yet passed he away like wind,
   and lo, he was quite gone:
  Yea and I sought him, but could find
   no sign of such a one.

Psalm xxxvij.

37 Mark and behold the perfect man,
   and mark till his decease:
For sure the end of such a one
   is everlasting peace.
38 But they that wilfully offend,
   shall be destroy'd together:
And this shall be the wicked's end,
   to be cut off for ever.
39 But righteous mens salvation
   is from the Lord above:
He, in their tribulation,
   their strength and stay doth prove.
40 And God shall help and succour them,
   and he shall save the just;
Delivering them from wicked men,
   because in him they trust.

PSALM XXXVIII.

ME, Lord, in wrath do not controul,
   nor scourge in fury fierce:
2 Thy heavy hand sinks down my Soul,
   thine arrows deeply pierce.
3 My flesh no soundness hath within,
   because thou art displeas'd:
My bones by reason of my sin,
   by no means can be eas'd.
4 The weight of mine iniquities,
   which o're my head doth roul,
Like to a heavy burden lies,
   too heavy for my Soul.
5 My wounds corrupt and putrifie,
   my folly makes it so:
6 And much bow'd down with misery,
   all day I mourning go.
7 My loyns are fill'd with loathsomness,
   my flesh hath no sound part:
8 I'm weak and bruis'd in such excess,
   I roar for grief of heart.

9 But, Lord, thou know'st my whole desire,
   my groans are in thy sight:
10 My heart doth pant, my strength doth tire,
   mine eyes have lost their light.

11 My lovers and my friends so dear
   stand distant from my sore:
My kinsmen unto me so near,
   come at me now no more.
12 Yea they that seek my life lay snares,
   and they that seek my wrong
Speak mischief, and their heart prepares
   deceits, even all day long.

13 But as a man both deaf and dumb,
   that neither speaks nor hears,
14 From whom no contradictions come,
   I stopt both mouth and ears.
15 For, Lord, my hope against my foe
   is wholly fixt on thee:
And thou, O Lord my God, I know,
   wilt hear and answer me.

16 For hear, said I, lest they should be
   puft up with wanton pride:
And magnifie themselves on me,
   when once my foot doth slide.
17 For I am ready now to halt,
   my sorrows still I see:
18 Wherefore I will declare my fault,
   my sin shall humble me.
19 But still my enemies are in heart
   increast, and waxen strong;
They hate my Soul without desert,
   and do me all the wrong.
20 They are my adversaries too,
   that good with ill repay;
Because I carefully pursue
   a good and godly way.

21 O Lord my God, forsake me not,
　far from me never be.
22 My Saviour, O defer no jot
　to help and succour me.

PSALM XXXIX. *Metre 1.*

I Will take heed unto my ways,
　　and keep my tongue, said I;
Bridling my mouth from sinful words,
　while wicked men stand by.
2 As dumb with silence thus I stood,
　and did not speak a word:
I held my peace from speaking good,
　then was my sorrow stir'd.
3 My heart within me waxed hot,
　while busied here about:
And as I mus'd the fire did burn,
　at last these words burst out.
4 Lord, make me understand my end,
　and days uncertain date;
That I may fully apprehend
　the frailty of my state.
5 Lo, thou hast made my days a span,
　mine age as nothing deem'd:
Sure all men are meer vanity
　at best estate esteem'd.
6 Sure each man walks in vainest show,
　they vex themselves in vain:
He heaps up wealth, and doth not know
　to whom it shall pertain.

The Second part.

7 And now, O Lord, what wait I for?
　my hope is fix'd on thee.
8 Save me from all my sins, lest I
　a scorn to fools should be.
9 But I was silent at these things,
　I spake not, but was dumb:

F 4　　　　　　　Because

Because I knew my sufferings
from thy good hand did come.
10 remove from me thy scourge and plague,
which I cannot withstand:
I am consumed by the blow
of thy correcting hand.
11 When thy rebukes correct for sin,
it makes man's beauty dye,
Like garments where the moth hath bin;
sure all are vanity.
12 Lord, hear my prayer, attend my cry,
regard my tears that fall:
I sojourn'd like a stranger here,
as did my fathers all.
13 O spare me, Lord, and give me breath,
my strength to me restore;
Before I go from hence by death,
and shall be seen no more.

PSALM XXXIX. *Metre* 2.

All People, &c.

1 Said I would my ways observe,
And keep my tongue lest that should swerve:
I'le bridle up my mouth with care,
while wicked men before me are.

As dumb with silence thus I stood,
I held my peace, yea even from good;
My sorrow being so represt,
was greatly stirred in my brest.

My heart within me waxed hot,
The fire did burn and ceased not,
whilst I was musing here about,
and at the last these words burst out.

Lord make me know and apprehend,
How short a time I have to spend;
and that within a little while
I shall be rid of all my toyl.

Psalm xxxix.

Lord, thou hast made the life of man
To be contracted in a span;
   And all mine age in thy account
   scarce to a moment doth amount.

And every man, undoubtedly,
Is altogether vanity;
   And at his very best estate
   is reckon'd at no higher rate.

Man walketh in a shadow vain,
And toils himself with needless pain:
   He heaps up wealth with wretched care,
   and knows not who shall be his heir.

The Second part.

Now, Lord, for what do I attend?
Truly my hopes on thee depend;
   Pardon my sins, that am brought low,
   and let not fools deride my woe.

I was as dumb, and spake no word,
Because thou did'st it, O my Lord!
   Remove thy stroke, I cannot stand
   to bear the blow of thy strong hand.

When thou rebukest man for sin,
A sad condition he is in;
   Thou mak'st his beauty like a cloth,
   fretted and eaten by the moth.

Sure every man, how great soever,
Is vanity, yea altogether;
   And reckon'd at no higher rate
   when valu'd at his best estate.

Lord hear my prayer, attend my cry,
Slight not my tears; for what am I?
   A stranger and a sojourner
   with thee, as all my fathers were?

O spare me, Lord, a little space,
That I may gather strength and grace,

before I lose this mortal breath,
and shall be taken off by death.

PSALM XL.

With expectation for the Lord,
  I waited patiently:
At length to me he did accord,
  and heark'ned to my cry.
2 He brought me from a dreadful pit,
  and from the miry clay:
And on a rock he set my feet,
  establishing my way.
3 He taught my mouth new songs to frame,
  our God to magnifie:
Many shall see and fear his Name.
  and on the Lord rely.
4 O blessed man whose hearts repose
  is God for all supplies;
Respecting not the proud, nor those
  that turn aside to lies.
5 Many great works, O Lord, are these
  which thou, My God, hast wrought;
Many thy gracious purposes,
  which are to us-ward thought.
None can sum up how great they be;
  and if I would express,
Declare, and speak of them to thee,
  I find them numberless.
6 No sacrifice nor such like thing
  didst thou at all desire:
Burnt-offering, or sin-offering
  thou didst of none require.
7 But thou hast opened mine ears;
  then, lo I come, said I:
The volume of thy book declares
  of me apparently.
8 My God, I come to do thy mind,
  and do it with delight;

Yea

Yea in my heart thy Law I find,
  for there thou didst it write.

The Second part.

9 Thy justice and thy righteousness
  in great resorts I tell :
Behold my tongue no time doth cease,
  O Lord, thou know'st full well.

10 Thy justice I have not conceal'd,
  my heart could not with-hold :
Thy faithfulness I have reveal'd,
  and thy salvation told.

11 With-hold not thou thy tender love
  from me, O Lord, therefore :
Let truth and mercy from above
  preserve me evermore.

12 For, Lord, with mischiefs manifold
  full sore beset am I :
My sins on me do take such hold,
  I even droop and die.

And surely many more they be
  than hairs upon my head :
Therefore my heart quite faileth me,
  and is discouraged.

13 But of thy mercy, gracious Lord,
  be pleas'd to set me free ;
And with great speed do thou afford
  salvation unto me.

14 Let them sustain rebuke and shame,
  that seek my Soul to kill ;
Drive back my foes, and blast their fame.
  that work or wish me ill :

15 Let this reward their shame repay ;
  confounded let them be
That in this manner scoffing say,
  Aha, aha, to me.

16 Let such as seek thy Name be glad,
  and joy in thee always ;

    Let such as love thy saving aid
      say still, to God be praise.
17 But poor and needy, Lord, am I,
      yet not of God forgot:
    Thou art my help and sure supply,
      my God, O tarry not.

PSALM XLI. *Metre* 1.

THe man is blest that prudently
      doth of the poor take care;
For God will sure deliver him,
      when greatest dangers are.
2 The Lord will keep him safe alive,
      and bless him in the land;
And thou wilt not deliver him
      into his enemies hand.
3 Upon his bed of languishing
      the Lord will hold his head;
And in his sickness strengthen him,
      and make even all his bed.
4 O Lord, said I, do thou extend
      thy mercy unto me;
And heal my Soul, for I have sin'd,
      and sore offended thee.
5 Mine enemies speak ill of me,
      and say, when shall he die,
That the remembrance of his name
      may perish utterly?
6 And if he come to visit me,
      he doth but vainly gloze:
His heart heaps up iniquity,
      and tells it where he goes.
7 My hateful foes lie whispering,
      and joyntly they combine
Against me, to devise my hurt
      is all their main design.
8 An evil and mischievous thing,
      say they, cleaves to him sore;

And now that he lies languishing,
  he shall rise up no more.
9 Yea, Lord, my peaceful friend, of whom
  I was so confident,
That at my table ate my bread,
  his heel against me bent.
10 But, Lord, be merciful to me,
  and raise me up agen;
That I may justly recompence
  the doings of these men.
11 And that thou favourest me, O Lord,
  by this good sign I see;
Because my foe may not insult,
  nor triumph over me.
12 But I in my integrity
  am stablisht by thy grace:
And thou for ever setteft me
  before thy glorious face.
13 The Lord the God of *Israel*
  be prais'd eternally,
From age to age for evermore;
  Amen, amen, say I.

PSALM XLI. *Metre* 2.

The man is blest by whom the poor
  is duly thought upon:
The Lord will sure his peace procure
  when troublous times come on.
The Lord will his preserver be,
  and him alive will save;
Great blessings he, O Lord, from thee
  on earth is sure to have.

He shall not be delivered
  unto his enemies will.
But on his bed be strengthened,
  when he lies weak and ill.
In my distress, I said, therefore
  be gracious, Lord, to me,

My Soul reſtore, and heal my ſore,
  though I have err'd from thee.

The Second part.

Mine enemies ſpeak ill of me,
  when comes his dying day?
And when ſhall we ſurvive to ſee
  his blaſted name's decay?
He viſits me with complements,
  his heart he fills with fraud
And vile intents, all which he vents
  when e're he goes abroad.

My haters all lie whiſpering,
  againſt my Soul combin'd,
Some hurtful thing on me to bring,
  deviſing in their mind.
An ill diſeaſe doth him ſurprize,
  and cleaves to him ſo faſt,
That there he lies, and ſhall not riſe,
  but breaths, ſay they, his laſt.

My truſted friend fed at my board,
  againſt me lift his heel:
But help me, Lord, that when reſtor'd
  they may thy juſtice feel.
Pity me, Lord, for well I know
  I am belov'd of thee:
I find it ſo, becauſe my foe
  triumphs not over me.

I am upholden by thy grace
  in mine integrity:
Thou giv'ſt me place before thy face,
  and that perpetually.
The Lord the God of *Iſrael's* Name
  be ever praiſed then;
And all his fame let us proclaim
  for evermore, *Amen.*

PSALM XLII. *Metre* 1.

Like as the Hart doth pant and bray,
   the well-springs to obtain:
Even so my Soul doth pant and pray
   to see God's house again.
2 I thirst for God, the living God:
   O when shall I draw near
The place of his most blest abode,
   and in his sight appear?
3 My tears have been both night and day
   my meat, wherewith I pine,
While constantly to me they say,
   where is that God of thine?
4 Remembring this my grief renew'd,
   and melts my Soul in woe:
For with the zealous multitude
   I had been us'd to go.
  I went with them to God's own house,
   with voice of joy and praise;
Where multitudes did follow us,
   observing holy-days.
5 O then my Soul, why should'st thou be
   cast down in thy distress?
O wherefore art thou mov'd in me,
   with such unquietness?
  Hope still in God's deliverance,
   for yet again shall I
Praise him for his sweet countenance,
   and help I have thereby.
6 My God, my Soul in sorrow sinks,
   yet think on thee I will,
From *Hermon* and from *Jordan's* brinks,
   and from the little hill.

The Second part.

7 Deep calls to deep, as waves do roul,
   and clouds come down in showers;

And floods of sorrow drown my soul,
  and all my vital powers.
8 Yet will the Lord command for me.
  his kindest love by day;
His song shall be by night with me,
  to God my life I'le pray.

9 I'le say to God my rock most strong,
  why hast forgot me so?
Why go I mourning all day long,
  oppressed by my foe?
10 ha, Lord, methinks there doth abide,
  within my bones a sword;
While daily they do thus deride,
  where is thy God, thy Lord?

11 Why art thou then cast down my Soul,
  and troubled in my brest?
God is thy rock whereon to roul,
  in him take up thy rest.
For yet again shall I advance
  that glorious Name of his:
The comfort of my countenance,
  and my dear God he is.

PSALM XLII. Metre 2.

Ye Children, &c.

1 Like as the thirsty Hart doth pant,
  When he doth brooks of water want;
    so sighs my Soul, O Lord, for thee.
2 My Soul thirsts for the living God;
  When shall I enter his abode,
    his beams of beauty there to see?
3 Tears are my food both night and day,
  While, where's thy God? they daily say.
4   My very Soul in tears I shed,
  When I remember how in throngs
We fill'd his house with praise and songs,
  and I their solemn dances led.

Psalm xlij.

5 My Soul, why art thou so deprest,
So tost and troubled in my brest?
   O hope in God for evermore.
For yet again shall I confess
His favours with much thankfulness,
   and comforts which he shall restore.
6 Yet now my Soul within me faints,
My God, consider my complaints;
   for I will think upon thee still;
Even from the vale where *Jordan* flows,
Where *Hermon* his high forehead shows,
   and also from the little hill.

The Second part.

7 Deep unto deep with noise do call,
When as thy spouts of water fall,
   and while thy dreadful tempest raves:
For all thy floods fall from the Skies,
The billows after billows rise,
   to swallow me amidst the waves.
8 Yet will the Lord by day command
His loving kindness near at hand;
   his songs by night shall lodge with me;
A musick sweet amidst my cares:
And then will I present my prayers,
   God of my life, even unto thee;
9 And say, my God my rock, O why
Am I forgot and mourning dye,
   and by my foes am brought to dust?
10 Their words like weapons pierce my bones,
While still they eccho to my grones,
   where is thy God, thy only trust?
11 My Soul, why art thou so deprest,
Troubled and tost within my brest;
   bow'd down and sunk beneath thy load?
O hope in God, and on him wait,
For I his praise shall celebrate,
   who is my Saviour and my God.

PSALM

PSALM XLIII. Metre 1.

Judge me, O God, and plead my cause
  against a nation vile:
O save me from the tyrants jaws,
  and such as practise guile.
2 For of my strength thou art the God:
  why do I mourning go,
Cast off by thee, and undertrod
  by my imperious foe?
3 O send out light and truth divine,
  to lead and bring me near
Unto that holy hill of thine,
  and tabernacles there.
4 Then to thine Altar I will press,
  O God, my wond'rous joy:
O God my God, thy Name to bless
  my harp I will employ.
5 Why art thou then discouraged
  within me, O my Soul?
And why art thou disquieted?
  let faith thy fears controul.
Hope still in God thy help to be,
  whom I shall ever praise:
My health of countenance is he,
  and my dear God always.

PSALM XLIII. Metre 2.

O praise the Lord, &c.

1 Judge me, O God, and plead my case
    Against a nation void of grace:
      O save thou me
    From men unjust, and those that trust
      in treachery.
2 God of my strength, thou art my stay,
    Why dost thou cast me clean away?
      why do I go
    So mournfully, oppressed by
      my cruel foe?

3 Send

Pſalm xliij.

3 Send out thy light and word moſt true,
  And let them lead and bring me to
    thy holy hill;
  That dwelling place, wherein thy grace
    abideth ſtill.

4 Then to God's Altar I will go,
  To God from whom my comforts flow;
    there I'le give laud,
  And honour thee with pſaltery,
    O God, my God.

5 Why art thou then caſt down my Soul?
  Why do ſuch waves within thee roul?
    and why art thou
  With fear and dread diſquieted
    within me now?

  Hope in the Lord thy God always;
  For I ſhall ever give him praiſe
    for his great aid,
  Who doth advance my countenance,
    and is my God.

PSALM XLIV.

WE have, O God, heard with our ears,
    our fathers have us told
  What works thou didſt in days of theirs,
    and in the times of old.

2 How thy hand drove out heathen men,
    and quite caſt out they were,
  Thy hand ſo ſore afflicted them,
    to plant our fathers there.

3 For by their ſword they never got
    poſſeſſion of the land:
  Their own puiſſance ſav'd them not,
    but it was thy right hand.
  It was thine arm and ſhining face,
    from whence their help did riſe;
  Becauſe our fathers found ſuch grace,
    and favour in thine eyes.

4 My

4 My great and powerful King art thou,
  even thou alone, O God :
 Command thou that deliverance now
  for *Jacob* may be had.
5 Through thee we will push down our foes,
  and through thy Name, O God,
 Whoever have against us rose,
  shall quite be undertrod.
6 For I will never trust, O Lord,
  unto my bended bow ;
 Nor yet conceive I that my sword
  can save me from my foe.
7 But thou hast sav'd us from our foes,
  and fully set us free :
 Yea, thou hast put to shame all those
  of whom we hated be.

The Second part.

8 In God we all day long do boast,
  and ever praise thy Name :
9 Yet now thou go'st not with our host,
  but casts us off with shame.
10 Thou mak'st us from the foe to fly,
  turn back, and quit the foil :
 And they that hate us mortally,
  inrich themselves by spoil.
11 Thou gavest us into their hands,
  as sheep ordain'd for food ;
 And scattered'st us in heathen lands,
  among a barbarous brood.
12 Thou sell'st thy people now for nought,
  taking no price nor pay :
 So that thy people are not bought,
  but wholly given away.
13 Thou makest us a meer reproach
  unto our neighbours near ;
 Yea a derision unto such
  as round about us are.

Psalm xliv.

14 Among the heathen we are spread,
   as by-words of disgrace;
A scornful shaking of the head,
   before all peoples face.
15 My sore confusion and disgrace
   before me still I see:
The shame of my abashed face
   hath also covered me.
16 Because the voice of blasphemy
   we hear with many taunts,
By reason of the enemy,
   and the avengers vaunts.

The Third part.

17 All this is come upon us, Lord,
   yet we forgat not thee;
Nor in the covenant of thy word
   have dealt deceitfully.
18 Our heart is not turn'd back, O God,
   nor have we gone astray:
Nor any other path have trod,
   but only in thy way.
19 Though thou hast crusht us in the place
   where Dragons draw their breath;
And covered us in this sad case
   with darksome shades of death.
20 Had we forgot our God's great Name,
   and help of Idols sought;
21 Should not our God search out the same,
   since he doth know our thoughts?
22 Yea, for thy sake, Lord, all the day
   are we kill'd up as sheep:
And counted as the flock which they
   for common slaughter keep.
23 Awake, O mighty Lord, awake,
   why sleep'st thou altogether?
Arise for thy dear servant's sake,
   cast us not off for ever.

24 O wherefore doſt thou hide thine eyes,
  forgetting our diſtreſs;
And look'ſt not on the miſeries
  which do our Souls oppreſs?
25 For down to duſt our Soul is trod,
  on earth as worms we craul:
26 Riſe for thy mercies ſake, O God,
  aid and redeem us all.

PSALM XLV. Metre 1.

MY ſtudious heart contemplating,
  good matter doth indite;
Touching the King I made a thing,
  which here I will recite,
My tongue is as a writer's pen,
  that writes with ſwifteſt ſpeed.
2 Much fairer than the Sons of Men,
  I ſay thou art indeed.
For grace is pour'd in plenteous ſtore
  into thy lips divine:
And God therefore for evermore
  hath bleſt thoſe lips of thine.
3 O gird thy Sword upon thy thigh,
  thou that excell'ſt in might;
Appear in thy great majeſty,
  and in thy glory bright.
4 And ride on in thy majeſty,
  with proſperous ſucceſs;
Becauſe of thy humility,
  thy truth and righteouſneſs.
And thy right hand, O mighty King,
  ſhall unto thee declare
Th' accompliſhing of many a thing
  moſt terrible and rare.
5 Thine arrows very ſharp ſhall be
  in all thy enemies hearts;
Subduing people under thee,
  ſore wounded with thy darts.

Psalm xlv.

6 O God, thou hast a lasting Throne,
  that nevermore decays:
And thy alone dominion
  a righteous Scepter sways.

7 Thy Soul loves truth, and lewdness hates,
  and God thy God therefore
Thee consecrates above thy mates,
  with Oyl of gladness store.

8 Of Cassia, Myrrhe and Aloes,
  do all thy garments smell;
Which out of these thy Palaces
  of Ivory please thee well.

9 Among thy noble female band
  Kings daughters were enroll'd:
At thy right hand the Queen did stand
  in purest Ophir-gold.

The Second part.

10 Hearken, O daughter, bow thine ear,
  consider and incline:
Forget what were thy people there,
  that fathers house of thine.

11 So shall the King desire to see
  thy beauty then much more:
For only he thy Lord shall be,
  whom thou must needs adore.

12 And there shall *Tyrus* daughter be,
  and many rich and great;
Presenting thee with gifts most free,
  thy favour to intreat.

13 The daughter of this Royal Line,
  within for to behold,
Doth with divine perfection shine,
  her cloathing's all wrought gold.

14 Be brought unto the King shall she
  in needle-work array'd:
And unto thee her Train shall be,
  and Virgin-mates convey'd.

15 With nuptial joys and festival
   they shall these Virgins bring;
Where met, they shall have entrance all,
   i'th' Pallace of the King.

16 In fathers stead thou shalt have sons,
   by new and heavenly birth:
And make those sons most mighty ones,
   and chief in all the Earth.

17 To ages all I'le keep in store
   the memory of thy Name:
Thy praise therefore for evermore
   shall all the Earth proclaim.

PSALM XLV. Metre 2.
To the proper Tune.

MY heart indites good things,
   To praise the King of Kings:
More swiftly than the writer's pen
   my tongue his praises sings.
O fair'st of humane race,
Thy lips are full of grace:
Therefore the Lord has blest thy word
   for ever to take place.

Thy Sword gird on thy thigh,
O mighty and most high;
Wear thou the Crown of bright renown,
   and ride on prosperously.
Truth, meekness, justice springs
From thee, O King of Kings;
And thy right hand shall understand
   to teach thee terrible things.

Full sharp shall be thy darts
In the Kings enemies hearts,
Whereby the people under thee
   fall by their own deserts.
Thy Throne, O God, abides,
Thy Rule a Scepter guides
Most exquisite, for thou lov'st right,
   and hatest all besides.

                                      And

And God thy God therefore
Anoints thee in such store
With Oyl of joy, like Saints on high,
   but infinitely more.
With all perfections clad
Thy gifts from Heaven had,
Like Cassia, Myrrh, and Aloes are,
   whereby to make thee glad.

Kings Daughters appertain
To thy most noble Train,
At thy right hand the Queen doth stand,
   deckt in her Ophir Chain.

The Second part.

Hearken, O Daughter dear,
Consider, and give ear;
Forget thy land, thy people, and
   thy fathers house most dear.
So shall thy beauty fair
Affect the King for care;
Since he's thy Lord to be ador'd,
   and that must be thy care.

And Tyrian Converts too
Shall bring their gifts to you;
The rich among the populous throng
   shall for thy friendship sue.
The Daughter of the King
Within all glittering,
You may behold in Cloth of Gold
   of God's embroydering.

The King shall have her brought
In Robes with needle wrought;
Her Fellow-Vir-gins following her,
   shall all to thee be brought.
With mirth shall they resort,
And in triumphant sort,
With joys enough be led into
   the King's Cœlestial Court.

Thou shalt have Sons brought forth
By new and heavenly birth,
To sit in seat of Princes great,
   and rule o're all the Earth.
And I will leave thy Name
For ages to proclaim;
Therefore shall people honour thee
   with everlasting fame.

PSALM XLVI. *Metre* 1.

God is our hope on whom we wait,
   our strength and refuge near,
A present help in every strait:
2 Therefore we will not fear;
No though the Earth should be displac't,
   and though the Mountains steep
Into the very Sea be cast,
   and buried in the deep.

3 Yea, though the Sea great noise doth make,
   and restless roars and raves;
And though the very mountains shake,
   with swelling of her waves.
4 There is a River flows apace,
   and maketh glad thereby
The City of God, the holy place,
   and Tents of the most high.

5 The Lord is in the midst of her;
   be mov'd she never may:
The Lord shall help her, and confer
   that help by break of day.
6 The Heathen raged furiously,
   the Kingdoms moved were:
His voice he uttered from on high,
   the Earth did melt for fear.

7 The Lord of hosts of *Israel*
   is evermore with his:
And lo, our tower impregnable
   the God of *Jacob* is.

Pſalm xlvj.

The Second part.

8 Come ſee, and ponder in your thought
 the works of God's own hand:
What deſolations he hath wrought
 in ſight of all the land.
9 He ceaſeth wars now every where,
 which Kingdoms did conſpire:
He breaks the bow, he cuts the ſpear,
 the chariot burns with fire.
10 Be ſtill, and underſtand, ſaith he,
 that I am God alone:
Among the heathen I will be
 the high exalted one:
On Earth I will be magnifi'd,
 in all my might and power.
11 The Lord of hoſts is on our ſide,
 and *Jacob*'s God our tower.

PSALM XLVI. *Metre 2.*

GOd is our ſtrength and ſtay
 when dangers do ſurround,
A preſent help alway,
 and ready to be found:
 Therefore we ſhall
Not be afraid though th' Earth be made
 to flit or fall.

And though the mountains high
 were carryed from the ſhore,
In deepeſt Seas to lie,
 and troubled waters roar:
 And though it make
The billows riſe with horrid noiſe,
 and mountains ſhake.

For there's a River here,
 whoſe ſtreams do flow abroad,
And ſhall moſt ſweetly cheer,
 and glad the City of God.

The holy Hill,
Where the moſt high in majeſty
abideth ſtill.

Within the midſt of her
doth God himſelf abide,
Her ſure deliverer,
ſo that ſhe ſhall not ſlide:
For God, I ſay,
Will bring her aid e're be diſplay'd
the break of day.

The Heathen rag'd with noiſe,
the Kingdoms moved were;
Then God put forth his voice,
the Earth did melt for fear:
This God of power
Hath here abode, and *Jacob's* God
is our high Tower.

The Second part.

O come behold and ſee
what works the Lord brings forth,
What deſolations he
hath wrought in all the Earth:
Whoſe mighty hand
Makes wars to ceaſe, and ſettles peace
in all the Land.

He breaks the ſpear and bow,
and quite cuts off the ſame;
The charet he doth throw
into the burning flame:
Be ſtill, ſaith he,
And know that I am God moſt high,
and known will be.

I will be magnifi'd
in all the Heathen Coaſts,
And all the Earth ſo wide
of me ſhall make their boaſts:
This God of power
Hath here abode, and *Jacob's* God
is our high Tower.

PSAL

PSALM XLVII. Metre I.

YE people all, with one accord
    clap hands and joyn in joys:
Shout ye, and sing unto the Lord
    with most triumphant noise.
2 For he's a high and dreadful one,
    to be ador'd with fear;
A mighty King with stately Throne,
    exalted far and near.
3 For us shall this Almighty King
    subdue the Heathen Lands;
And people in subjection bring
    to *Israel's* commands.
4 Our heritage where we must dwell,
    shall he select alone:
A glorious lot for *Israel*,
    his well-beloved one.
5 God is ascended up on high
    with shouts which shake the ground:
The Lord is gone up gloriously
    with trumpets chearful sound.
6 Sing praise to God, sing praise with mirth,
    sing praises to our King;
7 For God is King of all the Earth;
    all skilful praises sing.
8 God reigneth universally
    over the Heathen Lands:
Sits on his Throne of sanctity,
    and all the Earth commands.
9 The Princes of the Lands abroad
    do all of them flock hither:
All people serving *Abraham's* God,
    they and their Kings together.
For lo, the shields of all the Earth
    belong to God most high:
He is exalted and set forth
    exceeding gloriously.

PSALM XLVII. *Metre* 2.
Give Laud, &c.

1 Let all in sweet accord,
    clap-hands and voices raise
In honour of the Lord,
    and loudly sing his praise.
2   For God most high
Is King of Kings, and rules all things
    with majesty.

3 Whole nations of our foes
    he throws beneath our feet.
4 A happy lot he chose
    for us as he thought meet:
    The dignity
Of *Israel*, belov'd so well.
    by the most High.

5 God is gone up on high
    with shouts and trumpets sound,
Ascending gloriously.
6 O let him be renown'd;
    His praises sing,
And loudly raise your voice to praise
    our Heavenly King.

7 For God is Sovereign King,
    and Lord of all the Earth:
With understanding sing,
    and set his praises forth.
8   God reigns alone
O're Heathen men, sitting upon
    his holy Throne.

9 The Princes gather there,
    the Princes of all Lands:
And people far and near,
    whom *Abraham's* God commands,
    The shields are his;
Throughout the Earth of so great worth
    Jehovah is.

PSALM. XLVIII.

Great is the Lord, his praise no less,
  for so must we record
Here in his hill of holiness,
  and City of our Lord.
2 Mount *Sion* is a beauteous thing,
  the whole Earth's joy and pride:
The City of the mighty King
  is on her northern side.
3 The Lord within her Pallace there
  is known a refuge nigh:
4 For lo, the Kings assembled were,
  together they past by.
5 They saw it and they marvelled,
  for there they durst not stay;
But troubled and astonished,
  they made great hast away.
6 Great terror there fell on our foes,
  and grievous pangs of pain,
And sharp as women in their throws
  at any time sustain.
7 And as a furious eastern wind
  puts *Tarsbian* ships to wrack:
Such furious force our foes did find,
  when thy hand drove them back.

The Second part.

8 Now have we seen what we have heard
  recorded in our coasts,
Touching the City of the Lord,
  the Sovereign Lord of Hosts.
The City of our God, to wit,
  where this was testifi'd,
That God himself will stablish it,
  for ever to abide.
9 And these thy sure compassions, Lord,
  thy kindness and thy grace,

Most quietly did we record
within thy holy place;
10 For like thy name so is thy praise,
as far as land extends:
And store of righteousness always
thy right-hand comprehends.
11 Therefore let *Sion* plenteously
of heavenly joys partake:
And *Judah's* daughters leap for joy,
for thy just judgments sake.
12 Walk forth, and compass *Sion* mount,
and round about her go:
Her stately towers distinctly count,
and all their numbers know.
13 Mark ye her bulwarks very well,
her Pallaces regard:
That ye may certifie and tell
the ages afterward.
14 For this God doth and will abide
our God to our last breath:
For ever he will be our guide,
and our support till death.

PSALM XLIX.

All dwellers here on earth give ear,
   all people hearken hither:
2 All generally both low and high,
both rich and poor together.
3 My mouth behold shall now unfold,
and wisdom shall relate:
Yea, and my heart and inward part
shall knowledge meditate.
4 I will incline this ear of mine
a parable to hear:
And open my deep mystery
upon my harp most clear.
5 Why should the day of grief dismay,
and make me fear and doubt,

When

Psalm xlix.

When steps of my iniquity
shall compass me about.

5 Concerning those that trust repose
in wealth and worldly store,
And make their brags of heaped bags
replenisht more and more.
7 There's not a man of them that can
his brothers Soul redeem,
Nor for him may a ransome pay
sufficient in esteem:
8 (For that's of too great price to do,
and so must cease for ever.)
9 That always he alive should be,
and see corruption never.
10 He doth perceive all die, and leave
to others their estate :
The fool, the wise, the brutish dies,
for death's the common gate.

The Second part.

11 Their very heart and inward part
this thought doth entertain :
To wit, that all their houses shall
for evermore remain.
Their dwelling place from race to race,
as they conceive, shall stand :
They call the same by their own name,
to wit their house and land.

12 Nevertheless if man possess
great honour for a day,
'Tis quickly ceast, and like the beast
he perisheth straightway.
13 This way of theirs plainly appears,
a foolish way and weak:
Yet are they by posterity
approv'd in all they speak.
14 Like sheep in fold the grave shall hold
and death shall them devour:

And over them shall upright men
    at morning have the power.
And in the grave their beauty brave
    shall quite consume away,
And perish from their ancient home,
    which also shall decay.
15 But God will sure my Soul secure,
    when I this world shall leave:
On me the grave no power shall have,
    for God will me receive.
16 Be not afraid when one is made
    exceeding rich and great:
When some great name augments the fame
    of his fair dwelling seat.
17 Who once by death depriv'd of breath,
    shall no possessions have:
His pomp shall end, and not descend
    with him into the grave.
18 Though till he dy'd he magnifi'd
    his Soul for worldly pelf:
And worldly men will praise thee then,
    when thou befriend'st thy self.
19 But he shall go to them below,
    unto his fathers old:
And take his place with their vile race,
    and never light behold.
20 Man being high in dignity,
    yet understanding not,
In his decease is like the beasts
    which quickly die and rot.

P S A L M L. *Metre* 1.

THe mighty God, the Lord spake out,
    and gave the Earth a call,
From Suns up-rise, and round about
    to his far-distant fall.
2 From *Sion* beauties fairest fair
    hath God in glory shin'd.

3 Our God shall come, and shall not spare
   to utter all his mind.
 A flame of fire devouring quick
   shall go before his face:
 Tempestuous storms shall gather thick
   about his judgment-place.
4 He to the Heavens from on high,
   and to the Earth shall call;
 Gathering his people generally,
   that he may judge them all.
5 Gather to me my Saints, saith he,
   bring those before mine eyes,
 That have a covenant made with me
   by solemn sacrifice.
6 And then the Heavens shall record
   and make his justice known;
 Because that God, the righteous Lord,
   is Judge himself alone.
7 Hear, O my people, what I tell,
   and what I testifie
 To thy reproof, O *Israel*:
   God even thy God am I.
8 I will not say that thou didst sin
   for want of sacrifice:
 Thy burnt oblations still have bin
   renew'd before mine eyes.
9 No bullock will I take at all
   out of thy house to me;
 Nor any he-goat from thy stall,
   my sacrifice to be.
10 For mine alone are all the beasts
   wherewith the forrest fills:
 And all the cattel and increase
   upon a thousand hills.
11 What ever fowls the mountains yield,
   are all to me well known:
 And all wild beasts throughout the field,
   they also are mine own.

12 If any hunger I sustain'd,
   I would not tell it thee:
 The world and all therein contain'd
   belongeth unto me.

13 Will I desire to eat the flesh
   of strong bulls, dost thou think?
 Or will it God himself refresh,
   the blood of goats to drink?
14 Offer to God in sacrifice
   thanksgiving chearfully:
 And see thou pay thy vows likewise
   unto the Lord most high.

15 And then with courage call on me
   in any dangerous days;
 And I will sure deliver thee,
   and thou shalt give me praise.
16 But to the wicked, saith the Lord,
   what hast thou, wretch, to do
 To teach the Statutes of my word,
   or what belongs thereto?
 Why should thy wicked mouth relate
   what these my covenants be?
17 Seeing thou dost instruction hate,
   and cast my words from thee.
18 When thou a wicked thief hast seen,
   thou joynedst with him then:
 And a partaker thou hast been
   with the adulterous men.

19 Thou giv'st thy mouth the liberty,
   to utter all that's vile:
 Thy tongue is skill'd in treachery,
   to frame deceit and guile.
20 Thou sittest in the scorners chair,
   and speak'st against thy brother:
 Thou slanderest and dost not spare
   the son of thine own mother.

21 These

21 These wickednesses thou hast wrought,
   at which, though I did see,
I held my peace, and thou hast thought
   that I was just like thee.
But know, I will reprove thee yet
   for thy iniquities:
Thy sins in order I will set,
   most plain before thine eyes.

22 Now understand and think on this,
   ye that forget the Lord;
Lest I should tear you piece by piece,
   when none can help afford.
23 Who offers praise he honours me;
   and whoso walks aright,
Him will I surely cause to see
   God's saving health and might.

PSALM L. *Metre* 2.
To the proper Tune.

THe mighty God the Lord hath summon'd al',
   And call'd the Earth from Sun-rise to the fall.
From *Sion*'s perfect beauty God hath shin'd,
   Our God shall come, and not conceal his mind;
Before his face shall go a fire devouring,
And mighty Tempests round about him pouring.

Then shall he call to Heaven from on high,
And to the Earth his peoples cause to try,
   Gather my Saints at once before mine eyes,
   That are ingag'd with me by sacrifice:
And for his righteousness the Heavens shall shew it,
For God is Judge himself, he comes to do it.

Hear, O my people, I will testifie
Against thee *Israel*, God thy God am I,
   I will not blame thy want of Sacrifice,
   Or thy Burnt offerings still to cloy mine eyes:
No bullock from thy house do I desire,
Nor yet he-goats out of thy folds require.

For all the beasts which forrests do confine,
And cattle on a thousand hills are mine:
  I know the fowls which all the mountains yield,
  And mine are all the wild beasts of the field:
I would not tell it thee if I were empty,
For all the world is mine, and all its plenty.

The Second part.

Will I eat flesh of bulls, or dost thou think
That I desire the blood of goats to drink?
  Offer to God thanksgiving cheerfully,
  And pay thy vows to him that is most high;
Then in thy trouble call on me, and try me,
I'le be thy help, and thou shalt glorifie me.

But thus saith God to them that wicked are,
What right hast thou my Statutes to declare?
  Why shouldst thou take my covenant in thy mouth
  Who hat'st instruction, and contemn'st my truth?
Thou seest a thief, and with him thou consentest,
And with unclean adulterers thou wentest.

Thou giv'st thy mouth to evil, and thy tongue
Frameth deceit to do thy neighbour wrong:
  Thou sit'st and let'st thy slanderous speeches run
  Against thy brother thine own mothers Son:
These things thou didst, and I was silent at it,
Thou thoughtst me like thy self, and had forgat it.

But I'le reprove thee for thy thoughts so light,
And set thy sins in order in thy sight:
  Now think on this ye that forget God here,
  Lest I should tear you, when no helper's near.
Praise honours me, and upright Conversation,
Which whoso practise shall see God's salvation.

PSALM LI. *Metre* 1.

O Lord, consider my distress,
  and now with speed some pity take;
Blot out my grievous wickedness,
  good Lord, for thy great mercies sake;

2 Wash me, O wash me thoroughly,
  and purifie my heart within:
Wipe off my foul iniquity,
  and cleanse me fully from my sin.
3 For I acknowledge my offence,
  and my transgressions I confess:
And daily have a deeper sense
  of my most hainous wickedness.
4 Thee, thee alone I have contemn'd,
  committing evil in thy sight:
And if I were therefore condemn'd,
  yet were thy judgments just and right.
5 Behold, O Lord, for thou dost know
  that I receiv'd my shape in sin:
My mother hath conceiv'd me so,
  and I was bred and born therein.
6 Also behold, Lord, thou dost love
  the inward truth of upright hearts:
And wisdom coming from above,
  thou wrotest in my inward parts.

The Second part.

7 Purge me with hyssop, O my God,
  and then I shall be clean I know:
O wash me in my Saviour's blood,
  and I shall be more white than snow.
8 Make me to hear amidst my moans,
  the sweet and comfortable voice
Of joy and gladness, that the bones
  which thou hast broken may rejoyce.
9 Take all my sins clean off record,
  and hide them ever from thy view.
10 Create a clean heart in me, Lord,
  and a right spirit in me renew.
11 O cast me not away from thee,
  where I shall never see thy face:
Nor do thou take away from me
  thy sweet and sacred spirit of grace,

12 Restore to me those joys again,
   which I was wont in thee to find:
And thy sweet spirit let me retain,
   for to uphold my heart and mind.
13 And then shall sinners learn thy way,
   for they shall all be taught of me:
And such as now do go astray,
   shall be converted unto thee.

The Third part.

14 Deliver me, O God, from blood,
   O God of my salvation dear:
And then my tongue shall sing aloud,
   and make thy righteousness appear.
15 Then open thou my lips, O Lord,
   O thou that keepest *David*'s keys:
Then shall my busie tongue record,
   and shew forth thy most worthy praise.
16 For thou desir'st not sacrifice,
   nor is burnt-offering thy delight:
For were they valu'd in thine eyes,
   I would have set them in thy sight.
17 A wounded soul that feels its smart,
   is God's approved sacrifice:
A broken and a contrite heart,
   O God, thou never wilt despise.
18 Now, Lord, do good in thy good will
   to *Sion* and *Jerusalem*:
Build *Salem*'s walls, bless *Sion* hill,
   of thy good pleasure unto them.
19 Burnt-offerings then thou shalt accept,
   and whole burnt-offerings shall be paid,
In righteousness observ'd and kept,
   and bullocks on thy altar laid.

PSALM LI. *Metre* 2.

1 HAve mercy, Lord, and pity take
   on me in my distress:

For

Psalm lj.

For thine abundant mercy fake,
  blot out my wickedness.
2 O wash me clean from filthiness,
  and separate sin from me:
3 For my transgressions I confess,
  my sin I always see.

4 Against thee, Lord, and only thee,
  did I my sins commit:
That when thou speak'st and judgest me,
  thou mayest be clear and quit.
I did this evil in thy sight;
  wherefore, O Lord, thou shalt
Be said to pass thy judgment right,
  and I in all the fault.

5 My shape in sin, Lord, thou dost see,
  for I am form'd therein:
My mother hath conceived me
  in guiltiness and sin.
6 Lo, thou requirest truth sincere
  in every inward part:
Thou mak'st me know thy wisdom there,
  in secret of my heart.

7 Purge me with hyssop, and I know
  I shall be clean and free;
And whiter than the driven snow,
  if also washt by thee.
8 O then let joy and gladness speak,
  and make me hear their voice:
That so the bones which thou didst break,
  may feelingly rejoyce.

The Second part.

9 Lord, hide thine eyes from all my sin,
  and my misdeeds deface:
10 O God, make clean my heart within,
  renew my mind with grace.
11 O cast me not away from thee,
  thy presence shunning mine:

    Nor ever take away from me
      that holy spirit of thine.
12 The joys of thy salvation, Lord,
    restore to me again:
And thy free spirit to me afford,
    my Soul for to sustain.
13 And to transgressors I will teach
    thy ways, to penitent men:
And sinners, unto whom I preach,
    shall be converted then.
14 From guilt of blood acquit me, Lord,
    thou God and Saviour mine:
Then shall my song aloud record
    thy righteousness divine.
15 Unlock my lips, and then my task
    shall be thy praise to show.
16 For sacrifice thou dost not ask,
    which else I would bestow.
Burnt-offering is not thy delight,
    but other sacrifice.
17 A broken heart, a soul contrite
    thou wilt not, Lord, despise.
18 Now then, O Lord, of thy good grace
    do good to *Sion* hill:
Build up *Jerusalem*'s walls apace,
    and dwell among us still.

19 Then will we offer sacrifice
    of righteousness to thee:
And acceptable in thine eyes
    shall all our offerings be.
Yea, whole burnt-offerings and entire,
    in sacrifice shall they,
With bullocks fit for holy fire.
    upon thine Altars lay.

PSALM LII. *Metre 1.*

WHy boastest thou, O mighty man,
   thy mischiefs to fulfill?
For do thy malice what it can,
   God's mercy lasteth still.
2 Thy tongue deviseth villany,
   and wickedness unseen;
And working most deceitfully,
   is like a rasor keen.
3 Thou set'st thy mind (so void of grace)
   on evil more than good:
And rather would'st have lies take place,
   than truth be understood.
4 Thou lov'st all words that do devour,
   O subtle tongue and sly:
5 Likewise shall God by his great power
   destroy thee utterly.
Yea, from thy dwelling, O false tongue,
   the Lord's revenging hand
Shall take, and root thee from among
   the living in the land.
6 The just with fear shall plainly see,
   God's judgment in thy fall:
And for thy folly thou shalt be
   a laughing stock to all.
7 Behold the man that would not take
   the Lord for his defence:
But of his goods his God did make,
   and sin his confidence.
8 But I like a green olive-tree,
   in God's house shall have place:
And evermore my trust shall be
   in God's assured grace.
9 And since thy hand hath wrought all this,
   I'le spread thy praise, O God,
And wait upon thy Name, that is
   to all thy Saints so good.

PSALM LII. *Metre 2.*

1 WHy glorieſt thou in miſchief now,
    O man of mighty power?
God's goodneſs will continue ſtill,
    even every day and hour.
2 Thy tongue is ſtill deviſing ill,
    and miſchief comes thereby;
Yea it hath been a raſour keen,
    working deceitfully.
3 Thy wicked mind is more enclin'd
    to evil than to good:
And righteouſneſs thou loveſt leſs
    than lies to be purſu'd.
4 Deceitful tongue, thou lov'd all wrong,
    and words that do devour.
5 God ſhall therefore for evermore
    deſtroy thee by his power.

He ſhall I ſay take thee away
    out of thy dwelling place;
And pluck thee out even by the root,
    from all the living race.
6 The righteous there ſhall ſee, and fear,
    and laugh at him, and ſay,
7 Lo, this is he that could not ſee
    to make the Lord his ſtay.

But for defence put confidence
    in heaps of worldly pelf:
And in the ſin he lived in
    encouraged himſelf.
8 But like a green freſh olive ſeen
    within God's houſe am I:
And in the grace of God will place
    my truſt perpetually.
9 And I always will give thee praiſe,
    becauſe thou didſt all this:
And wait upon thy name alone,
    ſo good to Saints it is.

PSALM LIII. *Metre* 1.

THere is no God, the fool doth say,
  at least his heart saith so:
Corrupt are they, and vile their way,
  and all good works forgoe.
2 The Sons of Men th' Almighty view'd
  from Heaven, to descry
If any of them understood,
  and sought God faithfully.

3 Corrupt is all the multitude,
  they all are backward gone;
Not one of them doth any good,
  no verily not one.
4 Are all so brutishly misled,
  that wicked paths have trod?
They eat my people like to bread,
  they have not call'd on God.

5 But lo, they were affrighted sore,
  and mightily dismaid:
Although there was no cause wherefore
  to make them so afraid.
For all thy strong besiegers bones
  the Lord dispersi abroad:
And thou hast shain'd those wicked ones,
  because despis'd of God.

6 O that the sweet salvation then
  which *Israel* waits for still,
Were fully come to all good men
  from out of *Sion* hill.
For surely when the Lord sets free
  his captives now so sad:
Then *Jacob* shall most joyful be,
  and *Israel* shall be glad.

PSALM LIII. Metre 2.
Give Laud, &c.

The fool hath said in heart
   there is not any God;
They are in every part
   corrupt, and none doth good;
     Such atheism lurks
In every one that they have done
     most odious works.

The Lord from Heaven high
   look'd down on Earth below
On man's posterity,
   that he might see and know
     what paths men trod,
If any man did understand
     and seek for God.

But all were gone astray,
   even every mothers child;
All wand'red from the way,
   and filthily defil'd.
     So that they can
No good thing do, nor move thereto,
     no not a man.

Is all their knowledge gone
   that work iniquity?
They have not call'd upon
   the Lord that is most high:
     But they devour
My flock like bread, and on them fed
     with Tyrant-power.

They were in fear and dread,
   where was no cause of fear;
For God hath scattered
   their quarters here and there,
     That have encamp'd
Against our cause, and hence it was
     they were so damp'd

Lo, thou hast put to shame
 thy hateful enemies,
In God's Almighty Name,
 that did thy foes despise.
  And O that still
Salvation fell to *Israel*
 from *Sion* hill.

When as the Lord shall please
 to bring our bondage back,
And gives his folk the ease,
 and liberty they lack:
  Glad news shall we
In *Jacob* tell, and *Israel*
 full glad shall be.

PSALM LIV. *Metre* 1.

SAve me, O God, by thy great Name,
 and judge me by thy strength.
2 Attend my prayer, receive the same,
 and hear my words at length.
3 For strangers do against me rise,
 oppressors seek my blood:
And do not set before their eyes
 the fear of thee, O God.
4 Lo, God's my help, and stands with those
 that do uphold my heart.
5 He shall reward my envious foes
 according to desert.
Destroy them in thy righteousness:
 And freely I'le accord
With sacrifice thy name to bless,
 for it is good, O Lord.
7 For now hath God delivered me
 from all perplexing woes;
And let mine eye most plainly see
 his will upon my foes.

PSALM LIV. Metre 2.

Where righteousness, &c.

Lord save me by thy Name,
   and judge me by thy might,
O hear the prayer I frame,
   the words which I recite;
For strangers do arise,
   oppressors all agree
My Soul for to surprize,
   without regard of thee.

But thou art still my aid,
   the Lord will stand with those
By whom my Soul is stay'd
   against assaulting foes.
He shall repay my foe
   the evil that he doth,
Confound and overthrow
   those sinners in thy truth.

Then will I sacrifice
   most freely unto thee,
And praise thy name likewise,
   which is so good to me:
Though grief do me infold,
   he help'd me out of all;
And lets mine eyes behold
   my foes expected fall.

PSALM LV.

Vouchsafe O God my prayer to hear,
   and do not hide thy face:
But unto my request give ear,
   now suing for thy grace.
2 Attend unto me graciously,
   and hear my doleful cries:
I mourn in sense of misery,
   and make a troubled noise.

3 Because my enemies voice grows high,
   because lewd men oppress:

They cast on me iniquity
  in wrath and spitefulness.
My heart within me laboureth
  of pain that makes me sick:
The terrors of untimely death
  are fall'n upon me thick.

Trembling and fearfulness do fall
  on me in every part;
And horror coming therewithal,
  hath overwhelm'd my heart.
Oh that I had the faculty
  of flying like a dove:
Then would I fly away, said I,
  and to some rest remove.

Lo then I'd wander wide, and stay
  in desarts far to find,
And hasten my escape away
  from tempest, storm and wind.

The Second part.

Destroy, O Lord, do thou divide
  and separate their tongues:
For I have in the city spi'd
  strife, violence and wrongs.
o Both day and night they go about
  upon the city wall:
Mischief and sorrow both break out
  within the midst of all.

1 There is abundant wickedness
  within her very heart:
And from her streets, deceitfulness
  and guile do not depart.
2 For it was not an enemy
  that us'd me with such scorn;
For then I could more easily
  the injury have born.

Nor was it he that hated me,
  that lift his horn so high;

> For then I would have hidden me
> where he should not espie.
> 13 But it was thou, a man, that hast
> thy self so magnifi'd;
> Though my acquaintance once thou wast,
> my equal and my guide.
> 14 We did consult with sweet content,
> in most familiar kind:
> And to the house of God we went,
> in company combin'd.

The Third part.

> 15 Let death seize on them speedily,
> and send them quick to hell;
> For there is all iniquity
> among them where they dwell.
> 16 But as for me, my care shall be
> upon my God to call:
> And then shall he give ear to me,
> and send me aid withal.
> 17 Evening and morning and at noon
> I'le pray and cry aloud;
> And doubt not to be heard as soon,
> his ear's so easily bow'd.
> 18 He hath preserv'd my soul in peace,
> from battel in array;
> For there was found a great increase
> of strength with me that day.
> 19 My God shall hear and punish them,
> he that of old abides:
> But God's not fear'd of wicked men,
> because no change betides.
> 20 He hath put forth his treacherous hands
> against his peaceful friends;
> And broke his covenants solemn bands,
> to serve his wicked ends.
> 21 While he gave forth smooth butter'd words,
> his heart was bent to spoil;

And though his words were naked swords,
 they seem'd more soft than oyl.
22 Cast on the Lord thy burthen then,
 he shall thy Soul sustain:
For he will not let righteous men
 be mov'd, but still remain.

23 But they shall all be overthrown
 that wickedness commit:
For thou, O God, wilt bring them down
 into destructions pit.
To bloody and deceitful ways
 they that addicted be,
Shall not continue half their days;
 but I will trust in thee.

PSALM LVI. *Metre* 1.

Have mercy, Lord, on me,
 whom man would make a prey:
Behold how he oppresseth me,
 contending every day.
2 They that mine enemies be,
 would daily me devour;
For many fight against my right,
 O thou of highest power.
3 What time soever, Lord,
 I am of foes afraid,
Lo then will I trust faithfully
 in thy assured aid.
4 In God I'le praise his word,
 in God my trust shall be:
And fixed there I will not fear
 what flesh can do to me.
5 My words they utter wrong,
 and wrest them every day:
Their thoughts are still to work me ill,
 in every kind of way.
6 They all together throng,
 they hide themselves likewise:

My steps they watch, and lye at catch
    my Soul for to surprize.
7 Shall they escape so well
    in this their wicked path?
  Upon them frown, and, Lord, cast down
    this people in thy wrath.
8 Thou dost my wand'rings tell;
    let down thy bottle, Lord,
  And put in there each briny tear;
    are they not on record?
9 When I shall cry to thee,
    it puts to sudden flight
  My daunted foe, and this I know,
    for God defends my right.
10 In God enabling me,
    his word will I proclaim:
  Yea, in the Lord will I record
    his words due praise and fame.
11 In God alone have I
    repos'd my trust for aid:
  Let mortal man do what he can,
    I will not be afraid.
12 Thy vows upon me lie,
    Lord, I must pay the same:
  And I always will render praise
    unto thy holy Name.
13 For thou my Soul hast freed
    from death so near at hand;
  And wilt not thou uphold me now,
    and make my feet to stand?
  That I may still proceed
    to walk as in thy sight;
  And spend my days unto thy praise,
    with them that live in light.

PSALM

PSALM LVI. *Metre* 2.
All People, &c.

BE merciful, O God, to me;
Man would devour me but for thee;
  He daily doth against me fight
  By power to oppress my right.
My watchful enemies each hour
My life assail, and would devour:
  O thou most high, many there are
  That have conspired in this war.

Yet though encompast and afraid,
I fly for shelter to thy aid;
  For trusting to God's Word and Arm,
  I know no flesh can do me harm.
My words and meaning still they wrest,
Plotting close mischief in their brest:
  They joyn themselves; my steps they mark
  To overthrow me in the dark.

Shall they escape by wickedness?
This wicked people, Lord, suppress;
  In angry wrath upon them frown,
  See how they hunt me up and down.
O bottle up my tears, and look,
Are they not written in thy book?
  So soon then as to thee I cry,
  I know my foes shall faint and fly.

God's Word I praise and trust thereto,
Fearless I am what man can do;
  To thee, O Lord, I'le pay my vows,
  My knee in adoration bows:
For thou hast kept me from the grave,
My feet from falling thou didst save,
  That with the living in thy sight
  I may enjoy the cheerful light.

PSALM LVII.

BE merciful to me, O Lord,
   be merciful to me;
Because my Soul believes thy word,
   and puts her trust in thee.
Yea, to the shadow of thy wings
   I will for refuge fly,
Until these lamentable things
   shall quietly pass by.

2 I'le cry to God with earnest breath,
   even unto God most high;
Who faithfully accomplisheth
   all things for my supply.

3 And he from Heaven above shall send,
   and save me (by his power)
And me from his reproach defend,
   that would my Soul devour.

God shall send forth his truth and grace:
4   Though now my Soul doth dwell,
And lodge among a wicked race,
   set all on fire of hell.
Degenerate sons of-men I mean,
   whose malice being stirr'd,
Their teeth are spears and arrows keen,
   their tongue a sharp'ned sword.

The Second part.

5 Be thou exalted, O great God,
   above the Starry Skie:
And far above the earth abroad
   thy glory set on high.

6 My enemies have prepar'd a net,
   my steps to overthrow:
My Soul for which the same was set,
   is bow'd down very low.

And they have also digg'd a pit
   before me in the way:

But

But falling in the midst of it,
  themselves are made the prey.
7 My heart is fixed stedfastly,
  my heart is fixt, O God:
And I will sing with melody,
  and spread thy praise abroad.

8 Awake my glory, up I say,
  my Harp and Lute awake;
And I will wake before the day,
  sweet melody to make.
9 Thy praise, O Lord, will I set forth,
  where throngs of people be:
Among the nations of the earth
  will I sing praise to thee.
10 Because thy mercy doth ascend
  unto the Heavens high;
Thy truth as largely doth extend
  unto the cloudy Skie.
11 O God, let thy exalted Name
  above the Heavens stand:
Advance thy glory and thy fame
  above the Sea and Land.

PSALM LVIII. *Metre 1.*

O Congregation put in trust,
  and men of mortal seed,
Are all your judgments true and just?
  and are they so indeed?
2 Nay, in your hearts ye do devise
  to bind the cruel bands:
And in the earth ye exercise
  the violence of your hands.
3 The wicked from the very womb
  have erred on this wise;
Into the world no sooner come,
  but go astray by lies.
4 Such as the serpent's poison is,
  such poison just is theirs:

And as the addar stoppeth his,
  just so they stop their ears.
5 For the deaf addar will not hear
  the charmer's charming voice;
But deaf to all his charms appear,
  though they were ne're so choice.
6 Lord, break their teeth within their mouth,
  the great teeth of the stout,
Of the fierce Lions in their youth,
  O Lord God break them out.
7 As weak as water let them be;
  and when he aims to shoot,
Let all his whole artillery
  drop broken at his foot.
8 As snails within the shell consume,
  so, Lord, consume them quite;
And like abortives from the womb,
  which never see the light.
9 Before the pots can feel the thorns,
  his fury shall let drive;
And with his whirlwinds angry storms
  take them away alive.
10 The just shall joy, it doth them good
  to see the vengeance then;
And he shall wash his feet in blood
  of the ungodly men.
11 So that a man shall boldly say,
  sure just men have reward;
Sure there's a God that doth repay,
  and justice doth regard.

PSALM LVIII. *Metre* 2.

All People, &c.

DO ye, O Congregation,
  do ye speak righteousness indeed?
O mortal Generation,
  do ye with uprightness proceed?

Yea,

Psalm lviij.

Yea, ye in heart work wickedness,
   ye greatly tyrannize on earth;
Prone are the wicked to digress,
   estranged from their very birth.

As soon as they be born they err,
   by wicked lies they go astray;
Such as a serpent hath in her,
   such poisonous ill breath have they.
Deaf, addar-like, that as she lies
   she stoppeth close her wilful ear,
That charm a charmer ne're so wise,
   his voice, be sure, she will not hear.

O let the eager tusk that hangs
   on each side of their mouth be burst;
Break out, O God, the cruel fangs
   of these young Lions, keen and curst.
Melt them as running waters flow,
   and when the tyrant mischief heeds,
And shoots his shafts from bended bow,
   let them become as broken reeds.

So let them pass away on earth,
   as squalid snails to slime do run;
Or as a womans timeless birth,
   that they may never see the Sun.
Before they feel your thorns to prick,
   the living Lord shall them disperse,
The dead and dry, the keen and quick,
   as with a whirlwind very fierce.

The just shall see the vengeance then,
   rejoycing the revenge to see,
And in the blood of wicked men
   (victorious) wash his feet shall he:
Sure righteous men reap Vertue's fruits,
   and all men shall acknowledge so;
Sure he is God that executes
   most righteous judgment here below.

PSALM LVIII. Metre 3.
Ye Children, &c.

DO ye speak righteousness indeed,
O ye that are of mortal seed,
  O Congregation speak ye right?
Yea, ye in heart work wickedness,
Your hands with violence oppress,
  the Earth can scarcely bear your weight.
They are estranged from the way,
And from the womb they go astray,
  no sooner born than speaking lies;
As serpents poison, such is theirs;
Deaf adder-like they stop their ears,
  and will not hear in any wise.

They will not hear the charmer's voice;
Although his charms are wise and choice,
  they will not hearken to a word;
Lord break their keen and cruel fangs,
The eager tooth, the tusk that hangs
  in these young Lions mouths, O Lord.
As waters let them melt away,
And as a stream that hath no stay,
  and let his aimed arrows fail:
And when he bends his bow to shoot,
Let them drop broken at his foot,
  and let them melt as doth a snail.

So let them pass away on earth,
As woman-kinds untimely birth,
  that they may never see the Sun;
Before the pots can feel the thorns
He'l blast them, as with whirlwind-storms,
  alive, and in his wrath begun.
The righteous shall rejoyce to see
Vengeance on those that wicked be,
  and he shall wash his feet in blood;
So that a man shall then confess,
Sure there's rewards for righteousness,
  sure there's a just earth-judging God.

PSALM LIX. Metre 1.

MY God, do thou deliver me
 from all mine enemies;
And save me from their tyranny,
 that do against me rise.
2 From workers of iniquity,
 in mercy set me free:
From all their bloody cruelty,
 my God, deliver me.

3 For lo, they lie in wait for me,
 the mighty do combine
Against me undeservedly,
 and for no fault of mine.
4 They run and do themselves prepare,
 when I no fault do make:
Awake to help me by thy care,
 and perfect notice take.

5 Most mighty God of *Israel*,
 awake to judge the earth:
Spare none that wilfully rebel,
 but pour thy vengeance forth.
6 Lo, they return at evening-tide,
 and as a hungry hound
They make a noise on every side,
 and range the City round.

7 Their mouths belch out great blasphemy,
 lo, in their lips are swords:
For who, say they, do stand so nigh,
 that he should hear our words?
8 But thou, O Lord, shalt laugh at them,
 and they shalt be despis'd;
For thou shalt scorn the heathen men,
 and all th' uncircumcis'd.

9 Because of his great strength and power,
 Lord, I will wait on thee:
For God is my defence and tower,
 to which I always flee.

10 The

10 The God from whom my mercy flows,
   shall me betimes prevent;
And let me see upon my foes
   my very hearts content.

The Second part.

11 Lord, bring them down, but slay them not,
   disperse them by thy power;
And let it never be forgot,
   O Lord our shield and tower.

12 For their vile words and blasphemies,
   O trap them in their pride;
And for the curses and the lies
   which from their lips do slide.

13 Consume in wrath, consume them quite,
   that they may apprehend
Thou rul'st in *Jacob* by thy might,
   to th' earths remotest end.

14 Let them return at evening-tide,
   and like a hungry hound
Make a great noise on every side,
   and range the city round:

15 Wandring abroad with weary feet,
   seek up and down for meat;
And howl when they are hunger-bit,
   and have not what to eat.

16 But I with early diligence
   will sing aloud thy praise,
Who wast my refuge and defence,
   in all my dangerous days.

17 O thou my strength, I'le sing to thee,
   to praise thy love and power;
Who art a gracious God to me,
   my strong defence and tower.

PSALM LIX. *Metre 2.*

From all my cruel enemies,
   my God, deliver me;

From them that do against me rise,
   defend, and set me free.
And save me then from bloody men,
   and lewd men making strife:
For lo, they lie in secrecy
   to trap and take my life.

The mighty men with one accord,
   against me do combine;
Yet not for my transgression, Lord,
   nor any sin of mine.
They have begun, prepar'd to run
   in hast, without my fault:
Awake and see, and succour me
   against their fierce assault.

Thou therefore *Israel*'s righteous God,
   the Sovereign Lord of Hosts,
Awake and visit with thy rod,
   ev'n all the heathen Coasts.
And do not, Lord, thy grace afford,
   nor let them mercy find,
That do transgress by wickedness,
   with a malicious mind.

The Second part.

Let them return at evening-tide,
   as howling dogs are wont;
And round about on every side
   in every corner hunt.
Behold and see what blasphemy
   their belching mouths bewray;
Their lips have words as sharp as swords,
   for who shall see, say they?

But thou, O Lord, shalt laugh at them,
   and thou shalt entertain
Th' uncircumcised heathen men
   with laughter and disdain.
As for my foe that braves it so,
   with power and insolence;

On thee will I wait patiently,
  for God is my defence.

The Third part.

My gracious God shall me prevent
  with his compassions free,
And let me see my hearts content
  on enemies hating me:
Subvert them quite, and by thy might
  disperse, but slay them not:
O Lord our shield, some sign to yield,
  that may not be forgot.

For sinful words which mouths profain,
  and cursing lips let slide,
And for their lies, let them be ta'ne
  in height of all their pride.
Consume them Lord, as men abhorr'd,
  consume them quite and clean,
That every Land may understand
  great *Jacob*'s God to reign.

The Fourth part.

Let them return at evening-tide,
  as howling dogs are wont,
And round about on every side
  in every corner hunt.
Where wand'ring wide unsatisfy'd
  for meat, let them repine;
But lo, my tongue shall sing a song
  to praise thy power divine.

Yea in the morning I'le begin
  to sing aloud to thee;
And shew thy mercy which hath been
  a strong defence to me.
Thou wast my stay i'th dangerous day,
  to thee my strength I le sing;
God's my defence, and rock from whence
  my mercy hath her spring.

PSALM LX.

O God, thou didst us once forsake;
   and we were scattered then:
Such great displeasure thou didst take;
   O turn to us agen.
2 The earth sore broken with thy hand
   doth tremble, Lord, and quake:
O heal the breaches of our land,
   for it doth bow and shake.
3 Things that were hard and rigorous
   thou hast impos'd on thine:
And thou hast given drink to us
   of stupifying wine.
4 Yet gav'st thou them that feared thee
   the banner of thy aid,
Because of truth and verity,
   to be on high display'd.
5 Now, Lord, that thy beloved land
   delivered may be;
Save with the power of thy right hand,
   and hearken unto me.
6 In holiness Jehovah spake,
   my joy then shall not fail,
All *Shechem* to divide and take,
   and mete out *Succoth*'s Vale.
7 *Manasseh* must to me subscribe,
   and *Gilead* stand in awe:
My chiefest strength is *Ephraim*'s tribe,
   and *Judah* gives my Law.
8 On *Edom* I will set my foot,
   my wash-pot *Moab* shall be:
And thou, O *Palestina*, shout,
   and that because of me.
9 But who will lead me all the way
   unto the city strong?
And who will guide me, that I may
   to *Edom* go along?

10 Thou, Lord, that hadſt caſt off our coaſt,
  and thou, O God, even thou
That lately wentſt not with our hoſt;
  wilt thou not guide me now?
11 The help of man is vanity;
  Lord, help us in diſtreſs.
12 Through God we ſhall do valiantly,
  he ſhall our foes ſuppreſs.

PSALM LXI. Metre 1.

Regard, O Lord, when I complain,
  and make my ſuit to thee:
Let not my prayer aſcend in vain,
  but give good ear to me.
2 For from the earths remoteſt part
  I cry for ſome relief
To thee, O Lord, when as my heart
  is overwhelm'd with grief.

Conduct me to that rock of power,
  that higher is than I:
3 For thou waſt my ſafe hope and tower
  againſt the enemy.
4 And in thy tabernacle ſtill
  I gladly will abide;
Under thy ſecret wings I will
  continually confide.

5 The vows that did my ſoul engage,
  Lord, thou haſt heard the ſame:
And gav'ſt to me the heritage
  of thoſe that fear thy name.
6 To thine anointed thou didſt give
  prolonged days to ſee:
The many years that he ſhall live,
  like many an age ſhall be.
7 Before the Lord he ſhall abide,
  for ever to endure:
Thy truth and mercy O provide,
  which may preſerve him ſure.

8 So will I sing from day to day
    the praises of thy name:
That having vow'd, I daily may
    to thee perform the same.

PSALM LXI. *Metre* 2.

where righteousness, &c.

Lord hear my cry put forth,
    attend unto my prayer;
From th' ends of all the earth
    I now to thee repair.
My heart o're-whelm'd, I cry,
    O lead me to the rock,
That higher is than I,
    and can sustain the shock.

For thou hast been my fence,
    my shelter and my tower,
Against the violence
    of th' adversaries power.
Who drives me from thy tent,
    to wander far about,
(A kind of banishment
    unto a Soul devout.)

For fain would I abide
    within thy house for ever,
And so to have enjoy'd
    thy presence altogether.
And still I trust unto
    the shadow of thy wings,
That thou wilt bear me through
    my forest sufferings.

For thou, O God, hast heard
    my vows and my complaints,
And hast on me conferr'd
    the heritage of thy Saints.
The King's dear life defend,
    and thou, O Lord, engage

To make his time extend
  to many a joyful age.
Before thy blessed face
  he ever shall remain ;
Prepare thy truth and grace
  his Soul for to sustain.
So will I sing always,
  (as long as life allows)
Thy names deserved praise,
  and daily pay my vows.

PSALM LXII. *Metre* 1.

MY Soul with expectation
  depends on God indeed ;
Because my whole salvation
  doth still from him proceed.
2 He only is my rock of power,
  my saving health is he :
He is my high defence and tower,
  much mov'd I shall not be.
3 How long a time will ye devise,
  and labour what you can
To act mischievous villanies
  against an harmless man ?
Ye shall be sure of recompence,
  for God shall slay you all ;
Ye shall be like a tottering fence,
  and as a bowing wall.
4 His excellency to subvert
  they only do devise :
They bless with mouth, but curse in heart,
  and take delight in lies.
5 But thou, my Soul, still wait upon
  the high and holy one :
Because my expectation
  doth come from him alone.
6 He only is my rock of power,
  and my salvation prov'd :

He is my high defence and tower,
  I shall not once be mov'd.
7 In God is my salvation,
  and glorious dignity:
God is my strength and station,
  my rock and refuge nigh.
8 At all times trust in him alone,
  ye Saints, with one accord:
Pour out your hearts before his throne,
  our refuge is the Lord.
9 Sure mean men are but vanity,
  and great men are a lye;
Wholly more light than vanity,
  if them you weigh and try.
10 Trust not in wrong and injury,
  in robbery be not vain:
If wealth and riches multiply,
  set not your heart on gain.
11 Once God hath spoke, and made it known,
  and often have I heard,
That power belongs to God alone,
  and he must give reward.
12 And also that compassion
  belongs, O Lord, to thee:
And thou rewardest every one,
  just as his actions be.

PSALM LXII. Metre 2.
To the Tune of the old 121.

Truly my Soul doth wait on God,
  Because from him alone
Comes my salvation;
He only is my safe abode,
  My rock and refuge proved,
  I shall not much be moved.

How long will ye plot villany
  To make the righteous fall?
  Ye shall be slaughtered all;

Ye like a bowing wall shall be,
   And as a fence that totters,
   So perish all such plotters.

How to cast down the excellent,
   They only do devise;
   They take delight in lies;
They bless with mouth in complement,
   But inwardly are nursing
   Maliciousness and cursing.

My Soul wait thou on God alone,
   For from that hand of his
   My expectation is;
He only is my rock of stone,
   My health my refuge proved,
   I shall not once be moved.

The Second part.

In God is my salvation,
   He is to me a Crown
   Of honour and renown.
My rock, my strength, my station,
   And all my refuge ever
   Is God, that faileth never.

O trust in him, in him alone
   At all times evermore,
   Ye people rich and poor;
Pour out your hearts before his Throne,
   In all your fears and sorrows;
   God is a refuge for us.

Surely the men of low degree
   Are meerly vanity.
   And great men are a lye:
If in the ballance laid they be,
   Th' are lighter altogether
   Than vanity whatever.

Trust not in wrong and robbery,
   Think not a thought so vain,
   To thrive by ill-got gain;

Psalm lxiij.

If wealth and riches multiply,
  Yet do not so look on them
  To set your heart upon them.

God spake it once, yea twice I heard,
  That power belongs alone
  Unto the Holy One:
And mercy too is God's reward,
  And the reward's accruing
  To all men like their doing.

PSALM LXIII. *Metre* 1.

O God my God, I'le seek to thee
  with early care and hast:
For, Lord, my very soul in me
  doth thirst of thee to tast.
And in this barren wilderness,
  where waters there are none,
My flesh doth greatly long for thee,
  and thee I wish alone:

2 That I might see thy glorious power,
  and brightness of thy face;
As I have seen it heretofore,
  within thy holy place.

3 Because the loving-kindness, Lord,
  which is in thee always,
Is better to thy Saints than life,
  my lips shall give thee praise.

4 Thus will I bless thee all my days,
  and celebrate thy fame:
My hands I will devoutly raise
  in thy most holy Name.

5 With marrow and with fatness fill'd
  my longing soul shall be:
My mouth shall joyn with joyful lips,
  in giving praise to thee.

6 When on my bed I do record
  thy love with sweet delight,

And

  And meditate on thee, O Lord,
   I'th' watches of the night.
7 Because thou, Lord, hast been my help,
   I will lift up my voice:
  And in the shadow of thy wings
   I greatly will rejoyce.
8 My soul doth press hard after thee,
   for in thee I confide:
  And thy right hand upholdeth me,
   so that I shall not slide.
9 But they that seek my soul to slay,
   shall certainly descend
 Into the inwards of the earth,
   by some unhappy end.
10 The sword shall shed their guilty blood,
   and they shall fall thereby;
  And be the portion and the food
   of foxes, when they die.
11 But God's anointed shall rejoyce,
   his servants all shall glory
  In God that shall strike dumb my foes,
   and stop their lying story.

PSALM LXIII. *Metre* 2.

O God my God, whose blest abode
   I long for and inquire;
My Soul in me thirsts after thee
   with vehement desire:
For thee my flesh now longs afresh,
   in desarts that are dry,
In thirsty and in parched land
   where is no waters nigh.
That I might be brought out to see
   thy glorious power and grace;
As I sometime have seen it shine
   within thy holy place.
Since thy kind love is far above,
   the comforts of this life,

           How

How to proclaim thy praise and fame
    my lips shall be at strife.

The Second part.

Lord, I will praise thee all my days,
    I will extoll thy fame;
My hands will I lift up on high
    to thy most holy Name.
My Soul in me suffiz'd shall be,
    as if with fatness fill'd:
And thankful praise my mouth always
    with joyful lips shall yield.

When I record thy love, O Lord,
    upon my bed at night,
And meditate upon thee late,
    before the dawning light,
Since thou alone art he from whom
    my help proceeds and springs;
Therefore will I rest joyfully
    beneath thy shady wings.

The Third part.

My Soul doth press with eagerness
    to follow after thee;
And still I stand by thy right hand,
    for that upholdeth me.
But soon they must go down to dust,
    that seek my Soul to slay,
And falling by the sword shall die,
    and be the Foxes prey.

Yet for the King fresh joys shall spring,
    which from the Lord are had:
And all that swear by his true fear
    shall glory and be glad.
Whereas the mouth that speaks untruth,
    the righteous to defame,
By forged lies and falsities,
    the Lord shall stop with shame.

PSALM

PSALM LXIV. *Metre* 1.

Vouchsafe, O Lord, to hear my cry,
   and to my prayer give ear:
Preserve my life from th' enemy,
   of whom I stand in fear.

2 Lord, hide me from the secret snare
   that wicked men devise:
From them that wicked workers are,
   and do against me rise.

3 Who whet their tongues like sharpest swords,
   and bend their speeches so,
That they may shoot their bitter words,
   as arrows from their bow.

4 That they may shoot in secrecy,
   the perfect man to hit:
They do shoot at him suddenly,
   and do not fear a whit.

5 With courage they in ill proceed,
   and commune how to lay
Their privy snares, in hope to speed,
   for who shall see? say they.

6 They search out shrewd iniquities,
   they search with utmost art:
Their inward thought, how deep it lies
   in every wicked heart!

7 But God shall let his arrows fly,
   to shoot at them therefore:
And with an arrow suddenly
   shall they be wounded sore.

8 So shall they make their tongues to fall
   upon themselves that day:
And it shall make beholders all
   for fear to flee away.

9 All men shall fear that see this thing,
   they shall God's works declare,
Most prudently considering
   what these his doings are.

10 The righteous shall in God delight,
  confiding in his Name :
And all that are in heart upright,
  shall glory in the same.

PSALM LXIV. Metre 2.

O Lord Consider, &c.

Lord hear my voice in these my prayers,
  preserve me from the enemies snares;
From secret councels of the lewd,
  and from the Rebel-multitude ;

Who whet their tongue like sharpened swords,
  and bend their bow for bitter words,
At perfect men they aim their shot ;
  swiftly they shoot, and fear it not.

Hard'ned in sin, they vent their spleen,
  and talk of setting snares unseen :
They seek out mischief closely wrought,
  deep is each heart and secret thought.

But God shall shoot at them therefore,
  a sudden shot shall wound them sore :
So shall their tongues themselves betray,
  and all that see shall flee away.

All men shall fear th' avenging Rod,
  and shall declare the work of God :
For they shall wisely think upon
  the doings of the Holy One.

In streams of joy the just shall swim,
  be glad in God, and trust in him :
And all that are in heart upright,
  shall glory with a glad delight.

PSALM LXV. Metre 1.

Our silent praise, Lord, waits for thee,
  In *Sion*'s sacred Mount :
And unto thee the vow shall be
  perform'd with due account.

Thou art the God that hearest prayers,
   and there is none but thou;
Therefore all flesh to thee repairs,
   and every knee shall bow.

Iniquities have much prevail'd
   against us, we must say;
But yet thy mercy hath not fail'd
   to purge our sins away.
O blessed man whom thou dost choose,
   and bringest near to thee,
That he thy holy house may use,
   and there a dweller be.
We shall be satisfied and sped
   with goodness and with grace;
Wherewith thou hast replenished
   thy House and Holy place,

The Second part.

By dreadful things in righteousness
   thy answer shall be made
To our petitions and requests,
   O God our saving aid;
Who art the only confidence
   of Earth's remotest ends,
And theirs that are on Seas far hence,
   whose hope on thee depends.

Which by his power so infinite
   doth set the mountains fast;
Because that thou art girt with might,
   and power which is so vast:
Who stills the noise of raging Seas,
   and waves that rise and roar:
The Tumults too thou dost appease
   of people on the shore.
Far dwellers on the Coasts about,
   thy signs of Heaven affright:
Thou crown'st the mornings goings out,
   and th' evenings with delight.

Psalm lxv.

The Third part.

Thou visitest the earth, O Lord,
  and waterest every clod;
And hast it very richly stor'd
  with rain, the flood of God.
Which flood with water doth abound,
  their Corn thou dost prepare,
Having provided for the ground
  by thy so prudent care.

Upon her ridges yet agen,
  thy rain in plenty pours;
Her furrows thou dost settle then
  and make it soft with showers.
The springing of it thou dost bless,
  the year-time thou dost crown
With goodness, and with fruitfulness,
  thy paths drop fatness down.

Upon her pastures rain distills
  throughout the wilderness:
On every side the little hills
  no little joy express.
The pasture-fields fair flocks adorn,
  the valleys freshly spring;
And are so fill'd with crops of Corn,
  they shout for joy and sing.

PSALM LXV. Metre 2.

Have Mercy, &c.

O God, praise waiteth still
  for thee in *Sion* hill:
The vow will we perform to thee,
  and readily fulfill.
2 O thou whose titles are,
  The God that hearest prayer,
The God to whom all flesh shall come,
  to thee we do repair.

3 Our sins have born great sway,
   and much against us say:
But as for these, Lord, thou shalt please
   to purge them all away.
4 O blessed man is he,
   whom thou dost choose to thee,
And mak'st resort unto thy court,
   a dweller there to be.

Where all that do abide,
   shall fully be supply'd
With grace, of which the house is rich
   which thou hast sanctifi'd.
5 By fearful things display'd
   in justice for our aid,
O God of our protecting power,
   thy answer shall be made;

Who art our confidence,
   and all the earth's defence;
And also theirs whom th' ocean bears,
   and all the coasts far hence.
6 Whose strength sets fast the hills,
   and girt with power, he stills
7 The Sea that raves with boisterous waves,
   and mens rebellious wills.

8 Thy signs affright the stout,
   that dwell the earth throughout:
Thou dost display the break of day,
   and mak'st the evening shout.
9 Thou visitest the land,
   watering it with thine hand:
God's river which makes earth so rich,
   pours down at thy command:

It doth with water flow,
   and Corn thou dost bestow,
When as thou hast by thy fore-cast
   provided for it so.
10 Her ridges from aloft.
   thou waterest very oft:

Psalm lxv.

Her furrows all thou mak'st to fall,
  with showers thou mak'st it soft.
Her springing thou dost bless,
11 thou crown'st the year no less
With goodness free that comes from thee,
  thy paths drop fruitfulness.
12 They drop on desarts wide,
  the pastures are supply'd :
The rain distills on little hills
  made glad on every side.
13 The pastures flocks forth bring,
  with Corn the valleys spring :
And covered o're with stock and store,
  they shout for joy and sing.

PSALM. LXVI.

O All ye lands, in God rejoyce ;
  2 Sing forth his praise and fame :
Extol him both with heart and voice,
  and glorifie his Name.
3 How terrible, O Lord, say ye,
  in all thy works thou art !
Thy foes are forc'd to yield to thee,
  though with a feigned heart.
4 To thee shall all the earth bow down,
  and sing to thee, O Lord :
Thy holy Name's deserv'd renown
  in songs shall they record.
5 The works of God O come and see ;
  ye shall acknowledge then,
How terrible his actions be
  among the sons of men.
6 He turn'd the Sea to firm dry land,
  and where the Ships do swim,
We went on foot as on the sand,
  there we rejoyc'd in him.
7 He rules with power for evermore,
  his eyes all lands espie :

Let not rebellious men therefore
exalt themselves on high.

The Second part.

8 O all ye people, bless our God,
and let the chearful voice
Of his due praise be heard abroad,
while we in him rejoyce.

9 Who setting dangers all aside,
our Soul in life doth stay,
And suffering not our foot to slide,
upholds us in our way.

10 But thou hast try'd and prov'd us yet,
as doth the skilful tryer,
That proves his silver, casting it
into the hottest fire.

11 Thou broughtest us into the net,
where we intangled were:
And laid'st afflictions very great
upon our loins to bear.

12 Thou mad'st fierce men ride o're our heads,
we went through flames and floods:
But now thou hast thy people led
to places stor'd with goods.

The Third part.

13 Lord, I will go into thy house,
burnt-offerings I will bring:
And I will pay thee all my vows,
fulfilling every thing.

14 The vows which with my mouth I spake,
in all my grief and smart:
The vows I say which I did make
in anguish of my heart.

15 I'le offer thee burnt-sacrifice,
incense and fat of rams:
And I will offer thee likewise
fat bullocks, goats, and lambs.

Pſalm lxvj.

16 Come forth and hearken, every one
  that fears the living Lord :
 What he for my poor Soul hath done,
  I will to you record.
17 I call'd upon his ſacred Name,
  this mouth to him did cry :
 My tongue likewiſe extoll'd his fame
  with great alacrity.
18 I alſo watch'd leſt any way
  my heart ſhould ſin regard :
 For then I knew when I did pray,
  my prayer ſhould not be heard.
19 But God hath heard me verily,
  and did full well attend
 Unto my prayer and fervent cry,
  which did to him aſcend.
20 All praiſe to him, to him I ſay,
  that always had regard ;
 And never put my prayer away,
  nor ſent me home unheard.

PSALM LXVII. *Metre* 1.

HAve mercy on us, Lord,
  and grant to us thy grace ;
 And unto us do thou afford
  the brightneſs of thy face.
2 That all the earth may know
  the way to godly wealth :
 And all that live on earth below,
  may ſee thy ſaving health.
3 Let all the world, O God,
  give praiſe unto thy Name :
 O let the people all abroad
  extol and laud the ſame.
4 Throughout the world ſo wide,
  let all rejoyce with mirth :
 For thou ſhalt juſtly judge and guide
  the nations of the earth.

5 Let all the world, O God,
  give praise unto thy Name:
 O let the people all abroad
  extol and laud the same.
6 Then shall the earth increase,
  great store of fruit shall fall:
 And God our God shall grant us peace,
  and greatly bless us all.
7 Yea, God shall bless us all,
  and earth both far and near:
 And people all in general
  of him shall stand in fear.

PSALM LXVII. Metre 2.

All People, &c.

O God shew grace, and bless all thine,
  And cause thy face on us to shine:
Make known thy way to great and small,
Thy saving health to nations all.
Lord let the people praise thy Name,
Let all the people spread thy fame:
  O let the Nations of the Earth
  Be glad and sing for joy and mirth.
For thou shalt judge them righteously,
And govern all with Equity:
  Wherefore let all men praise thy Name,
  Let all the people spread thy fame;
Then shall the earth yield plenteousness,
And God our own God shall us bless:
  God shall us bless, and all men then
  Shall fear his Holy Name. *Amen.*

PSALM LXVII. Metre 3.

Give Laud, &c.

Lord bless us of thy grace,
  be merciful to thine,
And let thy pleased face
  upon thy servants shine,

That all may see
The saving health and heavenly wealth
that flows from thee.

Thy praise let all rehearse
with one united voice,
Sing in melodious verse,
exceedingly rejoyce;
Thy power obey,
Whose justice shall dispose of all,
and bear the sway.

Let all extol thy worth;
then store of fruits shall fall,
The Earth shall bring them forth,
and God shall bless us all:
God shall us bless,
And Earth's whole frame shall fear his Name
with awfulness.

PSALM LXVIII.

Let God omnipotent arise,
his scattered foes to chase:
And let his hateful enemies
fly from his angry face.
2 As driven smoke dispel them quite;
as fire melts wax away;
So let the wicked in his sight
quite perish and decay.
3 But let the just be fill'd with joy,
rejoycing in his sight:
Yea let them most exceedingly
rejoyce with all their might.
4 Sing unto God, sing forth his fame,
extol him with your voice,
That rides on Heav'n by I A H (his Name)
before his face rejoyce.
5 A father of the fatherless,
and judge of widows case

Is God, whose throne of holiness
  is in the highest place.
6 He stores the solitary cell,
  he frees the chain'd and bound:
But lets rebellious people dwell
  and starve in barren ground.

The Second part.

7 O God, when thou wast in the head
  of all thy peoples host,
When marching thou their camp didst lead
  along the desart coast.
8 The earth did at thy presence quake,
  in drops the Heavens fell:
Thy sight made *Sinai*'s hill to shake,
  O God of *Israel*.
9 O God, thou didst the drought asswage,
  sending a plenteous rain:
Whereby thy weary heritage
  was well refresht again.
10 Thy congregation setled there,
  for thou didst it restore:
Thou of thy goodness didst prepare
  a dwelling for the poor.
11 God gave the word of victory,
  and presently there came
Innumerable company,
  that published the same:
12 The Kings of Armies (overcome)
  were forc'd to flee away:
And even she that staid at home
  helpt to divide the prey.

The Third part.

13 Though ye have lien among the pots,
  ye shall be to behold
As wings of doves with silver spots,
  and plum'd with yellow gold,

Pſalm lxviij.

14 When the Almighty in our ſight
    gave Kings the overthrow,
 Victorious *Iſrael* ſhin'd as bright
    as doth the Salmon ſnow.
15 The hill whereon Jehovah dwells,
    as *Baſhan* hill we count:
 A lofty hill, that parallels
    the height of *Baſhan* mount.
16 Ye higher hills, why leap ye ſo?
    for this muſt be the hill
 Which God doth for his dwelling know,
    and ſo he ever will.
17 God's chariots twice ten thouſand fold,
    are Hoſts of chief account:
 The Lord's among them as of old
    in *Sinai*'s ſacred mount.
18 Thou haſt aſcended up on high,
    and thou, O Chriſt, didſt then
 Lead captive our captivity,
    receiving gifts for men.

 Yea alſo for rebellious men
    thou didſt thoſe gifts receive:
 That God the Lord might dwell with them,
    and they rebellion leave.
19 Bleſſed be God that doth us load
    with daily favours thus:
 Even that God that hath beſtow'd
    ſalvation upon us.
20 For our God is the God alone
    that doth ſalvation give:
 And thoſe that under death do grone,
    by him alone do live.
21 But God ſhall wound his enemies head,
    and in his kindled wrath
 Shall make his hairy ſcalp to bleed,
    that holds his ſinful path.

Pſalm lxviij.

The Fourth part.

22 I'le bring again, the Lord did ſay,
   from *Baſhan* when I pleaſe :
I'le bring my people ſafe away,
   even from the deepeſt Seas.
23 That thou mayeſt dip thy foot in blood
   of adverſaries ſlain :
And bathing in the crimſon flood,
   thy dogs their tongues may ſtain.
24 For they have ſeen, O God, this thing,
   they ſaw thy ſteps of grace,
The goings of my Lord, my King,
   within his holy place.
25 Before them went the ſinging men,
   the Minſtrels at their feet ;
Amongſt them were the Damſels then
   that tun'd the Timbrels ſweet.
26 God's praiſe in great Aſſemblies tell,
   bleſs him with one accord ;
Ev'n from the ſpring of *Iſrael*,
   O praiſe and bleſs the Lord.
27 There's little *Benjamin* their head,
   and *Judah*'s Councel by ;
And *Zabulon*'s Princes gathered,
   and thoſe of *Napthali*.
28 Thy God by his ſupream command
   hath ſtrengthened thee thus :
Strengthen, O God, by thy good hand
   what thou haſt wrought for us.
29 Thy Temple at *Jeruſalem*
   ſhall forreign Kings allure,
To come and bring their gifts with them,
   thy favour to procure.

The Fifth part.

30 Rebuke the ſpear-mens companies,
   and all the multitude.

Of bulls and brutish enemies,
  that are so fierce and rude.
Till all submit with one accord,
  and tributes bring from far;
O scatter thou those people, Lord,
  that take delight in war.

31 Then Princes out of *Ægypt* Lands
  to thee shall presents bring:
The Black-moores shall stretch out their hands
  to Christ our heavenly King.

32 Sing unto God most joyfully,
  ye Kingdoms of the earth:
O sing unto the Lord most high,
  and praise his Name with mirth.

33 To him that rides on th' utmost Heaven,
  the Heavens that were of old:
Lo, there his thund'ring voice is given,
  a mighty voice, behold!

34 Ascribe ye strength to our great God,
  whose excellency rare
Is over *Israel* plainly shew'd,
  whose strength the clouds declare:

35 O God, thou art a dreadful one,
  and so thou dost appear
From Heaven thy high and holy Throne,
  and in thy Temple here.
For *Israel*'s God and Saviour,
  he is the very same
That gives his people strength and power,
  and blessed be his Name.

PSALM LXIX.

Save me, O God, of thy free grace,
  for now the billows roul;
And pressing on come in apace
  unto my very Soul.
 I sink in deepest mire and mud,
  where is no standing ground:

  I am o'rewhelm'd with the flood,
   whose waters do abound.

3 Uncessant crying wearieth me,
 my throat is hoarse likewise :
  While, O my God, I wait for thee
  with sick and famisht eyes.
4 And they that hate me causelesly,
 I reckon to be moe
  Than are the very hairs (think I)
  which on my head do grow.

  And they that would destroy me, Lord,
  my wrongful foes are they,
  And mighty, so that I restor'd
  what I took not away.
5 O God, thou know'st my foolishness,
 and thou dost fully see :
  If I have done unrighteousness,
  it is not hid from thee.
6 Let none that wait upon thy Name,
 Lord God of hosts, I pray,
  Let none of them be put to shame
  for my sake any way.
7 Because for thy sake, O most high,
 I suffer this disgrace :
  For thy sake, Lord, especially
  hath shame o'respread my face.

8 A stranger now I am become
 to brethren of my own :
  One mother bare us in her womb,
  yet am I as unknown.
9 For zeal hath quite consumed me,
 which to thy house I bear :
  And the reproaches cast at thee,
  are fall'n to be my share.

    The Second part.
10 When I did weep, when I did fast
 for chastening of my Soul,

That in a scoff at me they cast,
      and did reproach me soul.
11 I put on sackcloth to my shame,
      for they my deed condemn:
   And when I wore it I became
      a proverb unto them.
12 They that did sit within the gate,
      discourst of these as crimes:
   And drunkards as they quaffing sate,
      did put me in their rhimes.
13 But as for me, O Lord, my prayer
      waits the propitious hour:
   Let me thy bounteous mercies share,
      and prove thy saving power.
14 Deliver me out of the mire,
      and me from sinking keep;
   From those that do my hurt desire,
      and from the waters deep.
15 Let not the flood prevail a whit,
      whose water overflows;
   Nor deep devour me, nor the pit
      her mouth upon me close.
16 Hear me, O Lord, for thou art good,
      and of a loving mind:
   Turn to me in the multitude
      of thy compassions kind.
17 And from thy servant do not hide
      thy face in this my need:
   I am opprest on every side,
      O hear me, Lord, with speed.
18 Unto my troubled Soul draw nigh,
      redeem and set it free:
   And from mine enemies tyranny
      do thou deliver me.
19 Thou know'st all my reproach and shame,
      thou seest my great disgrace:
   Mine enemies which procure the same
      are all before thy face.

The

The Third part.

20 My heart is broke with obloquy,
 and I am full of grief:
I look'd for some to pity me,
 but no man gave relief.

21 In vain on comforters I think,
 when gall they gave for meat:
And gave me vineger to drink,
 when as my thirst was great.

22 O turn their table to a snare;
 and that which should have bin
For to have made them well to fare,
 a trap to take them in.

23 Let darkness be before their eyes,
 and let them still mistake:
And cause their guilty loins likewise
 continually to shake.

24 Pour out thine indignation still,
 with force on them to fall:
And let thine anger terrible
 take hold upon them all.

25 And let their habitation
 be desolate and wast:
And in their empty tents not one
 inhabitant be plac'd.

26 For lo, they persecute him much
 whom thou hast smote before:
And talk unto the grief of such,
 as thou hast wounded sore.

27 And therefore sin unto their sin,
 and let them still transgress:
And let them never enter in
 into thy righteousness.

28 O let the book of life be rac'd,
 and thence their names be took,
And never with the just be plac'd
 in that most blessed book.

29 But I am poor and full of grief,
  Lord, to my Soul draw nigh:
 Let thy salvation give relief,
  and set me up on high.

30 I will take up a joyful song,
  God's praises to proclaim;
 Extol him with a thankful tongue,
  and magnifie his Name.

31 And this shall please the Lord likewise,
  and make a better proof
 Than oxe, or bull in sacrifice,
  that hath both horn and hoof.

32 Hereat the humble shall be glad,
  to see it with their eye:
 And lo your heart that seek for God,
  shall live and never die.

33 For lo, the Lord doth hear the cries
  which his poor servants make:
 Those prisoners he doth not despise
  that suffer for his sake.

34 Therefore let Heaven his praises sing,
  the Earth and all the Seas:
 And also every kind of thing
  that lives and moves in these.

35 For surely God will *Sion* save,
  and *Judah*'s Cities rear:
 That dwelling-houses men may have,
  and large possessions there;

36 His servants seed (the faithful race)
  inheriting the same:
 And it shall be the dwelling-place
  of them that love his Name.

PSALM LXX. *Metre* 1.
Have Mercy, &c.

MAke haft, O God, make haft
  my Saviour for to be:

And

And let no longer time be past,
  before thou succour me.
2 Let shame confound them all
  that for my Soul inquire:
Let them by just confusion fall
  that do my hurt desire.

3 And turn them back, O Lord,
  their shame for to repay:
And let repulse be their reward
  that say, aha, aha.
4 Let them that seek thee, Lord,
  be glad in thy great Name:
And let them all with one accord
  be joyful in the same.

Let them that love to be
  with heavenly help supply'd,
Continually say thus of thee,
  let God be magnifi'd.
5 But I am weak and poor,
  for speedy aid I call:
Thou art my help and Saviour sure,
  Lord, make no stay at all.

PSALM LXX. *Metre* 2.

O Lord consider, &c.

1 MAke hast, O Lord, and set me free,
    make hast, O God, and succour me.
2 Confound them with confounding shame,
    that seek my Soul, to hurt the same.
  Let them be turned backward still,
    turn'd back with shame that wish me ill.
3 Reward their shame that say, Aha,
    and let confusion be their pay.

4 All that seek thee, and all that love
    salvation coming from above,
  Full glad in thee let them abide,
    still saying, God be magnifi'd.

5 But I am needy, weak and poor,
   make haſt to help me, Lord, therefore:
My help and my deliverer
   thou art, O Lord, do not defer.

PSALM LXXI.

O Lord, I put my truſt in thee,
   when plunged in diſtreſs:
Let no confuſion ſeize on me,
   nor ſhame my Soul oppreſs.
2 Defend me in thy righteouſneſs,
   and reſcue me with ſpeed:
Encline thine ear with readineſs,
   and ſave me at my need.
3 Be thou my rock, where I may have
   all times a ſafe reſort:
'Twas thy command thy Saint to ſave,
   O thou my ſtrength and fort.
4 Save me, my God, from wicked men,
   and from their ſtrength and power;
From folk unrighteous, and from them
   that cruelly devour.
5 On thee, O God, my hopes attend,
   and upon none beſide:
My youth did upon thee depend,
   as its moſt faithful guide.
6 Thou haſt upheld me from my birth,
   thou tookeſt care of me
Even from the womb, thou brought'ſt me forth,
   my praiſe ſtill waits on thee.
7 Indeed I ſeem a prodigie
   to many carnal eyes:
But my ſtrong refuge is on high,
   on him my hope relies.
8 Therefore my mouth ſhall daily ſing
   the glory of thy Name:
And let it not ſpeak any thing,
   but of thy praiſe and fame.

The Second part.

9 My God, O cast me not away
  when age my limbs doth shake :
And when my vigour doth decay,
  do not my Soul forsake.
10 For they that bear me causeless hate,
  against me speak full ill :
And they that for my Soul lay wait,
  conspire against me still.
11 Lay hands upon him now they said,
  and let us all fall on :
For there is none to be his aid,
  his God from him is gone.
12 Therefore, O God, that seest my need,
  far from me do not be :
But Lord my God, make hast, make speed
  to help and succour me.
13 Confound them and consume them all,
  that do against me rise :
Let scorn and shame upon them fall,
  that do my hurt devise.
14 But I on thee my hopes have set,
  and laid them up in store :
Nor will I ever thee forget,
  but praise thee more and more.
15 My mouth shall all along the day
  shew forth thy righteousness :
All day thy saving joys display,
  for they are numberless.
16 Assisted by thy strength, O God,
  I will go safely on :
Thy righteousness I'le spread abroad,
  thy righteousness alone.
17 For from my tender infancy,
  O God, thou hast me taught :
And I have told continually
  what wonders thou hast wrought.

18 Forsake

18 Forsake me not now I am old,
 now that my hairs grow white:
Till I unto this age have told,
 and shew'd the next thy might.

The Third part.

19 Thy righteousness, O God, exceeds
 in the most high degree:
Thou hast performed wond'rous deeds,
 who can compare with thee?
20 Thou who hast shew'd me troubles sore,
 even thou my life shalt save:
And though I were intomb'd, restore
 and bring me from the grave.
21 My greatness thou shalt much increase,
 my comforts shall abound:
And with thy comforts and thy peace
 thou shalt inclose me round.
22 I will instruct each warbling string
 to make thy praises known:
Yea, O my God, thy truth I'le sing,
 O *Israel's* holy one.
23 A multitude of joys shall throng
 about my lips to sit;
While my glad Soul breaths out a song
 to him that ransom'd it.
24 My tongue shall also now proclaim
 thy justice all day long:
For they are quell'd and brought to shame,
 that seek to do me wrong.

PSALM LXXII.

Lord, give thy judgments to the King,
 that justice may be done:
And give the skill of governing
 unto his Princely Son.
2 Then shall he govern uprightly,
 and do thy people right;

Then

Then shall he judge with equity
the poor that have no might.

3 The lofty mountains he shall bless,
to bring the people peace:
The little hills by righteousness
shall yield a great increase.

4 And he shall judge the indigent,
and save the poor and weak:
And the oppressor fraudulent
in pieces he shall break.

5 And then from age to age shall they
regard and fear thy might:
So long as Sun doth shine by day,
or else the Moon by night.

6 He shall descend as soaking rain
upon the mowen grass:
As showers that water hill and plain,
whatever way they pass.

7 The just shall flourish in his days,
and all shall be at peace:
Until the very Moon decays,
and all its motions cease.

8 He shall be Lord of Sea and Land,
from shore to shore throughout;
From Sea to Sea on either hand,
and all the Earth about.

9 All those that in the desarts dwell,
before him bow they must:
His enemies he will compel
to stoop and lick the dust.

10 The Kings of *Tarshish*, and the Isles,
Sheba and *Seba*'s King,
Shall come with presents many miles,
and gifts to him shall bring.

11 Yea all the Kings and higher powers

Psalm lxxij.

12 For he the needy one shall save,
   when unto him they call;
The poor I say, and them that have
   no help of man at all.

The Second part.

13 Most mercifully he shall spare
   the poor whom power controuls:
And he will ever have a care
   to save poor needy souls.
14 From violence and fraud shall he
   their abject souls redeem;
And in his sight their blood shall be
   of singular esteem.
15 And he shall live, and they bring store
   to him of *Sheba*'s gold:
He shall be pray'd for evermore,
   and daily be extol'd.
16 Handfulls of Corn shall grow upon
   the pregnant mountains tops:
The fruit shall shake like *Lebanon*,
   so rich shall be the crops.

The Citizens of *Sion* hill
   shall flourish as the grass;
And in great peace and plenty still
   their happy days shall pass.
7 His name shall last, and be in mind
   till Sunnes surcease and rest:
And as a blessing to mankind,
   all Lands shall call him blest.
8 Praise ye the Lord of hosts, and sing
   to *Israel*'s God each one;
For he doth every wond'rous thing,
   yea he himself alone.
9 And blessed be his glorious Name
   to all eternity:
Let th' earth be filled with his fame;
   Amen, amen say I.

PSALM LXXIII.

TO *Israel* truly God is good,
  to each pure-hearted one.
2 But as for me I scarcely stood,
  my feet were almost gone.
3 For I was galled grievously,
  and mov'd with envy then,
Beholding the prosperity
  of these ungodly men.

4 For in their death no bands there are,
  their strength is firm and sure:
5 They have no plagues, no grief, no care,
  which other men indure.
6 Pride therefore, like brave ornaments,
  doth compass them about;
And like a garment, violence
  doth cover them throughout.
7 Their eyes stand out with very fat,
  of wealth they have such store;
What heart can wish, nor only that,
  but even a great deal more.
8 Corrupt they are and very vain,
  they speak with impious tongue;
Oppression proudly they maintain,
  and highly boast of wrong.
9 Against the Heavens all along
  their daring mouth dares talk:
And their unbridled lavish tongue
  throughout the earth doth walk.
10 Therefore God's people oft come up,
  and here they turn about,
Since waters of so full a cup
  to them are poured out.

The Second part.

11 And thus they say, how can it be
  that God should ever know?

And

Pſalm lxxiij.

And the moſt high diſcern and ſee
  the things that are ſo low?
12 Behold, theſe the ungodly are,
  that ſeem to live in peace;
And proſper in the world ſo far,
  whoſe riches ſtill increaſe.

13 Then ſaid I, I may gather hence,
  that I with too much pain
Have waſht my hands in innocence,
  and cleans'd my heart in vain.
14 For I was plagued for my ſin,
  even all day long, O God:
And every morning I have bin
  chaſtiſed with thy rod.

15 But when I had conceiv'd all this,
  I ſtill refrain'd my tongue;
Leſt I ſhould cenſure ſaints amiſs,
  and do thy children wrong.
16 Then I bethought me how I might
  This matter underſtand:
But lo, the labour was too great
  for me to take in hand.

17 Till in thy houſe I did attend,
  and there, O Lord, and then
I underſtood the wretched end
  of theſe ungodly men.
18 For ſurely in a ſlippery place
  thou cauſed'ſt them to ſit:
To caſt them down with great diſgrace
  into deſtruction's pit.

19 A moment brings their miſery,
  O great and wondrous change!
They are conſumed utterly
  with terrours great and ſtrange.
20 Juſt as a dream when men awake
  ſo Thou, O Lord, likewiſe

K   Awaking

Awaking for juſt Judgments ſake
their image ſhalt deſpiſe.

The Third part.

21 Yet thus my heart was griev'd hereby,
and pain my reins oppreſt.
22 So rude and ignorant was I,
and in thy ſight a beaſt.
23 Nevertheleſs I do remain
continually with thee:
By thy right hand thou doſt ſuſtain,
and ſtill upholdeſt me.
24 Thy Counſels, Lord, which I regard,
Thou mak'ſt to be my guide:
And ſhalt receive me afterward
in glory to abide.
25 For whom have I in heaven but thee?
nor is there any one
In all the earth deſir'd of me,
except thy ſelf alone.
26 My fleſh and heart do fail me ſore,
but God upholds my heart:
He is my ſtrength for evermore,
my portion and my part.
27 For they that farr eſtranged be,
lo, they and every one
That go a whoring, Lord, from thee,
ſhall quite be overthrown.
28 But it is good for me alway
that I to God draw near;
I truſt in God, that ſo I may
His wondrous works declare.

PSALM LXXIV.

WHy haſt Thou Lord, rejected us
and doſt thine anger keep
And keep'ſt it ever ſmoaking thus
againſt thy paſture ſheep?

Psalm lxxvi.

2 From times of old remember still
  where thy possessions fell :
The purchas't place of Sion hill,
  where thou wast wont to dwell.

3 Perpetual ruines are begun ;
  come help, O come apace :
See what thy foes have lewdly done
  within thy holy place.

4 Amidst thy congregations here,
  thine enemies rage and roar ;
And set for signs their ensigns there
  where thou wast serv'd before.

5 A man was famous formerly,
  for hewing down thick trees,
By lifting up his ax on high,
  to fetch his blow at these.

6 But now they rend and rase as fast,
  and all at once are broke :
The curious carved work defac't,
  with ax and hammers stroke.

7 Thy holy house they set on flame,
  defil'd, and cast to ground :
The dwelling-place of thy great name,
  where once thou wast renown'd.

8 They said in heart, come on, let us
  destroy them out of hand :
And they have burnt up every house
  of God in all the land.

9 Our signs are lost, our Prophets gone,
  thine oracles are dumb :
Among us all there is not one
  knows when an end shall come.

The Second part.

10 How long, Lord, shall the enemy
  breath such reproach and shame ?

Lord, shall our foes perpetually
 blaspheme thy sacred name?
11 Where-fore, O Lord, withdrawest thou
 thy hand, even thy right hand?
O from thy bosom pluck it now,
 thine enemies to withstand.

12 For God is *Israel*'s king of old,
 who hath salvation wrought:
And all the earth may well behold
 what help to his he brought.
13 Thou by thy strength didst part the seas,
 where liquid water spreads:
And in the very depth of these
 thou brok'st the dragons heads.

14 Leviathans heads thou didst divide,
 although his strength was great:
And thus thy people were suppli'd
 i'th' wilderness for meat.
15 The flood and fountain, Lord most high,
 thy power did cleave in two:
And mighty rivers thou mad'st dry,
 that *Israel* might go through.

16 The shining day and shady night,
 peculiarly are thine:
Thou hast, O Lord, prepar'd the light,
 and caus'd the sun to shine.
17 The earth with all the ends and coasts,
 thy mighty hand did frame:
Both summers heat and winters frosts
 By thine appointment came.

The third part.

18 Remember this O Lord Supream,
 and keep it on recotd,
How foes reproach and fools blaspheme
 thy sacred Name, O Lord.
19 Thy turtles soul which many hate,
 do not to them deliver:

Thy congregations poor estate
   do not forget for ever.
20 Regard thy covenant, rid and clense
   dark corners of our land,
So full of cruel robbers dens,
   as every where they stand.
21 O let not those that are oppreſt
   return again with ſhame :
But help the needy and diſtreſs't,
   and let them praiſe thy name.
22 Ariſe, O Lord, and ſtill maintain
   the cauſe that is thy own :
Remember well how fools diſdain,
   and daily ſcorns are thrown.
23 Think, Lord, how great their fury grows,
   how inſolent, how high :
The tumults of thy rebel foes
   increaſe continually.

PSALM LXXIV. *Metre 2.*

παραφραςικῶς, *Ye Children*, &c.

ARe we, O Lord, then quite forlorn,
   And can'ſt Thou thus for ever ſcorn,
   the people which Thou once did'ſt prize?
Didſt Thou in thy fair Paſtures keep,
And with ſuch care preſerve thy ſheep
   to be thine angers Sacrifice?
Didſt thou redeem us with ſuch pain
Only to ſell us back again,
   a People which Thou bought'ſt ſo dear?
Theſe didſt Thou purchaſe, and the Place,
That thou might'ſt both at once deface
   and never more inhabit there?

O do not ſo remember ſtill
Thy Sion, thy beloved Hill
   the dwelling place which did thee pleaſe :
Lift up thy feet and come In haſte

See how thine Enemies rob and waste
  within thy sacred Palaces.
The barbarous Soldier now doth roar
Where thou hast been ador'd before,
  their Ensigns in thy Temple are:
A man was famous formerly
For timber-work to build on high,
  but now is all lay'd wast and bare.

The Second part.

Thy Sanctuary's set on flame
The houses sacred to thy Name
  are all demolish't to the ground;
Their cruel hearts have all conspir'd,
The Synagogues of God are fir'd,
  and whatsoever was renown'd.
No more thy wonted signs appear,
No more our Prophets can make clear
  the destinies that are to come,
Not one can so much as forecast
How long these woful times may last,
  but thine own Oracles are dumb.

How long, Lord, shall the foe reproach,
How long shall Enemies incroach
  forever to blaspheme and dare?
Thy hand no longer now withdraw,
Thy hand that keeps the world in awe,
  O pluck it out and make it bare.
For, Lord, thou art my King alone,
From everlasting is thy Throne,
  and was established of old:
Thou work'st salvation in the midst
Of all the earth, and this thou didst
  in sight of *Israel* to behold.

The Third part.

The sea thou parted'st at one stroke,
And the fierce Dragons heads hast broke,

the Dragons which pursu'd thy sheep:
Pharaoh that proud Leviathan
And his stout Captains every man
   were overwhelmed in the deep.
Thou gavest him, and all his Host
To feed thy flock in desert Coast
   which saw them tumbled on the sand:
Thou did'st at once (as thou saw'st good)
Divide the fountain and the flood,
   and change large rivers into land.

The day that doth the world disclose,
The night ordain'd for our repose
   were form'd by thee, and both are thine,
On this great work thy pencil lay'd,
The colours both of light and shade
   and by thy beams the Sun doth shine.
And thou with an exact survey
The frontiers of the Earth did'st lay
   incroaching Nature so to bound:
Thou didst the pleasant Summer make
And Winter (which with frosts doth quake)
   to run in a perpetual round.

The Fourth part.

Remember this, O Lord supream
How foolish foes thy Name blaspheme,
   and scorn thee with reproaches rude.
Do not forsake thy Turtle so,
Nor let her soul still mourning go
   among the wicked multitude:
Though she should merit thy neglect
Yet thine own Covenant respect
   which thou in her defence didst swear:
For the dark places of the land
Full of the dens of robbers stand,
   and cruel men inhabit there.

O let not thine that are distress'd
Be doubly at one time oppress'd,

  add not unto their losses shame :
As they are needy and more poor
So if reliev'd their thanks are more ;
  O let them therefore praise thy Name !
Arise O God in thine own cause,
Plead in defence of thine own Laws,
  and force the fool his scorns to cease:
Can'st thou at once hold off and hear
Whil'st all their Tumults gather near,
  and do continually increase.

PSALM LXXV.

O God, we render thanks to thee,
  to thee we give the same :
For by thy wondrous works we see
  the nearness of thy name.
2 When I the congregation call,
  an upright judge I'le be.
3 The earth's dissolv'd, the men and all,
  her pillars hold by me.
4 But I admonisht them the while,
  ye wicked fools, said I,
Be not so vain, be not so vile,
  nor lift your horn so high.
5 Presumptuous horns do not advance,
  nor speak with haughty mouth :
6 Promotion doth not come by chance,
  from east, or west, or south.
7 But God is soveraign judge alone,
  and there can be no other :
He at his pleasure pulls down one,
  and setteth up another.
8 For in God's hand there is a cup,
  the liquour that it hath
Is wine as red as blood, fill'd up
  with mixtures of his wrath.
He pours it out, and he will make
  the wicked of the land

Wring out the very dregs, and take,
  and drink them at his hand.
9 To *Jacob*'s God I will each day
  declare fresh songs of praise.
10 The wicked's horns I'le cut away,
  but righteous mens I'le raise.

PSALM LXXV. *Metre 2.*

To thee, O God we bring
  a Crown of living praise,
To thee our thanks we sing,
  and hearts devoutly raise;
    Though thou art high;
Thy wonders show that we may know
    Thy Name is nigh.

When people flock to me,
  I'le be an upright judge:
And make them all agree
  and bear no kind of grudge;
    The Earth would fall,
Did not my reign with power sustain
    her pillars all.

The fool I did correct,
  and did his folly shame,
The wicked man I check't,
  his haughty pride to tame:
    From his high brow
The horn I broke; and to my yoke
    his neck did bow.

For neither from the East
  promotion doth betide,
Nor from the South or West,
  or any coast beside:
    That God bestows,
Whose soveraign power can in an hour
    Crown or depose.

With red and mixed wine
   a golden bowl he fills,
Whose virtue is Divine
   where-ever it distills:
      But of this cup
The dreggs remain for the profane
      to drink them up.

But I will still declare
   and spread thy praise abroad,
That shall be all my care
   to sing of *Jacob*'s God:
      Like him, I will
Debase the bad, but honour add
      to good men still.

PSALM LXXVI.

THe Lord is known in *Judah* well,
   and his most glorious name
Is very great in *Israel*,
   which doth extoll his fame.
2 The tabernacles of his grace
   at *Salem* you may see:
At *Sion* is the dwelling-place
   where he desires to be.
3 The burnisht arrows brake he there,
   the arrows of the bow:
The battel, sword, and shield and spear,
   the weapons of the foe.
4 Much brighter is thy glorious crown,
   more excellent each way,
And worthy of much more renown,
   then all the mounts of prey.
5 Lo, thou hast spoil'd the stout of mind,
   and they have slept their sleep:
Their hands the mighty could not find,
   their lives they could not keep.
6 O God of *Jacob*, thy reproof
   sent many a daring head,

Chariot, and horse with thundring hoof,
  to sleep among the dead.
7 Thou, thou alone commandest fear,
  as worthy of the same :
And who may in thy sight appear
  when once thy wrath doth flame ?
8 When thou didst make thy judgement come
  from heaven shining clear,
The earth that heard it was struck dumb,
  And all sat still for fear:
9 When as the Lord to judgment rose,
  and sent his judgments forth,
To save from their incensed foes
  all meek ones of the earth.
10 The fury that in man doth reign,
  unto thy praise redounds :
Remaining wrath thou shalt restrain,
  and set mens passions bounds.
11 Vow to the Lord your God, and pay,
  let all about his throne
Bring presents to him every day,
  for God's a dreadful one.
12 He tames the pride and jollity
  of princes in their mirth :
And very terrible is He
  to all the kings on earth.

Or,

The spirit of princes his proud foes,
  he cuts it clean away :
And terrible he is to those
  that earthly scepters sway.

II. *Metre.*

All people, *or,* O Lord, consider, &c.

1 In *Judah* God is known to his,
  His name is great in *Israel* :

2 His

2 His sanctu'ry at SALEM is,
   He doth in *Sion*-mountain dwell.
3 The bows and arrows brake he there,
   The battel, shield, and sword and spear.
4 Thou art more glorious every way,
   And excellent then mounts of prey.
5 The stout of heart are over-thrown,
   And they have slept their sleeps last night:
 And of the mighty men, not one
   Hath found his hands wherewith to fight.
6 O God of *Jacob*, thy reproof
   Spoil'd rattling wheel, and thundring hoof:
 Chariot and horse, at thy fierce blast,
   Into a sleep of death are cast.
7 Thou, thou alone art worthy fear,
   For who may stand before thine eyes?
 Who dares approach, who dares appear,
   When once thy burning wrath doth rise?
8 From heaven thou mak'st judgment heard;
   The silent earth was sore afeard
9 When God arose to judgment then,
   To save on earth all humble men.
10 Man's wrath shall surely praise thy name,
   Henceforth held in by thy restraints.
11 O make your vows, and pay the same
   Unto the Lord your God, ye saints.
12 Let all about him presents bring
   To him that daunts the proudest king:
 To him, I say, whose fear compells,
   And princes spirits curbs and quells.

PSALM LXXVII.

1 With my voice to God did cry,
   Even with my voice aloud;
 I cry'd to God, who graciously
   to me his ear hath bow'd.
2 I sought him in my woful day,
   my sore still ran all night:

Psalm lxxvij.

My weary soul did put away
all comfort and delight.

3 I thought on God in my distress,
yet trouble did remain:
And overwhelm'd with heaviness,
my soul did sore complain.

4 Mine eyes from sleep thou dost restrain,
and mak'st me still to wake:
I am so vext and full of pain,
my speech doth me forsake.

5 Then thought I on the days of old,
the years of ancient times;
Wherein God's mercies manifold
did overflow our crimes.

6 My song by night I call'd to mind,
I commun'd with my heart:
My soul made earnest search to find
some word to ease my smart.

7 Alas said I, what, will the Lord
cast off, and not restore?
And from henceforth will he afford
no favour any more?

8 Is all his mercy ceas't and gone?
must that no more prevail?
The promise of the holy one,
shall that for ever fail?

9 Hath God forgotten to express
his mercies wonted measure?
Is his dear love and tenderness
shut up in his displeasure?

10 Then said I, my infirmity
doth cause these doubts and fears:
I will recall what God most High
hath done in former years.

The Second part.

11 I will retain in memory
thy wonders manifold;

I will remember certainly
    thy wondrous works of old.
12 And I will also meditate
    of all thy works of fame:
  And I will chearfully relate
    how thou hast wrought the same.
13 Within thy sanctuary bright
    thy way, O God, is known:
  And there is none to match the might
    of our Almighty one.
14 Thou art the God by whose great might
    are wrought such wonders rare:
  And plainly in thy peoples sight
    thy works thou didst declare.
15 All *Israels* whole posterity
    are thy redeem'd indeed:
  Thy arm did set at liberty
    Jacob and *Joseph*'s seed.
16 The waters did thy visage see,
    they saw and were afraid:
  And at the very sight of thee
    the depths were sore dismai'd.
17 Excessive storms the clouds pour'd out,
    the skies sent forth a sound:
  Thy arrows also walk't about,
    and were dispersed round.
18 Thy thundering voice was heard on high,
    and from the heavens spake:
  Thy lightnings lightned earth and sky:
    the earth did move and quake.
19 Great waters and great seas there be,
    which thou didst tread and trace:
  Though none can now thy foot-steps see,
    nor know the certain place.
20 Thou ledst thy people on the sand
    amidst the seas so deep,
  By *Moses* and by *Aaron*'s hand
    like to a flock of sheep.

PSAL

PSALM LXXVIII.

Hearken, my people, to my law,
  encline your ears to hear:
And let my speech attention draw,
  and win a listning ear.
2 My mouth shall speak a parable,
  and sayings dark of old:
3 Which we have heard and known so well,
  and which our fathers told.
4 We will not from their seed conceal
  the wonders God hath done:
His praise and power we will reveal
  unto the age to come.
5 For God himself established
  in *Jacob* this decree:
This statute he determined
  in *Israel* for to be.

And charg'd our fathers every one,
  to hear what he decreed.
And to declare, and make it known
  to their ensuing seed.
6 That th'age to come and following race,
  his testaments might know:
Who should arise in fathers place,
  and them to theirs should show.
7 That they thereby might learn to set
  their hope in God above:
And might not God's great works forget,
  but keep his law in love.
8 And like their fathers might not be,
  degenerate and base:
A stiff and stubborn progenie,
  and a rebellious race.

A generation sure they were,
  whose heart was not set right:
Whose soul likewise was not sincere,
  and perfect in God's sight.

The Second part.

9 The sons of *Ephraim*, carrying bows,
   nor did they armour lack,
In day of battel with their foes,
   were forc't to turn their back.
10 God's covenant they observed not,
   nor would his laws regard:
11 His works and wonders they forgot,
   which he to them declar'd.
12 Great marvails had their fathers known,
   all acted in their sight:
In *Egypt* and the field of *Zoan*,
   performed by his might.
13 The sea for them he did divide,
   and did the chanel drain:
He heap't the waters on each side,
   and made for them a lane.
14 He led them with a cloud by day,
   and with a brighter light
Of flaming fire he shew'd the way,
   and led them all the night.
15 The stronger rocks he also clave
   within the desart dry:
And, drink as from great depths, he gave
   to them abundantly.
16 He made the stony rock to drown
   the desart where it stood,
And made the waters to run down
   like to a hasty flood.
17 Yet did they sin exceedingly,
   and more and more transgress,
Greatly provoking the most High
   within the wilderness.
18 Yea in their heart their sin was great,
   for (out of deep distrust)
They tempted God, by asking meat
   to satisfie their lust.

19 Yea

19 Yea against God they spake no less,
  and said profanely thus,
A table in the wilderness
  can God provide for us?

The Third part.

20 Behold he smote the rock indeed,
  and thence gusht waters great:
But can he give his people bread,
  and send them flesh to eat?
21 Therefore the Lord this thing discern'd,
  and caus'd his wrath to swell:
His anger against *Jacob* burn'd,
  and scorched *Israel*.
22 Since they did not on God rely,
  nor on that saviour wait,
23 Though he had charg'd the lofty sky,
  and opened heaven gate.
24 And showers of Manna he did rain,
  for them to eat their fill:
And gave them of the finest grain
  that heaven could distill.
25 So mortal man did freely eat
  the food of angels rare:
For God sent down that heavenly meat,
  enough and yet to spare.
26 A wind to blow in heaven he sent
  from Eastern parts design'd,
And by his power omnipotent
  brought in the southern wind.
27 He rain'd upon them living flesh,
  like summers dust for store:
And feather'd fowl he brought them fresh,
  as sand upon the shore.
28 In midst of all the camp throughout
  he let it gently fall:
And he disperst it round about
  their habitations all.

29 So they did eat their greedy fill;
  their own defire he gave;
30 Nor were eftrang'd from their own will,
  nor what their luft did crave.
But while the meat was in their mouth,
31 God's wrath upon them fell,
  And flew the flower of all their youth,
  and choice of *Ifrael*.
32 Yet for all this they finned ftill,
  their gracious God they grieve:
And let his works be what they will,
  they never would believe.
33 Therefore he made their deftiny
  their miferies to double;
Spending their days in vanity,
  and all their years in trouble.

The Fourth part.

34 But when he flew thefe wicked men,
  they back to God retir'd;
And fought him very early then:
  and after God inquir'd.
35 Remembring then that God alone
  was all the rock they had
And that redeemer they had none,
  except the higheft God.
36 Yet they diffembled all along
  and flatter'd with their mouth
They ly'd unto him with their tongue,
  and fought him not in truth.
37 For ftill their hearts hypocrify
  was manifeftly fhew'd:
And that they walk't not ftedfaftly
  in covenant with their God.
38 But he fo full of clemency,
  their injuries forgot;
And pardon'd their iniquity,
  and overthrew them not.

> Yea, many a time he pleas'd to turn
> destruction from their path:
> And would not let his anger burn,
> nor stir up all his wrath.

39 For graciously he call'd to mind
how that they were but flesh;
And like a transitory wind,
that doth not come afresh.

40 How often in the wildernes
did they provoke him sore:
And in the desarts did transgress,
and grieve him more and more?

41 Yea they turn'd back, as always prone
to tempt the Lord most high:
And limited the holy one
of *Israel* shamefully.

42 They were unmindful of his hand,
and of that famous day,
When from the foe in forrein land
he brought them safe way.

43 Nor did they keep his signs in thought,
which were in *Egypt* shown,
And mighty wonders he had wrought
within the fields of *Zoan*.

44 How he had turn'd the rivers there
to loathsom streams of blood:
So that no beast or passenger
could drink of lake or flood.

The Fifth part.

45 He sent of flies of divers sorts,
amongst them to devour:
And to destroy them in their courts,
he joyn'd the frogs in power.

46 He let the caterpillars eat
the fruit of all their soil:
And gave their labours hopeful sweat
to be the locusts spoil.

47 Their

47 Their pleasant vines with hail-stone showers
    were beaten down and lost :
And all their spreading sycamores
    were perish't with the frost.
48 Their cattel also he assaults
    with battering showers of hail :
And with the burning thunder-bolts
    he did their flocks assail.
49 Fierce anger, wrath, and discontent
    he let as fiercely fall
By evil angels, which he sent
    to vex and plague them all.
50 He making way for his fierce wrath,
    spar'd not their soul from death :
But made the pestilence a path
    to force their dying breath.
51 All *Egypts* first-born in one night
    He smote with dreadful hand,
The very chief of all their might,
    in *Cham*'s accursed land.
52 But made his people safely pass
    the danger of the deep :
And led them in the wilderness,
    like to a flock of sheep.
53 He led them safe and free from fear,
    amidst the briny waves :
But overwhelm'd their enemies were,
    the sea became their graves.
54 And them unto the borders brought
    of his most sacred land :
The mountain which himself had bought
    by power of his right hand.
55 The heathen folk he did expel,
    and did their lands assign
An heritage to *Israel*,
    dividing it by line :
And made his tribes dwell in their tents.
56 Yet tempt they God most high,

And kept not his commandements,
 but griev'd him vehemently:
57 Unfaithfully they backwards slide,
 their fathers dealt just so :
And they likewise were turn'd aside,
 like a deceitful bow.
58 With places which they built on high,
 they did the Lord displease :
And moved him to jealousie
 with graven images.

The Sixth part.

59 When God heard this, (as he must needs)
 he was exceeding wrath :
And *Israel* which had done such deeds,
 he did abhor and loath.
60 So that the tents of *Shiloh* were
 forsaken by him then :
The tents which he had placed there
 among rebellious men.
61 And sent into captivity
 his ark in forrain-land :
And gave his beauteous dignity
 into his enemies hand.
62 He gave his people to be slain
 by the devouring sword :
And caus'd his wrath to scorch amain
 the heritage of the Lord.
63 The fire of his incensed rage
 consumes their young men brave :
And honourable marriage
 their maidens might not have.
64 Yea, by the sword their priests did fall,
 and yet, alas ! there went
No widows to the funerall,
 their sad deaths to lament.
65 But then the Lord awoke anon,
 as one from sleep doth start :

And

    And shouted like a mighty man,
      when wine hath chear'd his heart.
66 And smote his foes i'th hinder parts
      to their perpetual shame :
    A vile disease for vile deserts,
      which on his enemies came.

67 And *Joseph*'s tabernacle was
      wholly refus'd by him :
    And yet he chose not in those days
      the tribe of *Ephraim*.
68 But chose the tribe of *Judah* there,
      even *Sion*'s sacred mount ;
    Above all other places dear,
      and high in his account.

69 And there his holy temple plac't,
      like pallaces on high :
    And like the earth, which he set fast
      to perpetuity.
70 He chose his servant *David* too,
      took him from folds of sheep,
    And set him other work to do,
      a flock of men to keep :

71 From following the great-bellied ewes,
      the Lord's own flock to feed ;
    His people *Israel*, and the *Jews*,
      that were of *Jacob*'s seed.
72 So *David* fed them faithfully,
      and govern'd all the land
    After his hearts integrity,
      and with a skilful hand.

PSALM LXXIX.

THe Heathen, Lord, come in amain,
    thine heritage to waste:
Thy holy temple they profane,
    Jerusalem is rac't.
2 Dead bodies of thy servants dear

And thy saints flesh hurl'd here and there,
  to every savage beast.
3 Their blood about *Jerusalem*,
  like water they have shed:
And none was left to bury them
  when they were slain and dead.
4 Our neighbours near do us deride,
  and mock us to our face:
And round about on every side
  they load us with disgrace.
5 How long, Lord, shall thine anger be?
  wilt thou still keep the same?
And shall thy fervent jealousie
  burn like unto a flame?
6 On Heathens pour thy fury out,
  which know thee not at all;
And on those kingdoms round about
  that on thy Name ne'r call.
7 For they have greedily devour'd
  thy servant *Jacob*'s race.
And quite laid waste with fire and sword
  his ancient dwelling-place.
8 O think not on our former crimes,
  prevent us (be not slow)
With tender mercy shew'd betimes,
  for we are very low.

The Second part.

9 Help us, O God our strength and stay,
  and that for thy names sake,
Save us, and purge our sins away
  and all the glory take.
10 Why say the heathen, where's their God?
  be known then in their sight:
Revenge on them thy servants blood,
  which they have spilt in spite.
11 The prisoners throbbing sighs receive,

    And by thy soveraign power reprieve
      the men condemn'd to die.
12 And let our neighbours have restor'd
      into their bosoms bold,
    The scorns they cast on thee, O Lord,
      restore them seven-fold.

13 So we thy flock and heritage
      will ever bless thy Name:
    And spread thy praise from age to age,
      and celebrate thy fame.

PSALM LXXIX. *Metre* 2.

Give Laud, &c.

Heathens are come, O God,
    thine heritage to spoil,
And have profanely trod
    On *Sion*'s sacred soil.
      and now, at once,
Jerusalem is made, by them,
      an heap of stones.

Thy servants they have slain,
    and their dead bodies given,
For meat to entertain
    the ravenous fowls of Heaven:
      and they have thrown
Thy Saints dear flesh for savage beasts
    to feed upon.

Their blood have they shed round
    about *Jerusalem*,
As water on the ground,
    and none to bury them,
      We are set out
A scorn to those our neighbouring foes
    all round about.

Psalm lxxix.

The Second part.

How long wilt thou, O Lord,
  be wroth, and not return?
Shall Jealousie be stirr'd
  perpetually to burn?
    O let it bee
Pour'd out on them (those Heathen men)
    that know not thee.

The Kingdoms let it scorch
  that call not on thy Name,
For they have rent thy Church,
  and quite devour'd the same:
    All *Jacob*'s race
They have defac't, and quite laid waste
    his dwelling place.

Remember in no case
  against us former crimes,
But let thy tender grace
  prevent us Lord betimes;
    For we with wo
And great decay, are, at this day,
    brought very low.

Thy help, O God, we claim
  now we are humbled thus:
For honour of thy Name
  O Saviour succour us:
    O purge and take
Our sins away, we humbly pray
    for thy Names sake.

Why should the Heathen say
  What! is their God now lost?
Be known Lord, in a way
  of Judgment, to their cost.
    And, in our sight,
Revenge, O God, thy servants blood
    spilt by their spite.

The Third part.

O let the Prisoners sighs
   before thee have access,
And speak Lord by the voice
   of thine Almightiness;
     O thou most high,
Deliver them whom they condemn,
    and doom to die.

And Lord repay it back
   with payment sevenfold
Into our neighbours lap
   Whoever durst be bold
     To cast one word
Of scornful shame upon thy Name
    O mighty Lord.

So we, O God, that are
   thy pasture, flock and store
Shall thankfully declare
   thine honour evermore;
     And ever shall
Thy praise proclaim, and spread thy fame
    to Ages all.

PSALM LXXX.

O Shepherd, thou that dost provide
   for *Israel*'s tribe and flock,
And dost the seed of *Jacob* guide,
   and lead'st him like a flock;
Thou glorious God, that dwell'st between
   the cherubims on high.
Give ear, and let thy light be seen
   to shine forth gloriously.

2 In *Ephraim*'s and *Manasseh*'s sight,
   and *Benjamin*'s appear:
In all our fight stir up thy might,
   to save us, Lord, draw near.

3 Turn us, O God, to thee again,
   for we too long have swerv'd :
Cause thou thy face on us to shine,
   and we shall be preserv'd.

4 Lord God of hosts, how long shall we
   be left to this despair ?
How long, Lord, wilt thou angry be
   at thy own peoples prayer ?

5 Thou giv'st thy people tears for bread,
   and tears likewise for drink :
Their table thus is overspread,
   their cup fill'd to the brink.

6 Thou mak'st us in our neighbours eyes
   mere subjects of debate :
With laughter do our enemies
   behold our sad estate.

7 Turn us again, Lord God of hosts,
   and cause (as we have crav'd)
Thy face to shine on *Israel*'s coasts,
   and then we shall be sav'd.

The Second part.

8 A noble vine of *Israel*
   thou didst from *Egypt* bring :
The heathen folk thou didst expell,
   and plant it there to spring.

9 Thou mad'st it room for *Israel*'s sake,
   by thy almighty hand :
And caused'st it deep root to take,
   and lo it fill'd the land.

10 The hills and mountains all abroad
   were covered with its shade :
And like the cedar-trees of God,
   her branches were display'd.

11 Her boughs extending far and wide,
   unto the sea she sent :
And to *Euphrates* river side
   her other branches went.

12 Why haft thou then with great decay
   broke down her hedges so,
That all that pass along the way
   do pluck her as they go?
13 And it is wasted by the boar
   that cometh from the wood:
The wild beasts of the field great store,
   devour it for their food.

The Third part.

14 Lord God of hosts, we beg of thee,
   return again to thine:
Look down from heaven, behold and see,
   and visit this thy vine.
15 The vineyard and the branches young,
   which thy right hand hath set,
And for thy self hast made so strong,
   do not, O Lord, forget.
16 It's burnt with fire, it is cut down,
   and in a wasting case,
At thy rebuke, Lord, at the frown
   of thy displeased face.
17 Uphold, Lord, in his high degree
   the man of thy right hand;
The son of man made strong by thee,
   and for thy cause to stand.
18 So will we not go back at all
   from thee, O Lord most high:
Then quicken us, and we will call
   on thy name constantly.
19 Lord God of hosts, our hearts incline,
   and turn us now again:
And cause thy face on us to shine,
   and safe shall we remain.

PSALM LXXXI.

O Sing aloud with chearful voice
    to God our strength and stay:
And make a very joyful noise
    to *Jacob*'s God this day.
2 O take a psalm for melody,
    and bring the timbrell hither,
The pleasant harp and psaltery,
    and joyn them all together.
3 Blow up the trumpet this new-moon,
    (a duty not the least)
At times appointed to be done,
    upon our solemn feast.
4 For this was made a statute-law
    for *Israel* of old;
And such as God himself did draw,
    for *Jacob*'s sons to hold.
5 This he ordain'd in *Joseph*'s house,
    passing through *Egypt* land:
Where I did hear the barbarous,
    but did not understand.
6 I eas'd him of the burden there,
    that on his shoulders lay:
His hands likewise delivered were
    from making pots of clay.
7 O *Israel*, thou didst call on me
    in thy distressful case:
I'rescu'd, and I answer'd thee
    in thunders secret place.
I prov'd thee also in the way,
    where thou would'st needs prove me:
Even at the streams of *Meribah*
    I try'd and proved thee.

The Second part.

8 O my dear people, come and hear,
    and I'le declare to thee:

O *Israel*, if thou wilt give ear,
  and hearken unto me;
9 There shall be in thee no strange god,
  nor ever at all shalt thou
Adore the gods that are abroad,
  to whom the Gentiles bow.
10 For I the Lord thy God am he
  who thee from *Egypt* led:
Open thy mouth in prayer to me,
  and thou shalt sure be sped.
11 But though that I did *Israel* chuse,
  my own select to be:
Yet *Israel* did my voice refuse,
  and would have none of me.
12 So then I gave them up unto
  their own hearts wandring thought,
To walk as they desir'd to do,
  as their own counsels taught.
13 O that my people had compli'd,
  and heark'ned unto me:
And *Israel* had not walk't aside,
  but kept to my decree.
14 I should have soon subdu'd their foes,
  and turn'd my powerful hand
To the subversion of all those
  that durst against them stand.
15 The haters of the Lord (be sure)
  had low submission made:
But *Israel*'s time should still indure,
  and never have decay'd.
16 With finest of the wheat should he
  have fed his chosen flock:
I would have satisfied thee
  with honey from the rock.

PSALM LXXXII.

IN the assembly of the Great,
   the Lord himself doth stand:
And sitteth in the judgment-seat
   with judges of the land.
2 How long shall partiality
   prevail among you then,
To make you judge unrighteously,
   and favour wicked men?

3 Defend the poor and fatherless,
   oppress'd by worldly might:
Aid such as suffer great distress,
   and see ye do them right.
4 The weak and poor deliver ye,
   and needy of the land:
And rid them from the tyrannie
   of every wicked hand.

5 They know not, nor will understand,
   in darkness they walk on;
All the foundations of the land
   out of their course are gone,
6 I said indeed that ye were gods,
   and sons of God most high:
And that ye had a mighty ods
   by princely majesty.

7 But ye as common men shall die,
   and ye shall fall one day
As fell those people formerly,
   whom vengeance swept away.
8 Arise, O Lord, thy self advance
   just judgment to pursue:
The earth is thine inheritance,
   all nations are thy due.

PSALM LXXXII. *Metre 2.*

GOd standeth in the throng
   with all the men of might,

The Gods he sits among
 determining the right:
  Why do ye then,
(So long a space) accept the face
  of wicked men?

The fatherless defend,
 and plead ye for the poor,
The hand of Justice lend
 th' oppressed to secure:
  To poor men stand,
And those that need let them be freed
  from lewd mens hand.

They do not, will not know,
 but in the dark walk on,
The Earth's foundations go
 to ruine, every one.
  Ye are, said I,
As Gods and Sons (the mighty ones)
  of the most High.

But like to other men
 ye shall be in your death,
And no more Princes then,
 after this mortal breath:
  O God arise,
Judgment make known, for thou dost own
  all Monarchies.

PSALM LXXXIII.

O God, no longer hold thy peace,
 but now thy silence break:
This still tranquillity surcease,
 and raise thy self to speak.
2 For now behold, thine enemies
 do rage tumultuously:
And those that hate thee do arise,
 and lift their heads on high.

Psalm lxxxiij.

3 Sly consultations they did take
   against us all at once:
  And they their Plots together make
   against thy hidden ones.
4 Come let us cut them off, said they,
   and leave no root behind:
  So that the name of Israel may
   no more be had in mind.
5 For they have all with one consent,
   consulted as one man:
  Confederate, and against thee bent
   with all the power they can.
6 The tents of all the Edomites,
   and many other mens:
  The Ishmaelites and Moabites,
   and all the Hagarens.
7 Gebal and Ammon do conspire,
   and Amalek combines
  With the inhabitants of Tyre,
   and with the Philistines.
8 Assur is also joyn'd with them,
   and all of them indeed
  Have joyn'd against Jerusalem
   with Lots incestuous seed.

The Second part

  Do to them, Lord, as in that day
   when Midians hoast was strook:
  As Jabin fell and Sisera,
   o'rethrown at Kishon brook:
10 Which miserably perished
    at Endor, and were found
   With carcases all scattered
    as dung upon the ground.
11 Like Zeeb and Oreb, O compell
    their noble peers to fall:
   As Zeba and Zalmunna fell;
    so let their princes all.

12 Those namely that have spoken thus,
   come on, and let us take
The houses of the Lord to us,
   and them our houses make.
13 Make them I pray thee, O my God,
   like wheels that still turn round:
Or like the stubble blown abroad,
   when whirlwinds sweep the ground.
14 And as the fire consumes a wood
   with fierce and furious flame;
And mountains where the trees once stood,
   are singed with the same:
15 So let thy whirlwind furiously
   pursue them, Lord, full fast:
And let thy tempests terrify,
   and fright them with thy blast.
16 Cover, O Lord, and fill their face
   with their deserved shame:
That they may humbly beg thy grace,
   and seek thy glorious name.
17 Yea, let them all confounded be,
   and troubled day and night:
Yea bring them all to infamy,
   and let them perish quite.
18 That men may know that thou alone,
   whom we Jehovah call,
In all the earth the onely one,
   art highest over all.

PSALM LXXXIV.

How lovely is thy dwelling place,
   O Lord of hosts, to me!
The tabernacles of thy grace,
   how pleasant, Lord, they be!
2 My soul doth long, yea faints to see
   the courts of thy abode:
My heart and flesh cry out for thee,
   the ever-living God.

Psalm lxxxiv.

3 The sparrow finds a room to rest,
    and save her self from wrong:
  The swallow makes her self a nest,
    where she may lay her young.
  Even nigh thine altars, Lord of hosts,
    my God and King most high:
  While I am banish't from thy coasts,
    and forc't farr off to fly.

4 But oh, how happy men they be,
    that may dwell all their dayes
  Within thy house to honour thee,
    and ever give thee praise!

5 And likewise blessed men are they,
    whose stay and strength thou art;
  That to thy house do mind the way,
    and seek it in their heart.

6 Who passing through the desarts dry,
    Do take unwearied pain,
  In digging wells for their supply,
    or use the pools of rain:

7 And so go on from strength to strength,
    till every one of them
  Appear before the Lord at length
    in his Jerusalem.

The Second part.

8 O God of hosts, vouchsafe to hear
    when I to thee do pray:
  O God of Jacob, lend an ear
    to that which I shall say.

9 O Lord our shield, of thy good grace
    be pleas'd to look upon,
  And graciously behold the face
    of thine anointed one.

10 For in thy courts thy name to praise,
    I count a day spent there
  Far better than a thousand dayes,
    a thousand dayes elsewhere;

The very threshold of thy house
     preferring far before
   The tents of the ungracious:
     to dwell there evermore.
11 For God the Lord is sun and shield,
     he grace and glory gives:
   And no good thing shall he withhold
     from him that purely lives.
12 O Lord of hosts, that man is blest,
     and happy sure is he,
   Whose heart by faith doth ever rest
     with confidence in thee.

PSALM LXXXIV. *Metre 2.*

Ye Children, &c.

1 O Lord of hosts, how lovely fair
     thy sacred tabernacles are:
2 And there my soul doth long to be
   Yea and my spirit pines away,
   Within thy courts to come and pray:
     my flesh and heart cry out for thee.
3 O living God, methinks I miss
   The sparrows and the swallows bliss,
     so happily inhabiting:
   For they may build their nests full throng,
   And near thine altar lay their young,
   O Lord of hosts, my God, my King.
4 O blessed are all those that may
   Dwell in thy house both night and day;
     for they will ever give thee praise.
5 And blest the man whose strength's in thee,
   Who though he cannot present be,
     yet sets his heart on thy sweet wayes.
6 That passing on by Baca's vale,
     Digg wells to serve when waters fail,
   or use the pools which rain doth fill.

7 From

7 From strength to strength they travel there,
  Until at last they all appear
before the Lord in Sion hill.

The second part:

8 O thou that art the God of war,
  Whose all the hoasts of creatures are,
depending on thy soveraignty,
  Vouchsafe thou, Lord, my prayer to hear,
Listen and lend a gracious ear,
  O God of Jacob's family.
9 O God our saviour and our shield,
  That dost to us protection yield,
behold us with a kind aspect:
  And now be pleas'd to look upon
The face of thine anointed one,
  and let thy beams on him reflect.
10 For in thy courts I count one day
  A thousand others to out-weigh:
nay I had rather keep a door
  Within the house of the most High,
Then dwell with all prosperity
  in sinners tents for evermore.
11 For God's a sun and shield divine,
  And doth with grace and glory shine,
and gives all good things to the just.
12 Blest is the man, O Lord of hoasts,
  That only thine assistance boasts,
And hath in thee repos'd his trust.

PSALM lxxxv.

Lord, thou hast dealt most favourably.
  with thy beloved land;
And Jacobs hard captivity
  brought back with powerful hand.
2 Thy peoples foul iniquities,
  which they have lived in,

Mark well the words that I do say,
  my supplication hear.

7 In time when trouble doth me move,
  to thee I do complain :
Because I know and plainly prove,
  thou answer'st me again.
8 For like to thee, O Lord, is none
  among the powers divine :
Nor are the works of any one
  to be compar'd with thine.

The Second part.

9 All nations made by thy great might,
  all whom thy hands did frame,
Shall come and worship in thy sight,
  and glorify thy name.
10 For, Lord, thou art a mighty one,
  and thou dost wondrous deeds:
And thou, O Lord, art God alone,
  from whom such power proceeds.
11 Teach me thy way of truth most right,
  and I'le observe the same :
And unto thee my heart unite,
  that I may fear thy name.
12 I will praise thee unfeignedly,
  O Lord, my God, that art ;
And I will ever glorify
  thy name with all my heart :
13 Because thy mercies shew'd to me
  in greatness do excel :
My soul by thee hath bin set free
  out from the lowest hell.
14 O God, the proud against me rise,
  and throngs of violent men
Have sought to make my soul their prize,
  but thee they mind not then.

15 But, Lord, thou art a God most kind,
   suffering no little space:
Compassions store in thee we find,
   and plenteous truth and grace.
16 O turn to me, and pitty me,
   and let thy servant have
The strength that is bestow'd by thee,
   Thy hand-maids son to save.
17 And shew me some good token now,
   that hateful foes may see
And be asham'd, because that thou
   dost help and comfort me.

PSALM LXXXVII.

The ground-works of God's city fair
   are very strongly stai'd:
Upon the holy mountains are
   his firm foundations laid.
2 God loves the gates of Sion best,
   his grace doth there abide:
He loves them more then all the rest
   of Jacobs tents beside.
3 Most glorious things are said of thee,
   O city of the Lord.
4 Rahab and Babylon shall be
   thy converts on record.
All those that know me, with desire
   hereof shall hear me tell:
How Ethiope, Palestine, and Tyre,
   were born in Israel.
5 And it shall be of Sion said,
   this and that man she bore:
And the most High will be her aid,
   and strength'n her evermore:
6 Counting the Gentile with the Jew,
   Recording every heir.

7 The singers and musicians too,
  and all my springs are there.

II. Metre.

LO! there the firm foundation lies
  Of Sion's sacred E D I F I C E
  upon the hills of holiness,
The Gates whereof the Lord doth love
All other buildings far above
  whatever Jacob doth possess.
Most glorious things are spread abroad,
Of thee, O city, lov'd of God,
  spoken to thy Eternal fame ;
Thou shalt have Convert many a one,
Ægypt, and also Babylon,
  hear, O my friends ! what I proclame.

Behold, both Tyre and Palestine
With Ethiopia shall be thine
  Sion brought forth this forreigner;
And said of Sion it shall be
This and that man was born in thee,
  And God most high shall stablish her.
The Lord in his eternal scroll
Shall Sion's citizens inroll,
  This man was born in Sion hill :
There's he that plays, there's he that sings,
And all my pure spiritual springs
  are found to flow within thee still.

III. Metre.

παφραστικῶς. *To the Tune of the Lord's Prayer.*

IN holy hills is Sion's floor,
    which God with grace and glory crowns,
God loves the gates of Sion more
    than all the rest of Jacob's Towns:
Most glorious things are fam'd abroad
Of thee, O city, lov'd of God,

For

For I will mention born in thee
   Egyptians, Babylonians, Moors,
Philiſtians, Tyrians there ſhall be
   told to my friends amongſt my ſtores.
For God hath ſaid that all on Earth
In Sion may renew their birth.

For God moſt high ſhall ſtabliſh her,
   and ſhall record each faithful ſoul,
When he is pleas'd to regiſter,
   and Sions converts to inroll.
There's he that plays, there's he that ſings,
And thence all heavenly comfort ſprings.

PSALM LXXXVIII.

Lord God of my ſalvation (dear)
   to thee I us'd to pray:
And bring my ſupplication near
   before thee night and day.
2 Now let my prayer have acceſs
   before thee, O moſt high:
Incline thine ear with readineſs,
   and hearken to my cry.
3 For, Lord, my ſoul is fill'd with wo,
   ſuch ſorrow now I have:
My very life is brought ſo low,
   that it doth touch the grave.
4 And I am counted one of them
   that to the pit deſcend:
And to be one among thoſe men,
   whoſe ſtrength is at an end.
5 As free among the ſlain and dead,
   lodg'd in oblivion's land;
No more by thee remembered,
   but cut off from thy hand.
6 Thou lay'ſt me in the loweſt pit,
   in deep and darkſom caves.

7 Thy wrath lies hard upon me yet,
   I'm prest with all thy waves.
8 My friends thou hast put far from me,
   and made them loath me sore:
 I am shut up in misery,
   and can come forth no more.
9 By reason of my misery
   mine eye sheds many a tear:
 Lord, I have daily call'd on thee,
   to thee my hands I rear.
10 Intend'st thou, Lord, said I, to show
   thy wonders to the dead?
 Shall dead men rise from graves below
   to make thy praises spread?
11 Shall we thy loving-kindness, Lord,
   within the grave express?
 Or can destruction best record
   thy truth and faithfulness?
12 Shall we in darkness understand
   thy wonders manifold:
 And in oblivion's cloudy land,
   thy righteousness behold?
13 But these my prayers and my cries,
   to thee, O Lord, I sent:
 And early ere the morning rise,
   my prayers shall thee prevent.
14 Why then, Lord, is my soul, I say,
   thus long cast off by thee?
 And wherefore dost thou hide away
   thy gracious face from me?
15 I am afflicted like to die,
   suffering from youth to age:
 I am distracted whilst that I
   indure such wrath and rage.
16 The fierceness of thy furious wrath
   is gone quite o're my head:

  And I do seem as one cut off
   with daily fear and dread.
17 They came about me every way,
   as waters breaking out:
  And altogether every day
   they compass'd me about.
18 And thou hast separated far
   from me my friends and lovers:
  And those that mine acquaintance are,
   a cloud of darkness covers.

II. *Metre.*

All People, &c. or, *O Lord Consider.*

Lord God of my salvation dear,
 I cry'd before thee day and night:
Unto my cry incline thine ear,
 And let my pray'r come in thy sight.
For, Lord, my soul is fill'd with wo,
 My life draws nigh unto the grave
Reck'ned with them that sink so low,
 And very little strength I have.

A freeman in this dead estate,
 As slain, and buried, and forgot:
As whom thy hand hath separate,
 And such as thou regardest not.
Thou lay'st me in the lowest ward,
 Where dark and deepest dungeons are:
Thy wrath upon me lyeth hard,
 And all thy bitter storms I bear.

My friends from me thou hast restrain'd,
 And made me loath'd in lovers eyes:
In prison I am fast detain'd,
 Mine eye laments my miseries.
O Lord, I daily call'd on thee,
 My humble hands I meekly raise:
Shall dead men, Lord, thy wonders see,
 Shall dead men rise to give thee praise?

Lord, can the grave thy grace express,
  Thy faithful truth destruction teach?
Thy wonders and thy righteousness
  Can dark and dumb oblivion preach?
Betimes, O Lord, will I direct
  My humble suits and cries to thee:
Why dost thou Lord my soul reject,
  Why dost thou hide thy face from me?

My tortur'd soul is pain'd to death,
  while from my youth I always bear
The heavy burdens of thy wrath,
  Thy terrours and distracting fear:
They clos'd me round as waters deep,
  They compass'd me at once, I say:
From me my lovers thou dost keep,
  And mine acquaintance hid'st away.

PSALM LXXXIX.

TH' eternal mercies of the Lord
  my song shall still express:
My mouth to ages shall record
  thy truth and faithfulness.
2 For mercy shall be built, said I,
  for ever to endure:
In heaven it self thy verity
  shall be establish't sure.
3 I made a covenant, saith the Lord,
  with David mine elect:
And to my servant past my word,
  and sware to this effect:
4 Thy seed will I establish fast,
  that it can never fall:
And build thy throne that it shall last
  to generations all.
5 The heavens shall praise thy wonders, Lord,
  and all thy faithfulness

Thy

Psalm lxxxix.

Thy congregations shall record,
and all thy saints confess.
6 For who in heaven can any way
with our Lord God compare?
Which of the glorious angels may
so bold comparison dare?
7 In saints assemblies evermore
must God have awful fear:
With reverence must they all adore,
that unto him draw near.
8 Lord God of hosts, what lord is he
with whom such strength is found,
Or who has faithfulness like thee
wherewith thou art girt round?
9 The restless raging of the seas
thou rulest at thy will:
Their swelling waves thou dost appease,
and mak'st them calm and still.
10 Thou brok'st in pieces Egypts land,
like one that slaughtered lies:
Thou hast with thy almighty hand
disperst thine enemies.

The Second part.

11 The heavens and the earth are thine,
the world so richly stor'd,
With all the fulness found therein;
thou founded'st them, O Lord.
12 The north and south no being had,
before thou didst them frame:
Tabor and Hermon shall be glad,
rejoycing in thy name.
13 O God, thou hast a mighty arm
of soveraign command:
Strong is thy hand, thy power is firm,
and high is thy right hand.

14 Justice

14 Juſtice and judgement on thy throne
   retain their dwelling-place :
Mercy and truth, conjoyn'd in one,
   ſhall go before thy face.

15 Bleſt is the people that doth know,
   and hear the joyful ſound :
Thy beams ſhall light them as they go,
   and ſhine about them round.

16 They in thy name ſhall all the day
   rejoyce exceedingly :
And in thy righteouſneſs ſhall they
   be lifted up on high.

17 For of their ſtrength thou art the crown,
   and of thy grace thou canſt
And wilt procure (with great renown)
   our horn to be advanc't.

18 For, Lord, thou doſt defend us well
   from every hurtful thing :
The holy one of Iſrael
   is our almighty King.

The Third part.

19 In viſion to thy ſaint was ſaid,
   (for then thou mad'ſt it known)
Lo, I my helping hand have laid
   upon a mighty one.
I have exalted very high
   one that is choſen forth
Of all the people generally,
   and one of greateſt worth.

20 My ſervant David I have found,
   and on his honoured head,
In token that he ſhould be crown'd,
   my ſacred oyl I ſhed.

21 With whom my hand ſhall go along,
   to ſtabliſh him full ſure :

My arm shall also make him strong,
  that he may still indure.
22 The enemy shall not oppress,
  nor make of him a prey:
Nor shall the son of wickedness
  afflict him any way.
23 I will beat down his furious foes,
  and quell them in his sight:
And I will greatly plague all those
  that bear him hate and spite.
24 But lo, my faithfulness and grace
  to him shall be the same:
His horn shall have the highest place,
  exalted in my name.
25 And I will make his power to reach
  unto the ocean wide:
And his right hand of power shall stretch
  unto the rivers side.
26 Thou art my father, he shall cry,
  thou art my God alone:
Thou art my rock to which I fly
  for my salvation.
27 And I will make him my first-born,
  by priviledge of birth:
And will exalt his glorious horn
  above all kings on earth.
28 My mercy will I make to last,
  preserv'd for him in store:
My covenant also shall stand fast
  with him for evermore.
29 His seed will I perpetuate,
  that it shall last alwayes:
His throne shall bear as long a date,
  as heavens eternal dayes.

The Fourth part.

30 If David's seed forsake my law,
  and walk not in my way:

31 If from my precepts they withdraw,
  and from my statutes stray:
32 They shall be sure that I their God
  to visit will begin;
  And scourge them with a smarting-rod,
  for their offence and sin.
33 Yet wholly to withdraw my love,
  their sin shall not prevail:
  Nor shall they so much anger move,
  to make my truth to fail.
34 My covenant I will never break,
  it shall contiuue still:
  And that which once my lips did speak,
  I'le certainly fulfill.
35 Once by my holiness I swore,
  that sacred oath and high;
  That having promised before
  to David, I'le not ly.
36 His seed for ever shall endure,
  while time it self shall run:
  His throne shall be establish't sure
  before me, as the sun.
37 And as the moon within the skie
  for ever standeth fast,
  A faithful witness there on high;
  so shall his kingdom last.

The Fifth part.

38 But now thou hast cast off, O Lord,
  and left me all alone:
  Yea in thy wrath thou hast abhorr'd
  me thine anointed one.
39 Thy covenant with thy servant made,
  thou hast again unbound:
  His crown thou hast ignobly laid
  and cast upon the ground.
40 Moreover thou hast broken down
  his hedges every one;

Pſalm lxxxix.

And his ſtrong holds in every town
  thy hand hath overthrown.
41 All they that paſs along the way,
  do ſpoil him every where;
He is a meer reproach and prey
  unto his neighbor's neer.
42 Thou haſt exalted the right hand
  of all his bitter foes,
And made his hateful enemies ſtand,
  rejoycing at his woes.
43 Moreover, Lord, his ſword ſo keen,
  thou now haſt blunted quite;
Nor art thou in the battle ſeen,
  to make him ſtand in fight.
44 His glory thou haſt made to ceaſe,
  and caſt his throne to ground:
45 His youthful dayes thou did'ſt decreaſe,
  and him with ſhame confound.
46 How long, Lord, wilt thou hide thy face,
  and not again return?
Shall thy fierce wrath ſo long a ſpace,
  like fire, conſume and burn?
47 Remember, Lord, how ſhort an hour
  I have for to remain:
Wherefore haſt thou imploy'd thy power,
  to make all men in vain?
48 What man alive ſhall not ſee death,
  but ſtill his life ſhall ſave.
And ſtay the hand that ſtops his breath,
  to bring him to the grave?
49 Lord, where's thy former clemency?
  thy kindneſs in our youth,
Which thou haſt ſworn ſo ſolemnly
  to David, in thy truth.
50 Remember, Lord, what great diſgrace,
  is by thy ſervants born

And

    And how my bosom doth imbrace
      the mighty people's scorn.

51 Reproaches which thine enemies,
    on me, O Lord, have thrown,
  And do the foot-steps scandalize
    of thine anointed one.

52 But blest for ever be the Lord,
    and blest be God agen ;
  And let the church with one accord
    resound amen, amen.

PSALM XC.

Lord thou hast been our dwelling-place
    from age to age on earth ;
2 Thou wast before the time and space,
    which gave the mountains birth :
  Or ever thou had'st fram'd or form'd
    the earth, or smallest clod,
  Or any part of all the world ;
    thou art eternal God.

3 Thou grindest man through grief and pain
    to very dust, and then
  Thou sai'st return to dust again,
    return ye sons of men.

4 Though life a thousand years do last,
    it seemeth in thy sight,
  As yesterday when it is past,
    or as a watch by night.

5 As with the floods that swiftly pass,
    thou carriest them away ;
  Even like a sleep, or like the grass
    which quickly doth decay ;

6 Which in the morning grows upright,
    but fadeth by and by ;
  And is cut down ere it be night
    all withered, dead and dry.

7 For by thine anger Lord our God
   are we consum'd and spent;
 And troubled with thy stinging rod
   of wrathful punishment.
8 Thou settest our iniquities
   plainly before thy face,
 And thy clear countenance descries
   our sins in secret place.
9 For all our days are past away,
   thine anger taking hold
 We spend our years from day to day
   as when a tale is told.
10 The date of all our dayes appears
    but threescore years and ten ;
 And they that live to fourscore years
   are surely stronger men :

 Yet pain and grief is all the strength
   which then they count upon;
 And also that cut off at length ;
   and we as blasts are gon.
11 To whom O God doth it appear
    what power thine anger hath,
 Even according to thy fear,
   so is thy dreadful wrath.
12 Lord teach us this religious art
    of numbring out our dayes;
 That so we may apply our heart
   to sacred wisdom's wayes.
13 Return, O Lord ; how long ere thou
    compassion on us take ?
 O let it, Lord, repent thee now,
   for thy dear servant's sake.
14 O fill us early with thy grace,
    that so we may rejoice ;
 And all our lives continued space,
   triumph in heart and voice.

15 According to the days wherein
    thou plagu'ſt us, make us glad;
  After the years which we have ſeen
    ſo ſorrowful and ſad:
16 O let thy bleſſed work appear
    unto thy ſervants true,
  And let thy glory ſhine moſt clear
    unto their children's view.
17 Shew us the beauty of thy face;
    and what we take in hand,
  Eſtabliſh, Lord, of thy good grace,
    And make it firm to ſtand.

II. *Metre.* Διαφορετικῶς.

The Firſt part.

Lord thou haſt been our dwelling-place,
    in generations all:
Thou waſt ere there was form or face
    of creature great or ſmall.
Before the mountains had their birth
    the world or ſmalleſt clod
Of all the vaſt and ſpacious earth,
    thou art eternal God.

But as for man that's made of clay
    he's ſoon unmade agen:
And falls to duſt, when thou doſt ſay,
    return, ye ſons of men.
Whereas again, a thouſand years
    to thy eternal ſight,
As yeſterday that's paſt, appears,
    or as a watch by night.

Like to a ſwift or haſty ſtream,
    thou mak'ſt man's life-time paſs:
Or like a tranſitory dream,
    Or like the ſpringing graſs.
Which in the morning flouriſheth,
    moſt pleaſantly up-grown:

And in the evening withereth,
   soon after it is mowen.

For in thine anger we are spent,
   and thus our time goes o're,
And in thy wrath so vehement
   we are afflicted sore.
Thou markest our iniquities
   as in the open Sun :
And thy clear countenance descries
   our sins in secret done.

For through thy wrath we faint and die,
   and all our days do fail,
Our years are spent as uselesly
   as when men tell a tale.

The Second part.

The time's but threescore years and ten
   that we continue here,
And if some stronger sort of men
   do live to fourscore year :
Their life is labour, strength is none,
   but sorrowful decay:
So soon is it cut off and gone,
   so fast we flee away.

Who knows, but in a weak degree,
   what power thine anger hath,
For greater than the fear can be,
   is thy most dreadful wrath.
Lord teach us the uncertainty
   and shortness of our dayes,
That so we may our hearts apply
   to wise and holy wayes.

Return, O Lord, how long a space!
   let it repent thee much,
Touching thy servants woful case
   whose suff'rings have been such.
O satisfie us speedily
   with thy compassions kind :

That all our days may yield us joy,
   and gladness cheer our mind.

As thou haft sent us sorrows keen
   so send us comforts glad
For dayes and years that we have seen
   so sorrowful and sad.
O let thy work appear unto
   thy servants every one,
Thy glory to their children shew
   when we are dead and gone.

The Lord our God shine on his church,
   and grace our joynt endeavour;
O prosper thou our handy-works,
   and stablish them for ever.

III. Metre. *To the Third New Tune.*

1, 2.

Lord, thou hast been our dwelling-place
In ages all, from race to race,
   and thou wast God before:
Before the mountains were brought forth,
Before the fabrick of the earth,
   True, God for evermore.

3, 4.

Thou to destruction turnest man,
And saist, Return, your life's a span,
   return to dust forthright:
A thousand years in thy survay
Are but as by-past yesterday,
   or as a watch by night.

5, 6.

As with a flood thou bear'st them hence
They're as a sleep which binds the sense,
   and feels not its decay:

As morning grafs doth fpread and fpring,
But is cut down at evening,
  and withereth ftraight-way.

7, 8.

For by thine anger we are fpent,
And by thy wrathful punifhment,
  we are afflicted fore:
Thou fetteft our iniquities
Apparently before thine eyes,
  and keep'ft them on the fcore.

8, 9.

Our fecret fins are fet in fight,
Before thy countenance fo bright
  and thou doft them behold:
For all our days thine anger wafts,
We fpend our years as idle blafts,
  as if a tale were told.

The Second part.

10.

Mans age is threefcore years and ten;
And if a ftronger fort of men
  can fourfcore count upon:
Yet is their ftrength but grief and toil,
For all's cut off within a while,
  and quickly we are gone.

11, 12.

Who knows what power thine anger hath?
For as thy fear fo is thy wrath,
  and greater if we knew:
So teach us, Lord, to count our dayes,
That we may follow wifdom's wayes,
  and bring our hearts thereto.

13, 14.

Return, O Lord, no tarrying make,
Repent thee for thy servant's sake,
   whose sufferings have bin sad:
O satisfie us speedily
With thy sweet grace, that we may joy,
   and all our dayes be glad.

15, 16.

O comfort us, and give relief
According to our dayes of grief
   and years that made us grone:
Thy work, Lord, let thy servants know,
Thy glory to their children show,
   when we are dead and gone.

17.

And let the beauty all abroad,
The beauty of the Lord our God
   be on us still to shine:
And stablish, Lord, our handy-works
The handy-work of thy true church,
   establish it to thine.

PSALM XCI.

Who dwelleth in the secret place
   of him that is most high,
In shadow of th' Almighty's grace
   abides continually?
2 Thus of the Lord I will report,
   my gracious God is he;
He is my refuge and my fort,
   in whom my trust shall be.

3 He surely shall be thy defence,
   both from the fowler's snare,
And from the noisom pestilence,
   which doth infect the air:

4 His feathered wings shall cover thee,
  and be thy confidence ;
 His truth thy trusty shield shall be,
  and buckler for defence.
5 Thou shalt not need to be afraid,
  for terrors of the night ;
 Nor for the arrow be dismaid,
  that in the day makes flight.
6 Nor shalt thou fear the pestilence,
  that walks in darksom way ;
 Nor that destructive violence
  that wasts at height of day.
7 And at thy side as thou doest stand,
  a thousand dead shall be ;
 Ten thousand strook at thy right hand,
  and yet thou shalt be free.
8 Only shalt thou stand by and see,
  beholding with thine eyes,
 What wicked mens reward shall be,
  for their iniquities.

The Second part.

9 Because thou mad'st, the Lord most high,
  thy dwelling-place to be ;
 The same to whom I alwayes fly,
  to shield and succor me :
10 There shall no evil thing befall
  to thee in any case ;
 Nor shall there any plague at all
  come nigh thy dwelling-place.
11 For he shall charge his heavenly host
  to bear thee in their arm ;
 And watch the way wherein thou goest
  and keep thee safe from harm.
12 And they shall be thy guard and guide,
  O dear beloved one,
 Lest that thy foot should slip aside
  or dash against a stone.

13 The lion thou shalt tread upon
　the aspe and lion's whelp,
　The dragon thou shalt trample on
　by God's great power and help.
24 Because he set his love on me,
　therefore saith God will I
Deliver him, and set him free
　from all adversity.

I'le set him up in high degree,
　because he knew my name:
15 With prayer he shall call on me
　I answering the same.
His horn with honor I will raise,
　be with him in temptation,
16 Suffice him with the length of dayes,
　and shew him my salvation.

II. *Metre.*

Ye Children, &c.

The secret place of God most high,
　Whoever dwells in faithfully,
Shall in th' Almightie's shade abide:
　Thus of the Lord I will report,
He is refuge and my fort,
　My God, in whom I will confide.
Sure he shall keep thee by his care,
　Both from the fowler's subtil snare,
And from the noisom Pestilence:
　His feathers safe shall cover thee,
Under his wings thy trust shall be,
　His truth thy shield and sure defence.
Thou shalt not need to take a fright
　For any terror of the night,
Nor for the shaft that flies by day:
　Nor darkness-walking Pestilence,
Nor the destructive influence
　That doth at Noon-tide wast and slay.

A

Psalm xcj.

A thousand, and ten thousand shall
   At thy left side and right hand fall ;
Yet shall it not come nigh to thee :
   Only (when dangers do surprize)
Thou shalt behold it with thine eyes,
   What wicked mens reward shall be.

The Second part.

Because the Lord, that is most high,
(Who is my refuge constantly)
   Thou hast thy habitation made ;
There shall no evil thing befall,
   Nor shall there any plague at all,
   Thee, or thy dwelling-place invade.
For to his blessed Angels, He,
   Shall give a charge concerning thee,
In all thy wayes to have thee kept ;
   That still upholden in their arm,
Thou shalt not dash thy foot for harm,
   Against a stone where thou hast stept.

Upon the lion thou shalt tread,
   And trample on the Dragon's head,
   The Adder, and the Lions whelp ;
Because he set his love on me,
   I'le set him high, I'le set him free,
   Because he knew where lay his help.
Upon me boldly he shall call,
   And I will answer him in all,
   I will be with him in distress :
I will relieve, and raise him high,
   Suffice him with long life will I :
   And shew him endless happiness.

PSALM XCII.

TO praise the Lord most thankfully
   it is an excellent thing,

     And to thy name, O thou most high,
       sweet psalms of praise to sing.
2 To shew the kindness of the Lord:
       before the morning light,
    Thy truth and justice to record
       when it doth draw to night.
3 Upon an instrument likewise
       whereto ten strings are bound,
    Upon your harps and psalteries
       with sweet and solemn sound;
4 For thou hast made me to rejoice
       in things archiev'd by thee,
    And I triumph in heart and voice
       thy handy work to see.
5 How great, O Lord, who can express
       thy works and thoughts profound,
    Which are a deep so bottomless
       that none can search or found:
6 The bruitish man discern's no whit
       nor see's thy mighty hand;
    And fools profane are far unfit
       this thing to understand.
7 When wicked men as grass do spring,
       and evil doers all
    Appear most fat and flourishing,
       it shews their utter fall.
    Then is their final ruine nigh,
       and at the very door;
8 But thou, O Lord, thou art most high,
       and that for evermore.

         The Second part.

9 For lo, O Lord, behold and see,
       behold thy foes shall fall,
    The workers of iniquity
       shall be dispersed all.

10 But like unto an unicorn,
　with high advanced head;
So shalt thou, Lord, exalt my horn,
　and fresh oil on me shed.

11 My own desire upon my foes,
　mine eye shall surely see:
The same mine ear shall hear of those
　that rise to trouble me.

12 But like the palm the just shall be,
　so flourish and come on:
And like unto the cedar tree,
　that grows in Lebanon.

13 Those that within the house of God
　are planted by his grace,
In our God's courts shall spread abroad,
　and flourish in that place:

14 And in their age much fruit shall bring,
　and fat, as e're was seen;
And pleasantly both bud and spring,
　with boughs and branches green.

15 The Lord's uprightness to express,
　who is a rock to me;
And there is no unrighteousness
　in him, nor none can be.

II. Mettre.

Have mercy, &c.

To bless and praise the Lord
　it is an exc'llent thing,
To magnifie thy Name most high,
　in praises when we sing,
I'th' morning to record
　thy loving kindness dear,
And to express thy faithfulness
　when th' evening draweth near.

On lute and pfaltery,
   and harps moft folemn found;
For Lord through thine own works divine,
   thou mad'ft my joyes abound.
I triumph to defcry
   the works which thou haft wrought,
How great and rare, O Lord, they are,
   how deep is every thought?

A bruitifh man knows not,
   no fool perceives this thing:
For often when ungodly men,
   as morning grafs do fpring,
Then is the final lot
   of their deftruction nigh,
But thou doft reign the moft fupream
   to all eternity.

For lo! O Lord, thy foes,
   for lo thy foes fhall fall:
Thy truth affures of wicked doers,
   they fhall be fcattered all.
But like the horn that grows
   on Unicorn's bold head;
So Lord thou fhalt, my horn exalt,
   and frefh oyl on me fpread.

The Second part.

Mine eye his wifh fhall fee,
   upon mine enemies:
The fame mine ear, of them fhall hear,
   that do againft me rife.
But like a Cedar tree
   which Lebanon forth-brings,
The juft fhall grow; and flourifh fo
   as laden Palm-tree fprings.
His Temple-plants fhall fpring
   in our God's courts each one,
And ftill produce, their fruitful juice
   in age, when they are grown.

Still fat and flourishing,
  God's justice to express,
My Rock is He, most pure and free
  from all unrighteousness.

PSALM XCIII.

The Lord doth reign with royalty,
  array'd in beauty bright;
The Lord is cloath'd with majesty,
  and girds himself with might.
The world is fixt, and still must hold,
  for thou decreed'st the thing.
2 Thy throne's established of old;
  thou art eternal king.
3 The floods have lifted up, O Lord,
  the floods, (whose tempest raves;)
Have lifted up their voice, and roar'd.
4 The floods lift up their waves.
The Lord on high is mightier far,
  than many water's noise;
Yea, mightier than the waters are,
  when foaming billows rise.
5 Thy testimonies precious
  are kept on sure record;
And holiness becom's thy house
  for evermore, O Lord.

II. *Metre.* The mighty God, *&c.*

The Waves suppressed.

The Lord doth rule and reign triumphantly,
The Lord is cloath'd with robes of majesty;
  The Lord is cloath'd with strength,
    With strength throughout,
  Wherewith he girts, and binds himself about:
The world is stablisht't on a sure foundation,
That it can not be moved from its station.

Thou hast of old established thy throne,
For Lord thou art the everlasting one :
   The floods, O Lord, the floods have lift aloft,
   The floods have lifted up their waves full oft ;
The floods have lifted up their waves and waters
But what's their power compar'd to their Creator'

The Lord on high is mightier evermore
Than all the noise of waters when they roar ;
   Yea, mightier far than all the waves combin'd,
   When seas are chafed by the eastern wind :
His testimonie's sure, and still persever ;
Holiness decks thy house, O Lord, for ever.

PSALM XCIV.

O Lord, to whom it doth belong,
   just vengeance to repay :
O God, the punisher of wrong,
   do thou thy self display.
2 Thou judg of all in general,
   thy self no longer hide :
Arise, dispense a recompence
   to all the sons of pride.

3 How long, O Lord, how long, I say,
   shall wicked men oppress !
How long a time shall such as they
   triumph in wickedness :
4 How long shall they pronounce and say
   hard things not to be born,
And all that plie iniquity
   still boast themselves with scorn.

5 Thy people, Lord, they break and bray,
   thy heritage they oppress,
6 Widows and strangers they do slay,
   and kill the fatherless.
7 And yet dare they presume to say
   the Lord shall never see.

This Jacob's God whom they applaud
  shall no discerner be.
8 O understand ye people rude,
  some knowledg now discern,
Ye fools among the multitude
  when will ye wisdom learn?
9 Shall he not hear that plants the ear,
  and also shall not he
That form'd the eye so curiously
  be able for to see?
10 He that doth Heathen men chastise
  shall not that God correct?
He that doth teach man to be wise
  is there in him defect?
11 The Lord can tell and knows full well
  what thoughts we entertain
For he doth scan the thoughts of man
  and finds them all but vain.

The Second part.

12 Blest is the man whom thou, O Lord,
  dost fatherly chastise,
And out of thy most holy word
  dost teach him to be wise.
13 That thou (most blest) may'st give him rest
  till stormy times be past,
And till the ditch be digg'd in which
  the wicked shall be cast.
14 For sure the Lord will not reject
  the people whom he takes,
The heritage to him select
  at no time he forsakes.
15 But sure regress to righteousness
  shall judgment have again,
And joyntly then true-hearted men
  shall wait upon her train.

16 Who will rise up in my defence
   against the vile and leud;
Who will for me stand up against
   the wicked multitude?
17 But that the Lord did help afford
   against these wicked men,
I had almost given up the ghost,
   and dwelt in silence then.
18 But when I said my foot doth slide,
   I now am like to fall,
Thy mercy, Lord, thou didst provide,
   to stay me therewithal.
19 Amid'st the crowd and multitude
   of various thoughts which roul
Within my brest, thy comforts rest
   and do delight my soul.
20 Lord, shall the throne of wickedness
   have fellowship with thee?
Which frameth mischief to oppress,
   by law and flat decree?
21 They gather all against the soul
   of righteous men and good:
And as for them they dare condemn
   the innocentest blood.
22 But lo, the Lord that saves all his,
   is my defence on high:
My God my rock and refuge is;
   and unto him I fly.
23 He'll recompence their own offence,
   and take them in their sin:
The Lord, I say, our God shall slay,
   and cut them off therein.

PSALM. XCV.

Come let us sing with joyful noise
  to our salvation's rock.
2 With Psalms of praise and shouts of joys,
  into his presence flock.
3 A God, a king of great command,
  a king of gods He is,
4 The Earth's great deeps are in his hand;
  the strength of hills is his.
5 Dry land and seas, lo! both of these,
  his hands did form and frame.
6 O come adore with bended knees
  the Lord our maker's Name.
7 For he's our God, and we the flock,
  of whom he hath command;
His people and his pasture-flock,
  and sheep of his own hand.
8 If ye will hear God's voice to day
  then harden not your heart,
As Israel did at Meribah,
  within the desert part.
9 When tempting infidelity
  did in their bosomes lurk,
What time your fathers tempted M E.
  prov'd me, and saw my work.
10 'Twice twenty years they griev'd my mind,
  and I of them did say,
This people errs with heart so blind,
  they have not known my way.
11 To whom I sware it in my wrath,
  then kindling in my brest,
That they should never tread the path
  that leads into my rest.

II. *Metre.*

II. *Metre.* Have mercy, &c.

O come sing we a song,
  a joyful noise be made
With joynt accord before the Lord,
  our rock of saving aid.
Into his presence throng,
  hearts truly thankful bring,
And make a noise exciting joys,
  sweet psalms unto him sing.

Great King, great God he is,
  whose power all Gods transcends,
The spacious lands are in his hands,
  the deeps he comprehends.
The strength of hills is his,
  the sea is his command,
He made the same: His hands did frame
  the dry and solid land.

O come bow down all we,
  before him let us fall;
Let us adore and kneel before
  the Lord that made us all.
For our great God is he,
  we are his people dear,
The pasture sheep which he doth keep,
  his voice this day now hear.

And harden not your heart,
  as once at Meribah
Ye did transgress i'th' wilderness,
  in that temptation-day.
As in the desart part
  your fathers tempted ME,
And prov'd my might: each Israelite,
  when they my works did see.

I forty years was griev'd
  with this lewd race, and say'd,

Psalm xcv.

they are indeed an erring feed,
  in heart and judgment stray'd.
Nor have they yet believ'd
  wherefore I did protest;
That never they should find the way,
  of entrance to my rest.

III. *Metre.* All People, &c.

Come let us sing with joyful noise,
  to God our rock of saving might:
With psalms of praise and shouts of joys,
  now let us come before his sight.
For he's a God of highest throne,
  a King above all Deities:
The earth's deep places are his own,
  the strength of hills is his likewise.

The sea is his, he did it frame,
  his hands did form the solid land:
O come adore our maker's Name,
  with bended knee and raised hand.
For he's our God, and none but he,
  we are his pasture people choice;
The sheep of his own hand are we,
  to day if ye will hear his voice.

Then harden not your heart, as they
  i'th' provocation did transgress,
And as in that temptation day,
  within the desart wilderness.
When as your Fathers tempted ME,
  prov'd me, and saw my work display'd:
Full forty years I griev'd to see
  this generation, and I said:

'Tis a people errs in heart,
  and hath not known my way most blest,
Such as I sware should have no part
  nor entrance into my rest.

PSALM XCVI.

Sing ye with praise unto the Lord,
  new songs of joy and mirth;
Sing to the Lord with one accord,
  all people of the earth.
2 Yea, sing unto the Lord, I say,
  and magnifie his name;
From day to day his praise display,
  his saving health proclame.
3 Declare his glory, do not spare,
  but let the heathen know,
How great and rare his wonders are,
  and this to all men shew;
4 For God a great God doth appear,
  and greatly prais'd must be;
And every where be had in fear
  above all gods must He.
5 For all the gods of heathen lands
  dumb idols do appear:
But God's own hands and quick commands
  made the celestial sphere.
6 Before him honor stands in sight
  with majesty and grace:
Adored might and beauty bright
  are in his holy place.
7 Ye people give unto the Lord,
  let every stock and tribe
Unto the Lord with joynt accord
  glory and strength ascribe.
8 Give glory to the Lord the King,
  due to his name on high:
Devoutly bring an offering,
  and to his courts draw nigh.
9 O Worship ye the Lord with fear
  in beauties holy place:

Psalm xcvij.

O earth appear from far and near
  before his awful face.
10 Tell heathen men the Lord doth reign,
  the world confirm'd shall be ;
  Nor shall again a shake sustein,
  so just a judg is He.
11 O let the heavens rejoice therefore
  and let the earth be glad ;
  The sea shall rore and all her store
  triumphant joys shall add.
12 Yea let the field and every thing
  therein lift up their voice :
  The trees shall sing, the woods shall ring
  and mutually rejoice.
13 Before the Lord for lo he comes
  the earth to judg and try,
  To us he comes with righteous dooms
  of truth and equity.

PSALM XCVII.

The Lord doth reign as sovereign king,
  let all the earth rejoice :
  The multitude of Isles shall sing
  with glad and pleasant voice.
2 Dark pitchy clouds and shady night
  are round about his throne :
  Most perfect judgment, truth and right
  dwell with the holy one.
3 A dreadful fire before him goes,
  which fiercely burning out,
  With furious flames consumes his foes
  and enemies round about.
4 His lightnings did most brightly blaze,
  and to the world appear :
  Whereat the earth did look and gaze,
  amaz'd with deadly fear.

5 The hills like wax did melt and thaw
  and could no longer stand:
 When they God's glorious presence saw,
  the Lord of sea and land.
6 The heavens high declare and shew
  his justice all abroad;
 That all the world may see and know
  the glory of our God.
7 Confusion to all those shall come,
  on graven gods that call,
 That boast themselves of idols dumb:
  ye gods adore him all.
8 Mount Sion heard with great applause,
  and was affected much;
 And Judah's daughters joy'd, because
  thy judgments, Lord, were such.
9 For thou, O Lord, art set on high
  and idols under-trod;
 And thou exalted wondrously
  above each other god.
10 Hate evil ye that love the Lord,
  he saves his Saints dear souls:
 He saves them from this wicked world,
  and adverse power controul's.
11 And light is sown for righteous men,
  and each shall reap his part;
 And gladness great springs up for them
  that are of upright heart.
12 Rejoyce ye righteous in the Lord,
  much joyfulness express;
 And give him thanks when ye record
  his perfect holiness.

II. *Metre.* *Tune,* Give Laud, &c.

God reigns and rules on high,
  with clouds and darkness clad,

Let

Let th' earth be fill'd with joy,
  and numerous I'les be glad,
    His truth is known,
And Judgment pure, the station sure
  of his high Throne.

Fire goes before his face,
  and flaming round about,
Burns up his foes apace,
  his lightning glanceth out,
    and these do make
The world shine bright, and at the sight
  the earth did quake.

At presence of the Lord
  like wax the mountains thaw'd
At presence of the Lord,
  by whom the Earth is aw'd:
    The Heavens express
How just is He, and all men see
  his gloriousness.

The Second part.

Confusion on them all
  which serve an Image carv'd,
That to dumb Idols fall,
  and boast what Gods they serv'd:
    Ye feigned Powers,
See that ye do bow down unto
  this God of ours.

O Lord thy Judgments voice
  made Sion hear and joy,
And Judah's Towns rejoyce,
  for, Lord, thou art most high,
    Thou hast the odds
Of all the Earth, and art set forth
  above all Gods.

Ye lovers of the Lord,
   hate all that evil is,
For he the souls doth guard
   of all dear Saints of his:
     And saveth them
From cruel spite and crushing might
   of wicked men.

For just men light is sow'n,
   and gladness richly stor'd
For each pure-hearted one,
   ye just joy in the Lord,
     Him praise and bless
At memory of his so high
   pure holiness.

PSALM XCVIII.

Sing to the Lord a new made song,
   for he hath marvels don;
His holy hand and arm most strong,
   the victory have won.
2 The Lord Almighty hath made known
   his saving health and might;
His truth he openly hath shown
   in all the heathen's sight.
3 Towards Israel's honored house hath he
   remembred truth and grace;
The earth did his salvation see
   declar'd in every place.
4 Make joyful noise unto the Lord,
   all dwellers on the earth;
Make noises loud, his praise record
   with songs of joy and mirth.
5 O sing unto the Lord, I say,
   and with the harp rejoice;
With solemn harp his praise display,
   and psalms melodious voice.

6 With trumpets shrill express your joys,
   with sound of cornet sing;
  And make a very joyful noise
   before the Lord the King.

7 O let the sea with billows swell,
   and all its fulness roar;
  The world likewise, and all that dwell
   upon the spacious shore.

8 Let floods clap hands with one accord,
   let hills express their mirth,
  And join in joyes before the Lord,
   who comes to judg the earth.

9 With righteousness and judgment then,
   shall he the people try,
  And justly judg a world of men
   with truth and equity.

II. *Metre.*

Give Laud, &c.

Now sing a new-made song
   to Christ the King of Kings,
Whose arm and right hand strong,
   hath wrought such wondrous things:
      His hand, I say,
His holy and victorious hand
      hath got the day.

The Lord hath now made known
   his saving health and might,
His righteousness is shewn
   in all the heathens sight,
      To Jacob's race
His truth extends: the earth's far ends,
   have seen his grace.

Let all that dwell on earth
   their high affections raise,

With universal mirth,
　and loudly sing his praise;
　　In God rejoice
With harp, I say, with harps sweet play,
　and Psalms sweet voice.

The chearful trumpet sound,
　the shrill-voic't cornet bring:
Let all with joy abound
　before the Lord the King:
　　Roar out ye seas,
The world and all the dwellers shall
　rejoice with these.

Floods clap your thronging waves,
　ye hills cause your mirth,
He, who his people saves,
　now comes to judge the earth,
　　The world He shall
With judgment try, and equity
　dispence to all.

PSALM XCIX.

The Lord doth reign as king of kings,
　let all the people quake,
He sits upon the Cherubims;
　let th' earth be mov'd and shake.
2 The Lord that doth in Sion dwell,
　is wondrous high and great:
The people he doth far excell
　and sits in soveraign seat.
3 Let all men praise and magnify
　thy great and dreadful name:
For it excels in sanctity,
　and most deserveth fame.
4 The princely power of our king
　loves judgment, truth and right,
Thou rightly rulest every thing
　in Jacob through thy might.

5 The Lord our God exalt ye now,
    and worship him alone :
  Before his footstool bend and bow,
    for he's a holy one.
6 Moses and Aaron with his priests,
    and Samuel on him call :
  Among his Saints these made requests,
    and he did answer all.
7 He in the cloudy pillar spake
    and shewed to them his will :
  The laws and statutes he did make
    they laboured to fulfill :
8 O Lord our God thou didst them hear,
    and wast a pardoning God :
  Thy mercy did to them appear
    though thou didst use thy rod.
9 The Lord our God exalt ye still,
    bow down before his throne,
  And worship at his holy hill,
    for He's a holy one.

II. *Metre.* All People, &c.

The Lord doth reign, let people quake,
  on Cherubims he sets his seat :
O let the earth be mov'd and shake.
2 The Lord in Sion is so great.
  Above all people he is high.
3 His greatness let them magnifie ;
  And let them praise his dreadful name,
    for high and holy is the same.
4 The king's firm strength doth judgment love,
    thou dost establish equity :
  Thou execut'st it from above,
    and rul'st in Jacob righteously.
5 The Lord our God exalt therefore
    and reverently his name adore ;

  At footstool of his holy throne;
   for he's a high and holy one.

6 Moses and Aaron also were
  among his priests and men of fame,
And Samuel among them there
  that call'd upon his holy name.
They call'd, and he did answer make;
7 In cloudy pillars to them spake,
  They to his testimonies clave,
   and kept the ordinance that he gave.
8 Thou answered'st them, O Lord our God,
  thou wast a pardoning God likewise,
Though thou took'st vengeance with thy rod,
  and their inventions did'st chastise.
9 The Lord our God exalt ye still,
  and worship at his holy hill;
Because the Lord our God alone,
  he is the high and holy one.

PSALM C.

ALL people that on earth do dwell,
  Sing to the Lord with chearful voice:
2 Him serve with fear, his praise forth-tell,
  Come ye before him and rejoice.
3 The Lord ye know is God indeed,
  Without our aid he did us make:
We are his flock, he doth us feed,
  And for his sheep he doth us take.

4 O enter then his gates with praise,
  And in his courts do ye proclame
Your thankfulness to him alwayes,
  And ever bless his holy name.
5 Because the Lord our God is good,
  His mercy is for ever sure:
His truth at all times firmly stood.
  And shall from age to age endure.

         II. *Metre.*

II. Metre.

Have mercy, &c.

All men of mortal birth,
  that dwell in all the earth,
2 O make a noise to God with joys,
  and serve the Lord with mirth:
 O come before his throne
 with singing ev'ry one:
3 For certainly the Lord most high,
  ev'n he is God alone.

He made us, and not we,
  not we our selves, but he,
We are his flock, and pasture-flock,
  he made us so to be.
4 With praise come to his gate,
  and in his courts relate
 His laud and fame, and bless his name,
  his honor celebrate.

5 For God is good for ever,
  his mercy faileth never;
 His truth doth last all ages past,
  and so abideth ever.

III. Metre.

Now Israel old. 124.

Make joyful noise to God, O all ye lands,
  Observe the Lord with gladness and delight
  With chearful singing come before his sight.
Know that the Lord is God who all commands,
Tis He that made us, and not our own hands.

His people and his pasture sheep are we,
  Enter his gates, your gratitude proclame,
  Come to his courts with praise, & bless his Name:

For God is good, his mercies conſtant be,
His truth endures to all eternity.

PSALM CI.

Mercy and judgment are my ſong
    which Lord I'le ſing to thee;
2 And wiſely walk in perfect way,
    until thou viſit me.
And I will walk with upright heart,
    within my houſe, O Lord;
3 Not any thing will I behold
    that is to be abhorr'd.

I hate their work that turn aſide,
    to me it ſhall not cleave.
4 I will not own a wicked man,
    the froward heart I leave;
5 I'le cut him off that ſlandereth
    his neighbour privily:
I'le not endure the proud in heart,
    nor him that looketh high.

6 I will look out the faithful men,
    that they may dwell with me:
And whoſo walks in perfect way
    my ſervant he ſhall be.
7 Whoſo is bent to uſe deceit,
    I will abandon quite:
The liar I will not abide
    to tarry in my ſight.
8 The wicked I will ſoon deſtroy,
    and rid the land of them;
And cut away the wicked ones
    from God's Jeruſalem.

II. *Metre.* All People, &c.

Mercy and judgment now I ſing
To thee, O Lord, from whom they ſpring,

I will behave my self each day
With prudence in a perfect way.
O when wilt thou draw near to me
That I established may be:
    Then will I walk in thy true fear,
    Within my house with heart sincere.

I will not set before mine eye
Temptations to iniquity.
    I hate their work that virtue leave,
    It shall not to my conscience cleave.

The froward heart from me shall go,
I will no wicked person know:
    I will cut off the slandering tongue
    That doth his neighbour secret wrong.

The proud in heart I will not brook,
Nor him that hath a lofty look:
    My fixed eye shall ever stand
    Upon the faithful of the land.

I'le mark the men that most excell,
That they may in my presence dwell:
    For He that walks in perfect wayes
    Shall be my servant all his dayes.

My house shall harbour none that cheat,
So much do I abhor deceit:
    And him that doth in lies delight,
    I will not suffer in my sight.

Yea, all the wicked of the land
I will destroy with timely hand:
    And purge the city of our Lord,
    Of all that are to be abhorr'd.

PSALM CII.

Lord hear my prayer and let my cry,
    come speedily to thee,
2. In day of my calamity
    Hide not thy face from me.

Incline me

Incline thy gracious ear to me
 in this my day of need,
And when I call and cry to thee
 Lord answer me with speed.
3 For like as smoke consumes away,
 so do my dayes exspire,
My bones are burnt and do decay
 like to a hearth with fire.
4 My heart is smitten like the grass
 quite withered and dead;
And I, alas! do quite let pass
 to eat my needful bread.
5 By reason of my doleful grones
 and pain that I am in,
My grief breaks forth, so that my bones
 do cleave unto my skin.
6 Lo, I am like a pelican
 in mournful wilderness,
And like a hated owl I am
 in deserts comfortless.
7 I watch and am quite desolate
 and sparrow-like alone,
Which separated from her mate
 on houses top doth mone.
8 Mine enemies have all the day
 reproached me with scorn,
And mad men in their frantick way
 are all against me sworn.
9 So that I have in stead of bread
 the ashes eaten up,
And with my drink the tears I shed
 are mingled in my cup.
10 Because of thy severity
 and of thy angry frown;
For thou hast lifted me on high
 and then hast cast me down.
11 The days wherein my life doth pass,
 are like a flitting shade;   And

And I am like the withering grass,
  which instantly doth fade.
12 But thou, O Lord, shalt still endure
  for ever constantly,
And thy remembrance shall stand sure
  to all posterity.

The second part.

13 Thy tender bowels now shall stir,
  to bring poor Sion home;
For lo, the time to favor her,
  yea, the set time is come.
14 For even in her very stones,
  thy servants take delight;
The ruins under which she groans,
  find favour in their sight.
15 And so the heathen every where,
  shall reverence thy name;
And all the kings on earth shall fear
  thy glory and thy fame.
16 Whenas the Lord builds up again,
  fair Sion's broken wall,
His glory shall appear most plain
  and visible to all.
17 The prayer of the destitute
  he shall regard and prize,
Their earnest and their humble suit
  the Lord will not despise.
18 And this for ages yet to come,
  shall rest upon record;
People created in the womb
  shall one day praise the Lord.
19 For from his sanctuaries height
  the Lord hath cast his eye;
From heaven did his perfect sight
  the spacious earth descry.

20 To hear the prisoners doleful grones
  and lamentable cry ;
 And to relieve oppressed ones
  that are condemn'd to die.
21 That so the LORD's most holy name
  may be declar'd to them ;
 And they proclaim his praise and fame
  throughout Jerusalem
22 Whenas the people far and nigh
  shall all be gathered there.
 And kingdoms meet unanimously
  to serve the Lord in fear.
23 But while I waited in the way,
  my strength he hath decay'd ;
 Yea, he hath shortened my day,
  then thus to him I said :
24 Oh ! take me not away, my Lord,
  in midst of all my dayes :
 Thy years all ages shall record,
  thy time no whit decayes.
25 The earth's foundation thou hast laid
  of old, as now it stands ;
 The glorious heavens thou hast made
  the work of thine own hands.
26 But they shall perish and decay,
  while thou continueth still ;
 They shall wax old and wear away,
  just as a garment will.
 As vestures thou shalt change their frame,
  and changed they shall be ;
27 But thou art evermore the same,
  Thy years no end shall see.
28 And Lord thy faithful servant's race
  for ever shall endure ;
 Their seed likewise before thy face
  shall be establisht sure.

PSALM

PSALM CIII.

Bless thou the living Lord, my soul,
  his glorious praise proclaim :
Let all my inward powers extol,
  and bless his holy name.
2 Forget not all his benefits,
  but bless the Lord, my soul :
3 Who all thy trespasses remits,
  and makes thee sound and whole.
4 Who did redeem and let thee free
  from death's infernal place :
With loving kindness crowned thee,
  and with his tender grace.
5 Who fills and satisfies thy mouth
  with all good things of his,
And makes thee to renew thy youth,
  just as the Eagles is.
6 The Lord doth fully execute
  justice and righteousness,
And judgment, for the destitute
  whom wicked men oppress.
7 To Moses he did first reveal
  the wayes that they should go ;
And made the sons of Israel
  his mighty acts to know.
8 The Lord is merciful we know,
  and graciously enclin'd ;
To anger he is very slow,
  compassionate and kind.
9 Continually he will not chide,
  nor evermore contend ;
His anger shall not long abide,
  but quickly have an end.
10 He doth not unto us dispence,
  as our deserts have bin :

    Nor giveth us a recompence
      according to our sin.
11 For as the heaven is far above
      the earth's inferior frame;
    So is his mercy and his love
      to them that fear his name.

12 As far as is the sun's uprise
      in distance from his fall,
    So far our foul iniquities
      he separates from us all.

The Second part.

13 As fathers are compassionate
      unto their children dear,
    So doth the Lord commiserate
      his saints, that do him fear.
14 For he doth know our brittle frame,
      our mould and fashion just;
    He well remembers whence we came,
      and that we are but dust.
15 And as for man his dayes (alas!)
      do soon decline and yield;
    He flourisheth but as the grass,
      or flower of the field.
16 For it is gone, and quickly too,
      when some bleak wind goes o're;
    And then the place whereon it grew
      shall never know it more.
17 But unto all eternity
      God's goodness doth endure;
    To ages all successively
      his righteousness stands sure.
18 To such as keep his covenants,
      and fear his holy name;
    Remembring his commandements
      to execute the same.

Psalm civ.

19 The Lord within the heavens high
   hath firmly fixt his throne;
And over all things generally
   his kingdom rules alone.
20 All ye his angels bless the Lord,
   ye that in strength excell;
That do his precepts with regard,
   minding his word so well.
21 Bless ye the Lord, O! bless him still,
   O all ye hosts of his;
His ministers that do fulfil
   what ever his pleasure is.
22 O bless the Lord ye works of his,
   wherewith the world is stor'd;
Where ever his dominion is,
   my soul bless thou the Lord.

PSALM CIV.

O Bless the Lord, my soul, and say,
   my God thou art full great;
Bright honour is thy rich array,
   and majesty thy seat.
2 With light thou coverest thee about,
   as with a princely robe;
And like a curtain stretchest out
   the bright celestial globe.
3 With watery seas his roof he ceils,
   and there his rafters binds,
He makes the clouds his chariot-wheels,
   and walks on winged winds.
4 He makes his winged messengers
   of pure spiritual frame:
He makes his glorious ministers
   a burning fiery flame.
5 He laid the whole foundation
   of all the earth so sure,

That

    That still it keeps its station,
      and ever shall endure.
6 Which first was covered with the flood
      as with a garment large,
    The waters o're the mountains stood,
      until they heard thy charge.

7 And then at thy rebuke they fled,
      thy thundering voice they fear'd;
    Hasting away for fear and dread,
      and straight, dry land appear'd.
8 And now dispersed far and wide,
      by hill and dale they go,
    Unto the place thou didst provide,
      to that same place they flow.

9 Their passage thou dost now restrain,
      and settest them their bound,
    That they may never turn again
      to cover all the ground.

The Second part

10 The Lord doth send the fruitful springs
      into the vales below;
    And all along the hills he brings
      their fruitful streams to flow.
11 And they give drink to every beast,
      which in the field doth ly:
    Wild asses there, among the rest,
      do quench their thirst thereby.

12 By them the feathered nation
      do comfortably house,
    And have their habitation
      to sing amongst the boughs.
13 And from his chambers richly stor'd,
      he watereth all the hills.
    The fruit which these thy works afford,
      the earth with plenty fills.

14 For cattel he makes grafs to fpring,
  and herbs, for man's own ufe;
Convenient food for every thing,
  he makes the earth produce.
15 To glad man's heart he makes the foil
  bring forth the grape for wine;
Heart's ftrengthening bread and fuppling oil,
  to make his face to fhine.
16 The trees of God (though many a one)
  no moifture ever want;
The Cedars of mount Lebanon,
  which he himfelf did plant.
17 Wherein the birds do make their nefts,
  the ftork too (as for her)
She hath her houfe wherein fhe refts,
  upon the ftately firr.
18 For wilder goats, the mountains tops
  are made a refuge fit;
And in the clefts of hollow rocks
  the little conies fit.
19 He did appoint the changing moon
  the feafons for to fhew;
And when his time is to go down
  the fun doth likewife know.
20 Thou makeft darknefs, and behold
  dark night is over-fpread;
And then the forreft beafts are bold,
  to creep forth to be fed.
21 The lion aud the lions whelp
  come roaring all abroad
After their prey, and feek their help
  and fuftenance from God.
22 The fun arifeth in the sky,
  they flock together then,
And lay them down moft quietly
  within their fecret den.
23 Then man goes forth with cheerful mind
  his labors to begin,

And plies his work of every kind,
  till evening calls him in.

The Third part.

24 How many are thy works, O Lord,
  in wisdom all compos'd;
The earth by thee is richly stor'd
  with treasures there inclos'd:
25 So is this great and spacious deep
  replenisht therewithall,
Where things innumerable creep,
  and beasts both great and small.
26 The ships go also here away,
  Leviathan here keeps,
Whom thou hast made to sport and play
  within the tumbling deeps.
27 On thee do all these creatures wait,
  expressing their desires,
That thou maist give them needful meat,
  when-as the time requires.
28 That which thou giv'st (as thou seest best)
  they gather for their food;
Thy liberal hand thou openest,
  and they are fill'd with good.
29 Thou hid'st thy face, and by and by
  in misery they mourn;
Thou tak'st away their breath, they dye
  and to their dust return.
30 Thy spirits power thou sendest forth,
  they are created then;
And so the face of all the earth
  thereby renews agen.
31 The glory of the Lord most high
  for evermore shall be;
And in his works of majesty
  greatly rejoice shall he.

32 His look can make the earth to quake,
   His gentle touch and stroke
Can cause the solid earth to shake,
   and make the mountains smoke.
33 Unto the Lord will I sing praise,
   while I have life and breath;
And glorify him all my days,
   and honour him till death.
34 My thoughts of him shall be so sweet,
   as nothing else can be,
And all the streams of joy shall meet
   when, Lord, I think on thee.
35 Let sinners perish from the earth,
   and leud men be no more;
But let my soul God's praise set forth,
   praise ye the Lord therefore.

PSALM CV.

O Render thanks unto the Lord,
   and call upon his name;
Among the people, O! record
   his deeds deserving fame.
2 Sing unto him whose power exceeds,
   sing psalms to him with joy:
To talk of all his wondrous deeds,
   your busy tongues imploy.
3 O make your boasts with one accord
   in God's most holy name;
Let every soul that seeks the Lord
   be joyful in the same.
4 Seek ye the Lord, for him inquire,
   his strength and power implore:
His face and favor O! desire
   and seek it evermore.
5 What he hath wrought, to mind recall
   in each mysterious deed;

His wonders and the judgments all,
  which from his mouth proceed.
6 O ye the seed of Abraham,
  who serv'd him with respect;
Ye children which of Jacob came,
  his chosen and select.

7 He is indeed the Lord our God,
  his judgments are set forth,
And manifested all abroad
  throughout the spacious earth.

8 He calls to mind his covenant,
  and never he repents;
The word of his commandement
  to thousands of descents.

9 Which covenant the Lord did make
  to Abraham and his heir;
The solemn oath which he did take,
  and unto Isaack sware.

10 And he confirm'd the same as well
  to Jacob for a Law,
A covenant which from Israel
  he never would withdraw.

11 Saying, I will my Church advance,
  and give into her hand
The lot of her inheritance
  all Canaans fertile land.

12 When they of faithful Israel's seed
  but few in number were,
Yea, but a very few indeed,
  and also strangers there.

13 When shifting habitation
  they went at God's command,
From nation unto nation,
  flitting from land to land.

14 He did not suffer any man
  to wrong them where they came,
But for their sakes he soon began
  the mighty kings to blame.

15 Saying

Psalm cv.

15 Saying to those that sate on thrones,
  let no presumptuous arm
Once touch my dear anointed ones,
  nor do my Prophets harm.
16 He call'd for famine on the land,
  and brake the staff of bread;
17 But he beforehand sent a man,
  by whom they should be fed.

Even Joseph for a servant sold,
  subjected to controul;
18 Whose feet the heavy chains did hold,
  the iron pierc't his soul.
19 Until the time and period,
  which Joseph had foretold,
Try'd was he, by the word of God,
  as fire doth try the gold.

20 Then gave the king commandement
  that loosed he should be,
The ruler of the people sent
  to loose and set him free.
21 He made him ruler of his house;
  and Lord of Egypt Land;
And all his substance precious
  committed to his hand.

22 To bind his disobedient Peers,
  his Princes to compell,
And for to teach his Senators
  the way to govern well.
23 And then did aged Israel stir,
  and into Egypt came;
And Jacob was a sojourner
  within the land of Ham.

24 And he did greatly multiply
  his people Israel there,
And made them stronger, verily,
  than all their enemies were.
25 He turn'd their hearts to be as foes,
  his people they abhorr'd;

And

  And craftily they dealt with those,
   the servants of the Lord.
26 His servant Moses then he sent,
   and Aaron whom he chose:
27 His signs and wonders eminent
   in Egypt they disclose.
28 Darkness he sent where they did dwell,
   and made it dark indeed;
  His messengers did not rebel
   against his word decreed.
29 He turn'd their waters into blood,
   and slew their fish thereby:
30 The land brought forth a loathsom brood
   of frogs abundantly,
  Kings chambers swarmed with the same,
31 Then spake the Lord of hosts,
   And divers sorts of flies there came,
  and lice in all their coasts.
32 He gave them hail in all the land,
   and flaming fire for rain;
33 He let no vine nor figtree stand
   unsmitten in the plain.
  He brake the trees in all their coasts;
34 He spake, and locusts came,
   And caterpillers, mighty hosts,
  whose number none can name:
35 And ate up every herb and flowr
   which in the land was found;
  And utterly they did devour
   the fruits of all the ground.
36 He also smote within one night
   The first-born in the land,
  The very chief of all their might
   he smote with dreadful hand.
37 He brought them forth, and furnish't well
   with silver and with gold,

Nor did the tribes of Israel
  one feeble person hold.
8 All Egypt was exceeding glad,
  when they did thus depart,
So much the fear of Israel had
  surprised every heart.
9 He spread a cloud in open sight
  to be a shady tent;
And all the night did fire give light
  to Israel as they went.
10 He brought them quails whereon they fed,
  for flesh they askt to have,
And satisfi'd them with the bread
  which he from heaven gave.
11 He opened the rock from whence
  fresh waters gusht apace
(As if a river ran from thence)
  in dry and desert place.
12 For into his remembrance came
  the holy promise made
Unto his servant Abraham,
  Which promise cannot fade.
13 And then he brought his people forth
  with joy for their release;
And all his chosen ones with mirth
  and shouts of joyfulness.
14 And unto them delivered
  the heathen people's lands,
And they alone inherited
  the labor of their hands.
15 That they the better might observe
  the statutes of his word,
And from his precepts might not swerve,
  O! magnify the Lord.

PSALM CVI.

Praise ye the Lord, to him give thanks,
 for good and kind is he,
For lo, his mercy doth indure
 to all eternity.
2 His mighty acts who can recite
 according to their worth,
His praises that are infinite
 who fully can set forth?

3 Blessed are they that judgment keep,
 and he that doth observe
The perfect rule of righteousness,
 and doth at no time swerve.
4 Think on me Lord with favor free,
 such as thy people find;
With thy salvation visit me,
 and have me in thy mind.

5 That I may see that nations good,
 whereof thou hast made choice,
And glory with thy heritage,
 and in their joy rejoice.
6 But we have sinned grievously,
 the father and the son,
We all have wrought iniquity,
 and lewdly we have done.

7 Our fathers, though they saw thy works,
 yet did not understand
Thy wonders and thy miracles,
 perform'd in Egypt land:
Nor did they keep in memory
 thy great abundant grace:
But did provoke him at the sea,
 the red sea was the place.

The Second part.

8 Yet did he save them every one,
  for honour of his name:
 That he might make his power known,
  and spread abroad his fame.
9 The red sea also dried up
  at his severe command,
 And so he led them through the deep,
  as through the desert land.
10 He sav'd them from their haters hand,
  and safely let them go:
 Redeeming them from Egypt land,
  and from their cruel foe.
11 The waters overwhelm'd their foes,
  not one escap't away:
12 Then they believ'd the word he spake,
  and sang his praise that day.
13 But all his works so wonderful
  they presently forgot;
 And for his counsel and his will
  they duly waited not.
14 But being in the wilderness,
  did lust exceedingly,
 And in the desert place no less
  they tempted God most high.
15 He gave them also their request
  at full, without controul;
 But wasting leanness therewithal
  he sent into their soul.
16 They envied Moses in the camp,
  and yet not him alone,
 But Aaron too, who had the stamp
  of consecration.
17 The earth then opened suddainly,
  proud Dathan to devour

  And all Abiram's company
   it covered in that hour.
18 And in their congregation
   a fire was kindled then,
  The very breath and flame whereof
   burnt up those wicked men.

19 They made a calf their deity,
   when they in Horeb were,
  And worship'd superstitiously
   the molten image there.
20 And thus they chang'd their glorious God
   into a molten mass,
  Form'd in the likeness of an ox
   that feedeth upon grass.

21 But God, that was their Saviour,
   they utterly forgot,
  The works which he in Egypt did,
   they now remembred not.
22 Most wondrous works he brought to pass
   in Ham's accursed land;
  And dreadful things by the red sea
   perform'd by powerful hand.

23 Therefore he thrate to ruine them,
   and would have made it good,
  Had not his chosen Moses then
   before his presence stood.
  He stood before him in the breach
   to turn his wrath away;
  Or else he had destroy'd them quite,
   and they had fallen that day.

24 Yea, they despis'd the pleasant land,
   and trusted not his word;
25 But murmuring in their tents they stand,
   not hearkening to the Lord.
26 Therefore he lifted up his hand
   against them every one,
  That in the desert wilderness
   they might be overthrown.

27 To overthrow their seed also
  among the nations rude,
 And scatter them in all the lands
  among the multitude.
28 For now they join'd themselves likewise
  to filthy Baal Peor,
 And are the dead God's sacrifice,
  for such those Idols were.
29 Thus they provok'd the Lord to wrath,
  with that abhorred sin,
 Of new-found out idolatry,
  and so the plague broke in.
30 Then stood up zealous Phinehas,
  and did those sinners slay
 By judgment just (for such it was)
  and so the plague did stay.
31 And it was counted unto him
  a righteous act indeed,
 To all the generations
  of his ensuing seed.
32 They vext him also at the lake,
  so called from their strife,
 That Moses suffered for their sake
  the shortning of his life:
33 Because their provocations
  his patient spirit stirr'd,
 So that he utt'red with his lips
  an unadvised word.
34 They did not utterly destroy
  the nations of the land,
 Concerning whom the Lord most high
  did give a strict command.
35 But were among the heathen spread,
  whose works they learned there,
36 And all their idols worshipped,
  which were to them a snare.

37 Yea, they did slay in sacrifice
 their daughters and their sons:
 Offering to divel-deities
 their harmless little ones.

38 Their sons and daughters blood they shed,
 and them with guilty hand
 To Canaan's idols offered,
 and blood defil'd the land.

39 Thus was it their own works and deeds
 that did defile them so,
 And with their own inventions
 a whoring they did go.

40 Therefore the anger of the Lord
 against his folk did flame:
 His own inheritance he abhorr'd
 by reason of the same.

41 Into the hands of heathen men
 he gave them for a prey:
 Their hateful foes rul'd over them,
 and forc't them to obey.

42 Their enemies with cruelty
 opprest them in the land;
 And they were humbled shamefully
 under their enemies hand.

43 He did release them many times,
 but they provok't him so,
 What with their counsels and their crimes,
 that they were brought full low.

44 He did regard them ne'retheless,
 and had a gracious eye
 To their affliction and distress,
 whenas he heard their cry.

45 His covenant he for them renew'd
 repenting in his mind,
 According to the multitude
 of his compassions kind.

46 He made them to be favored
 and pitied of all those,
 By whom they were as captives led,
 when they were bitter foes.
47 Save Lord our God and gather us
 from heathens now adayes,
 That we thy holy name may bless,
 and triumph in thy praise.
48 Bless Israel's God, the Lord most high,
 and let all flesh record
 His praises to eternity,
 Amen, praise ye the Lord.

PSALM CVII.

O Render thanks unto the Lord,
 for good and kind is he;
 Because his mercy doth endure
 to all eternity.
2 Let the redeem'd in every land,
 the Lord's redeem'd, say so:
 Those whom he rescu'd from the hand
 of their injurious foe.
3 And gathered them out of the lands
 both from the east and west.
 And from the north, and from the south,
 unto a place of rest.
4 In wilderness they wandered
 in solitary way;
 And found no place inhabited,
 nor town wherein to stay.
5 Hungry and thirsty all the while,
 not having what to eat;
 So that their very soul began
 to faint for want of meat.
6 Then did they cry unto the Lord,
 when trouble did oppress;

Whose favour did relief afford
 to them in their distress.

7 And led them forth the readiest way,
 a dwelling-place to find,
 A city for their safe abode,
 according to their mind.

8 Let them therefore praise God's great name,
 for his great goodness then,
 And for his works of wondrous fame,
 to all the sons of men.

9 For he doth fully satisfy
 the longing soul with food,
 And filleth every hungry soul
 with blessings that are good.

10 Such as in shades of darkness ly,
 where death doth seem to reign,
 Bound in the bands of misery,
 as with an iron chain.

11 Because they did rebelliously
 transgress against God's word;
 And did contemn that counsellor,
 who is the highest Lord.

12 Therefore he did their heart bring down,
 with labour and with pain;
 And down they fell, and there was none
 to help them up again.

13 Then did they cry unto the Lord,
 when anguish did oppress,
 And he did save them speedily
 out of their deep distress.

14 From shade of death and darksom night,
 which they could not break through,
 He brought them out to life and light,
 and brake their bands in two.

The Second part.

15 O! that all men would praise the Lord
   for his great goodness then,
  And for his wondrous works declar'd
   unto the sons of men.
16 For he hath broken by his might
   the brazen doors and gates,
  And he hath cut in sunder quite
   the iron barrs and grates.
17 Fools fall into affliction
   by falling into sin;
  And through their own iniquities
   they are insnar'd therein.
18 Their soul whom thy hand visiteth,
   abhors all kind of meat;
  And they draw near the gates of death,
   their sickness is so great.
19 Then in their trouble do they cry
   unto the Lord for aid,
  Who saveth them from their distress,
   according as they prai'd.
20 He sent his word of power supreme,
   and did them heal and save;
  And graciously delivered them,
   even from the very grave.
21 Oh! that all men would praise the Lord
   for his great goodness then,
  And for his works most wonderful,
   unto the sons of men.
22 And let them offer sacrifice
   of praise unto the Lord;
  And with the shouts of joy likewise
   his wondrous works record.

The Third part.

23 They that descend to sea in ships,
 imployed for their gain
In necessary merchandize
 upon the watery main;
24 These men do God's rare works behold,
 and no men more than these
Do see his wonders manifold
 within the deepest seas.
25 For by the word of his command
 he makes fierce winds to rise,
And lifteth up the rouling waves
 unto the very skies.
26 They mount to heaven, then they roul
 down to the deeps below;
And by and by their very soul
 doth melt because of woe.
27 They reel and stagger to and fro,
 like drunkards in their fits,
And like unto distracted men
 are put besides their wits.
28 Then in their trouble did they cry
 unto the Lord for aid;
Who did redress their misery,
 according as they prai'd.
29 The storm is chang'd into a calm
 by his command and will;
So that the raging waves thereof
 are now exceeding still.
30 Now winds and waves do rage no more,
 which they are glad to see,
And so he brings them to the shore
 where they desir'd to be.
31 Oh! render praises to the Lord
 for his great goodness then,

And for his works most wonderful,
  unto the sons of men.
32 And in the congregation great
  let them exalt his name;
And in the honor'd Elders seat
  advance his praise and fame.

The Fourth part.

33 The Lord did make it barren soil,
  where floods did once abound,
And turns the very water-springs
  to dry and thirsty ground.
34 A fruitful land to barrenness
  he turn's, because of sin,
When he reward's the wickedness
  of those that dwell therein.
35 Again the very wilderness
  to standing pools he brings,
And turns the dry and desert ground
  to plenteous water-springs.
36 And there he makes the hungry dwell,
  that so they may provide,
And get them cities furnisht well,
  wherein they may abide.
37 That they may plant the pleasant vines,
  and sow the fruitful field;
And may receive the rich increase,
  which every year shall yield.
38 Such blessings are on them conferr'd
  that they are much increast;
So that of all the numerous herd
  they do not lose a beast.
39 Yet for their sin they are brought low,
  and minished again;
Expos'd to wicked tyranny,
  affliction, grief, and pain.

40 He powres on great-ones great disgrace,
   and causeth them to stray
In solitary desert place,
   where is no beaten way.
41 Yet setteth he the poor on high,
   and him from harm doth keep:
And multiplies his family
   like to a flock of sheep.
42 This thing the righteous shall descry,
   rejoycing in the same:
And it shall force iniquity
   to stop her mouth with shame.
43 Whoso hath wisdom from above
   these matters to record,
Even they shall understand the love
   and kindness of the Lord.

PSALM CVIII.

O God, my heart is now prepar'd,
   so also is my tongue:
I will advance my voice, O Lord,
   and praise thee with my song.
2 Awake my viol and my harp,
   sweet melody to make:
And in the morning I my self
   right early will awake.
3 Among the people shall thy praise
   be published by me:
Among the heathen folk, O Lord,
   will I sing praise to thee.
4 Because thy mercy, Lord, is great
   unto the heavens high:
Also thy truth extends it self
   unto the cloudy sky.
5 Above the starry firmament,
   extoll thy self, O God,

And, Lord display upon the earth,
  thy glory all abroad.
And that thy dear beloved ones
  delivered may be:
Save them, O Lord, by thy right hand,
  and therein answer me.

The Second part.

7 God in his holiness did speak,
  my joy I cannot hide:
The vale of Succoth I'le mete out,
  and Shechem I'le divide.
8 Gilead is mine, Manasseh mine,
  and Ephraims tribe together
Shall be the chief of all my strength,
  and Judah my law-giver.
9 My servile wash-pot Moab is,
  on Edom I will tread:
And in my triumphs with a shout,
  Philistia shall be led.
10 But who will undertake to be
  my leader and my guide,
To Edom, and the city there
  so strongly fortifi'd?
11 Lord, wilt not thou that didst cast off
  our armies heretofore?
And with the hosts of Israel
  wilt thou go forth no more?
12 Lord, give us help from trouble then,
  because no other can:
And it is very vanity
  to hope for help from man.
13 We shall do very valiant acts,
  assisted by our God.
And by his power our enemies
  shall all be under-trod.

PSALM

PSALM CIX.

O God my praise, hold not thy peace;
2 For false and wicked tongues
Against me speak, and never cease
their clamours, lies, and wrongs.
3 With words of spite and causeless fight,
they compass me alway;
4 Even for my love my foes they prove,
but I make haste to pray.
5 They did reward me ill for good,
and hate for love they show.
6 Therefore set thou some tyrant lewd,
to triumph o're my foe.
Let Satan stand at his right hand,
7 And when his doom comes in,
Appoint that he condemned be,
and turn his prayer to sin.
8 His office let another take,
cut short his wicked life:
9 His children wretched orphans make,
with widow-hood vex his wife.
10 Let all his sons be vagabonds,
and beg for to be fed:
In places that are desolate,
let them seek out their bread.
11 Let the unjust extortioner
catch all he hath away:
And that which he hath laboured for,
let be the strangers prey.
12 Stir up no friend that may extend
relief in his distress:
And let there none have pity on
his children fatherless.
13 Cut off his whole posterity,
before thy wrath asswage:

Their name extinguish utterly,
   in the ensuing age.
14 His fathers fault let that be brought
   before the Lord for ever:
His mothers crime by length of time,
   let be extinguisht never.

15 Before the Lord continually
   let them be all brought forth:
That he may cut their memory
   for ever from the earth.

16 Since he forgot and cared not,
   compassion to impart:
But sought to break the poor and weak,
   and slay the broken heart.

17 As he lov'd cursing and despite,
   let it come to him so:
As blessing did not him delight,
   so let it from him go.

18 And as he had arrai'd and clad
   himself with curses vile:
Let it like drink within him sink,
   and soak his bones like oyl.

19 Let it be to him like the coat,
   that never is laid by:
And like the girdle girt about
   his loins continually.

20 Let God dispense this recompence,
   mine enemies to controul:
That are incens't to speak against
   mine inoffensive soul.

The Second part

21 O God the Lord, do thou for me,
   even for thine own names sake:
Because right good thy mercies be,
   my freedom undertake.

22 For I indeed do stand in need,
   with misery sore distrest:
My grieved heart with wounds doth smart,
   and bleeds within my breast.
23 I'm gone like suns declining shade,
   like wandring locusts tost:
24 My knees through fasting weak are made,
   my flesh its fat hath lost.
25 Yea, I became to them a shame,
   on me they gaze and stare:
26 Their heads they nod, help, Lord my God,
   and me in mercy spare.
27 That they may know this is thy hand,
   that thou hast done the deed.
28 And when they curse, do thou command
   a blessing to succeed.
Let shame surprize my foes, that rise
   my soul for to destroy:
But yet afford thy servant, Lord,
   abundant cause of joy.
29 And let mine adversaries all
   be cloathed with disgrace:
Let shame and self-confusion fall
   upon mine enemies face.
So that their own confusion
   may cover them throughout,
As if it were a mantle there,
   to compass them about.
30 And I will greatly praise the Lord,
   with joyful mouth and tongue:
Yea, and I will his praise record
   amidst the thickest throng.
31 For he shall stand at our right hand,
   and for our sake controul
The doom of them that would condemn
   the poor mans harmless soul.

PSALM

PSALM CX.

THe Lord unto my Lord thus spake,
    Sit thou at my right hand,
Till I thy foes a foot-stool make,
    whereon thy feet shall stand.
2 The Lord shall out of Sion send
    thy kingdom's powerful rod:
Amidst thy foes shalt thou extend
    thy government, O God.
3 Thy people shall come willingly
    in that thy day of grace;
Yielding a fruitful progeny
    in beauties holy place.
Thy converts there shall not be few,
    which in thy youth shall come,
As plenteous as the pearls of dew,
    that drop from mornings womb.
4 The Lord hath sworn, what he did speak,
    repent him he will never:
By order of Melchizedek
    thou art a priest for ever.
5 The Lord that is at thy right hand,
    shall in his wrath make way:
And strike through kings that dare withstand,
    in his revengeful day.
6 He shall sit judge of heathen men,
    and smite great numbers dead,
And wound the very chief of them,
    o're many Countries spread.
7 And he shall drink of that same brook,
    which runneth in the way:
Therefore shall he his head lift up,
    to triumph and bear sway

II. Metre.

II. Metre.

All People, or, *O Lord Consider,* &c.

The Lord unto my Lord thus said,
   Sit thou at my right hand on high,
Until thine Enemies be made
   a footstool for thy majesty.
The Lord shall send from Sion hill
   the scepter of thy soveraign might,
Rule thou amidst thine enemies still,
   thy people yielding to thy right.
Thy holy beauteous church, O Christ,
   shall bring thee store of Converts true,
As when the womb of morning moist
   o're-spreads the earth with drops of dew.
For thus the Lord Almighty swore
   and this his oath he will not break,
Thou art a Priest for evermore,
   By order of Melchisedek.
The Lord that stands at thy right hand
   in day of's wrath shall kings confound,
Judging in many a Heathen land,
   and heads of many countries round.
And he shall fill, in that same day,
   each place with bodies of the slain,
Drinking the torrent in the way,
   and so lift up the head again.

III. *Metre.* Ye Children, &c.

The Lord unto my Lord thus spake,
   Sit at my right hand till I make
   a very foot-stool of thy foes.
2 The Lord shall send from Sion's tower
   The soveraign sceptre of thy power:
   rule thou amidst them that oppose.

Pſalm cxi.

3 Thy people ſhall come willingly,
  In day of thine authority,
    within fair Sions ſacred walls :
Where thy firſt converts ſhall abound,
  As thick as dew upon the ground,
    which from the womb of morning falls.

4 The unrepenting God thus ſwore,
  Thou art a prieſt for evermore,
    by order of Melchizedek.
5 And God at thy right hand ſhall ſlay
  Proud kings in that his wrathful day:
6 And all the heathen he ſhall check,
  With corpſes he ſhall ſtrew the ground,
  And heads of many countries wound,
    filling the places with the dead.
7 And he ſhall make no longer ſtay,
  But drink the torrent in the way :
    therefore ſhall he lift up the head.

PSALM CXI.

א Applaud the Lord, whom I will praiſe
    with my whole heart and might :
ב Both in the ſecret of the juſt,
  and in the churches ſight.
ג 2 Great are the works of our great God,
  and every one no doubt
ד Delighting in them from their heart,
  with care do ſearch them out.
ה 3 His work moſt honourable is,
  and glorious no leſs :
Unto eternity endures
  his truth and righteouſneſs.
ו 4 Surely he made his wonderous works,
  ſtill to be had in mind:
ח Choice favours hath the Lord in ſtore,
  and he is good and kind.

ט 5 To them that fear his holy name
  he giveth meat good store :
י Jehovah will be mindful of
  his covenant evermore.
כ 6 Clearly hath he declar'd to his,
  his works of powerfulness :
ל Leaving to them the heritage,
  which heathens did possess.
מ 7 Most perfect are his handy-works,
  his judgments very pure :
נ Not one of his commandements,
  but are exceeding sure.
ס 8 Stablisht they are for evermore,
  so that they cannot fade :
ע And even in truth and righteousness
  each one of them is made.
פ 9 Plenteous redemption he hath sent,
  to make his people free :
צ So is his covenant evermore
  confirm'd by his decree.
ק Know ye that holy is his name,
  and to be had in dread.
ר 10 Religious fear of God likewise,
  is wisdoms well-spring head.
ש Sound understanding have they all,
  that carefully indeavour
ת To practise his commandements :
  his praise endures for ever.

PSALM CXII.

PRaise ye the Lord, for blest are such
  as fear the Lord aright,
And love his laws exceeding much,
  and do them with delight.
2 His seed shall multiply on earth,
  and prosper mightily :

And God shall pour his blessings forth
  on his posterity.
3 Of wealth and riches in his house,
  there shall be plenteous store:
His memorable righteousness
  endures for evermore.
4 Unto the man immaculate,
  in darkness riseth light:
Gracious he is, compassionate,
  and every way upright.
5 A good man shews much kind respect,
  and lends to him that needs:
And with discretion will direct
  all his affairs and deeds.
6 Surely he shall not moved be,
  while time to time can add:
In everlasting memory
  the righteous shall be had.
7 For any evil tidings told,
  he shall not be afraid:
His faithful heart which makes him bold,
  on God is firmly stai'd.
8 His heart is so established,
  afraid he shall not be;
Till his desire accomplished
  upon his foes he see.
9 He hath disperſed liberally,
  and given to the door:
He shall to perpetuity
  be stil'd a righteous doer.
Exalted high his horn shall be,
  with honour thus atchiev'd;
10 The wicked man this thing shall see,
  and be extreamly griev'd.
Yea, he shall gnash his teeth for spite;
  and pining melt away:

And his desire shall perish quite,
the wicked mans, I say.

II. *Metre.* All People, &c.

Praise ye the Lord with one accord
The man is blest that fears the Lord:
   That takes delight continually
   In the commands of God most high.

His seed on earth shall have great place
And he be happy in his race:
   Riches and wealth his house shall store,
   Renown'd for goodness evermore.

Unto the upright man likewise
Great light in darkness doth arise:
   Gracious is he in God's own sight,
   Full of compassion and upright.

A good man favour shews and lends,
And with discretion spares and spends:
   Surely he never shall be mov'd
   That hath his wealth so well improv'd.

The righteous person had shall be
In Everlasting MEMORIE:
   No tidings ill shall him affright,
   His faith is fixt on God's great might.

His heart is well established,
He shall not be dismay'd with dread:
   Until he faithfully disclose
   His expectation on his foes.

He gives with bounty to the poor
His Name endures for evermore
   His horn shall be exalted high
   With honour and with dignity.

The wicked man this thing shall see,

III. Metre. *To the proper Tune.*

The man is blest that fears the Lord
Delighting greatly in his word :
Mighty on earth his seed shall be,
And blessed his Posterity :
    Riches and wealth his house shall fill,
    And his renown continue still.

Unto the man that is upright,
In darkness there ariseth light,
He is a gracious righteous one
And full of kind compassion :
    A good man's kind, he lends and spares,
    Discretion guiding his affairs.

For certain mov'd he shall be never,
The just shall be in fame for ever ;
His stablish'd heart on God is staid,
Of evil tidings not afraid,
    His faith is fix'd, his pain is past,
    Until he see his enemies cast.

He hath dispersed of his store,
And given plenty to the poor,
His righteousness remaineth sure,
And shall for evermore endure :
    His horn shall be exalted high
    With honour and with dignity.

The wicked man shall see this thing
And it shall wound him like a sting ;
Yea, it shall make him gnash his teeth
And pine away for very grief :
    Thus wicked mens desires shall die,
    The Lord then praise and magnifie.

PSALM CXIII.

Praise ye the Lord, praise ye his Name
  ye servants of the Lord,
His Name be now and ever blest,
  of all with one accord.
From Sun's uprise within the Skies,
  unto the going down,
Must we proclaim the Lord's great fame,
  and give his Name renown.

The Lord is high o're nations all,
  His fame surmounts the sky,
And who is like the Lord our God,
  whose dwelling is on high?
Yet from that place he doth abase
  Himself to see and know
The things that move in Heaven above,
  and in the Earth below.

He lifts the poor out of the dust,
  and from the dunghil brings
The needy sort to Princes seats,
  to sit with Israel's kings.
The barren he doth make to be
  a house-keeper well stor'd,
With joy to breed her fruitful seed;
  wherefore praise ye the Lord.

II. *Metre.*

Ye children which do serve the Lord,
  Praise ye his name with one accord:
2 Both now and ever bless his name.
3 Even from the rising of the sun,
  Till it return where it begun,
    extoll and magnifie his fame.
4 The Lord all people doth surmount,

   His glittering glory we may count
   above the heavens to extend.
5 For who in all the world abroad,
 Is like unto the Lord our God,
   whose dwelling doth all height transcend?
6 He doth abase himself we know,
 Things to behold both here below,
   and also in the heavens high.
7 The poor and needy sort he brings
 Even from the dust to sit with kings,
   in thrones of princely majesty.
8 Among his people thus doth he
 Place them with princes in degree,
   that lately from the dunghil came.
9 The barren he doth make to bear,
 And with great joy her feed to rear:
   praise ye therefore his holy name.

PSALM CXIV.

When Israel out of Egypt went,
   their dwelling to exchange:
And Jacob's house remov'd their tent
   from folk of language strange:
2 His sanctuary Judah was,
   he rul'd in Israel.
3 The sea saw that and fled apace,
   and Jordan backwards fell.
4 The mighty mountains then did skip,
   like joyful flocks of rams:
 The little hills did likewise trip,
   like little wanton lambs.
5 What ail'd thee, O thou sea, to fly?
   why didst thou courage lack?
 And why wast thou so suddenly,
   O Jordan, driven back?
6 Ye mighty mountains, that ye skipt,
   like to the nimble rams:

> Ye little hills, because ye tript,
> like to the wanton lambs?
> 7 O earth, in God's great presence quake,
> even Jacob's God that brings
> 8 The stony rock to standing lake,
> the flint to water-springs.

II. Metre. *Ye Children, &c.*

> When Israel went from Egypt land,
> And Jacob's house by powerful hand
> from people of a barbarous tongue;
> 2 Judah was then his holy place,
> And Israel his dominion was,
> who led them safely all along.
> 3 The sea saw that and fled amain,
> And Jordan wheel'd about again,
> and forced back his waves profound:
> 4 The rocky mountains skipt like rams,
> The little hills like timorous lambs,
> and could not stand their stedfast ground.
>
> 5 What ail'd thee, O thou sea, to fly?
> What drove you back so hastily,
> ye rouling waves of Jordan's floud?
> 6 What made you mountains skip like rams?
> And you, O little hills, like lambs,
> to quake and tremble as ye stood?
> 7 Tremble, O earth, before the face
> Of that great God of Jacob's race,
> tremble before him awfully.
> 8 He turns hard rocks to standing lakes,
> And fountains of hard flint he makes,
> by his great power and majesty.

PSALM CXV.

Psalm cxv.

Even for thy mercy marvellous,
  and for thy truths dear sake.
Why should the heathen utter this,
  now where's their God, say they?
But our God in the heavens is,
  what he will do he may.

Their idols gold and silver be,
  which mens own hands did make.
Lo, they have eyes, but cannot see,
  and mouths, but never spake.
Have ears, but do not hear a jot,
  noses, but feel no scent:
Proportion'd hands, but handle not,
  and feet, but never went.

Nor ever speak they through their throat,
  Such are their makers (just)
And so are all that on them dote,
  and in them put their trust.
O Israel, trust thou in the Lord,
  thy help and shield is he.
O Aaron's house, trust in his word,
  a help and shield to thee.

1 And ye that fear the Lord each one,
  be careful that ye build
Your confidence on him alone,
  who is your help and shield.
2 The Lord hath thought upon us well,
  his people he will bless:
Even all the house of Israel,
  and Aaron's house no less.

3 Whoever fear the Lord therefore,
  he'll bless them great and small:
4 God shall increase you more and more,
  you and your children all.
5 You are the blessed of the Lord,
  whose quick commandment came,

And made the heavens at a word,
　and earths inferiour frame.
16 The heaven, even the heavens high,
　are all of them the Lords:
But he to mans posterity
　the spacious earth affords.
17 The dead indeed praise not the Lord,
　they give him no renown:
Nor any do his praise record,
　to silence that go down.
18 But we that are alive therefore,
　will bless the living Lord,
From this time forth for evermore,
　do ye his praise record.

　　　II. *Metre*. All People, &c.

Not unto us, Lord, not to us,
　but give the glory to thy Name,
For thy sweet mercy marvellous,
　and thy truth's sake which we proclaim.
2 Why should the Heathen speak abroad
　Now where's their God? let Israel shew?
3 But our God hath in heaven abode,
　and done whatever he pleas'd to do.
4 Their Idols gold and silver are,
　the handy-works of men they bee:
5 Have mouths but nothing can declare,
　and they have eyes but do not see.
6 And they have ears joyn'd to their head
　but hear not those that on them call:
And they have noses fashioned,
　but yet they do not smell at all.
7 And they have hands but handle not,
　and feet drawn forth for greater note.

The makers that did them compose
are like to them, and much akin,
and so is every one of those
that put their confidence therein.

The Second part.

O Israel trust thou in the Lord
  thy helper and thy shield to be:
10 O Aaron's house trust in his word,
  thy helper and thy shield is he.
11 Ye that fear God O trust in him,
  your help and shield is God most high.
12 Mindful of us the Lord hath been,
  and he will bless us bounteously.

He'll bless the house of Israel,
  and all that sit in Aaron's seat;
13 All that fear him may know full well,
  that God will bless them small and great.
14 God shall increase you more and more,
  you and your children (from the birth)
15 Ye are the blessed stock and store
  of him that made both heaven and earth.
16 The heavens even the heavens high spheres
  they are the Lord's, each one of them,
But all the earth and all it bears
  he giveth to the sons of men.
17 The dead do never praise the Lord,
  nor any that go down to th' pit,
18 But we will his high praise record
  henceforth for ever, So be it.

PSALM CXVI.

I Love the Lord unfeignedly,
  because he pleas'd to hear
My supplication and my cry,
  with an attentive ear.

2 Becaufe he hath inclin'd the fame
   fo gracioufly to me :
Therefore will I call on his name,
   whil'ft I alive fhall be.
3 The pangs of death did me infold,
   and compaffed me round :
The pains of hell on me gat hold,
   I grief and trouble found.
4 Then did I call moft earneftly
   upon the Lord's great name :
Releafe my foul, O Lord, faid I,
   I humbly crave the fame.
5 The Lord's a very gracious one,
   and full of righteoufnefs :
And tenderer compaffion
   no bowels can exprefs.
6 The Lord preferveth carefully
   all thofe that fimple be :
For I was funk in mifery,
   and he recovered me.
7 Return, my foul, that art fet free,
   return unto thy reft :
For largely hath the Lord to thee
   his benefits expreft.
8 Becaufe that thou my foul haft freed,
   which elfe in death had flept :
Mine eyes from tears delivered,
   my feet from falling kept.
9 Now will I walk before the Lord,
   as alwayes in his fight :
Among the living to record
   his praife in land of light.
10 For I believed help would come,
   therefore I fpake no lefs :
Though I was plunged for a time,
   in very deep diftrefs.

Psalm cxvj.

The second part.

11 At other times in haſt I ſaid,
   tuſh, all men liars be.
12 O then what ſhall I give to God,
   for all his gifts to me?
13 The cup of ſweet ſalvation,
   lo, I will take it up:
And God's great name I'le call upon,
   with that ſame bleſſed cup.
14 The ſolemn vows which I did vow
   unto the Lord moſt high,
Thoſe will I pay and offer now,
   whil'ſt all his ſaints ſtand by.
15 Of great account undoubtedly,
   and precious in God's eyes
The death of his dear ſaints ſhall be,
   when any of them dies.
16 Truly I am thy ſervant, Lord,
   I am thy hand-maids ſon,
Thy ſervant that obeys thy word,
   whoſe bonds thou haſt undone.
17 To thee, Lord will I ſacrifice
   the ſacrifice of praiſe:
To call upon thy name likewiſe,
   my thankful voice I'le raiſe.
18 The vows I ſay which I did vow,
   unto the Lord moſt high,
I will among his people now,
   perform them openly.
19 In God's own courts I'le offer them;
   there in thy houſe, O Lord,
In midſt of thee Jeruſalem:
   his praiſe do ye record.

PSALM CXVII.

PRaise praise the Lord with one accord,
   all nations tongues and lands,
Whose marvailous kind love to us
   for ever firmly stands.
So likewise doth his blessed truth
   it lasts for evermore,
That faithful word of God the Lord,
   praise ye the Lord therefore.

II. *Metre.*

Have mercy, &c.

Praise God ye nations all,
   all people praise his name
Whose grace to us so marvailous.
   deserves eternal fame.
His truth to great and small
   abides on sure record:
For evermore, do ye therefore
   give praise unto the Lord.

III. *Metre.*

Give Laud, &c. *A Praxis for the old* 148 *Ps.*

Give laud and praise the Lord,
   ye lands and nations all;
For he confirms his word
   with grace to great and small;
     On firm record
His truth abides, and never slides;
     Praise ye the Lord.

IV. Mitre.

A Praxis for the old 124 Psal.

Praise ye the Lord all nations, tongues and lands,
Because we find
   His mercies marvailous, And loving kind—
     ness very great to us:
His faithful word
   for ever firmly stands,
Praise ye the Lord,
   all nations tongues and lands.

PSALM CXVIII.

Give thanks to God, for he is good,
   his mercies still indure:
2 Let Israel say this very day
   his mercies still are sure.
3 Let Aarons house confess this day,
   his mercy still prevails.
4 Let them that fear the Lord now say,
   his mercy never fails.
5 I call'd on God in my distress,
   and largely he reply'd.
6 I fear not man do what he can,
   for God is on my side.
7 Whoe're they be that succour me,
   the Lord takes part with those:
   And I my full desire shall see
   upon my hateful foes.
8 It is far better to depend
   upon the Lord alone,
   Then to repose our confidence
   in any mortal one.
9 Better it is to trust in God,
   and cast on him our care:

Then to repose our trust in those
  that powerful Princes are.

The Second Part.

10 All nations compass me about,
  but in Gods name alone
I trust that I shall easily
  destroy them every one.
11 They compast me about, I say,
  they compast me about:
But in the name of God shall I
  destroy and root them out.
12 They swarm'd like Bees but are extinct
  as thorns that fiercely flame:
For soon I shall destroy them all,
  in Gods almighty name.
13 My foe, thou hast thrust sore at me,
  thinking to make me fall:
But so the Lord assisted me,
  that I escaped all.
14 The Lord is all my fortitude,
  he is the song I sing:
And is become the rock from whom
  my saving health doth spring.
15 The voice of saving health and joy,
  in just mens dwellings is:
The Lords right hand doth valiantly,
  that strong right hand of his.
16 The right hand of the Lord, I say,
  it is exalted high:
The Lord's right hand none can withstand,
  it works so valiantly.
17 I shall not die, for I shall live,
  and living shall declare
The works of our almighty Lord,
  how wonderful they are.

The Third part.

18 The Lord indeed that chasteneth me,
   hath chastened me sore:
Yet hath not he abandon'd me
   to death, when at death's dore.
19 Open to me the sacred court,
   the gates of righteousness:
And thither I will now resort,
   God's praises to confess.
20 This is the blest and sacred gate
   of God the Lord, I say,
Where righteous men shall enter in,
   to praise the Lord alway.
21 Lord, I will praise thy holy name,
   for when to thee I pray'd,
Thou heard'st my voice, and art become
   my rock of saving aid.
22 The stone which by the builders was
   refused with disgrace,
Is now become the corner stone,
   and set in chiefest place.
23 This is the work of our great God,
   and wondrous in our eyes.
24 This is the day the Lord hath made,
   to fill our hearts with joyes.
25 Save now, I do beseech thee, Lord,
   I pray thee earnestly,
Now to afford thy help, O Lord,
   and send prosperity.
26 Blessed be he that comes to us
   in God's great name alone:
And we from Sions sacred house,
   do bless you every one.
27 God is the Lord who light affords,
   which this high day adorns:

Come, bind the sacrifice with cords
  unto the altars horns.
28 Thou art my God whom I'le exalt,
  my God whom I will praise.
29 Give thanks to God for he is good,
  his mercy lasts always.

PSALM CXIX. I. Metre.

The First part.

א A Blessed people sure are they
    that undefiled are;
And walk in God's unspotted way,
  and keep his Laws with care.
א And blest are they that care to keep
  his Testaments entire,
And they that for the Lord do seek
  with all their hearts desire.
א Assuredly they do no sin
  of purpose so to do:
But love God's laws and walk therein,
  and closely cleave thereto;
א A strict command thou giv'st us hence,
  from which we may not swerve,
That we with care and diligence
  thy statutes should observe.
א Assist me therefore, O my Lord,
  and so direct my way,
That I may keep thy holy word,
  and never go astray.
א And then can no confusion fall
  nor shame on me reflect:
While unto thy Commandments all
  I have a due respect.
א An upright heart shall be prepar'd
  for thy sincerer praise,
When unto me thou hast declar'd

Psalm cxix.

All care that can be will I take
  to keep thy holy word;
O do not utterly forsake
  nor leave me quite, O Lord.

The Second part.

9 What may a young man think to do,
  to cleanse his way, O Lord?
Surely by taking heed thereto,
  according to thy word.
10 Lord, I have sought thee from my heart,
  and from my heart I pray,
That I may not at all depart,
  or wander from thy way.
11 I hid thy word within my heart
  from sin to keep me free:
12 A blessed one, O Lord, thou art,
  thy statutes teach thou me.
13 The judgments of thy mouth divine,
  I with my lips have told:
14 Rejoycing in those wayes of thine,
  more then in heaps of gold.
15 Upon thy precepts I will muse,
  thy wayes I will respect:
16 Thy statutes with delight peruse,
  and not thy word neglect.

The Third part.

17 Deal bounteously in gifts of grace
  with me thy servant, Lord;
That I may live and run my race,
  and keep thy holy word.
18 Open, O Lord, and clear mine eyes,
  that I may then behold
What wonderful great mysteries
  thy statutes do unfold.

19 I do confess my self to be
  a stranger here below:
 O do not hide thy laws from me,
  which I should fully know.
20 My soul doth break with fervency,
  and only for this cause,
 Of longing so continually
  after thy sacred laws.
21 As for the proud presumptuous men,
  which from thy statutes stray,
 Thou hast, O Lord, rebuked them,
  and cursed is their way.
22 Remove reproaches and contempts,
  remove them, Lord, from me:
 For I have kept the testaments
  which I have learnt of thee.
23 And though great princes also sate,
  thy servant to condemn:
 Thy statutes I did contemplate,
  and boldly spake of them.
24 Thy testimonies also are
  my very hearts delight:
 Nor need I other counseller,
  to guide my wayes aright.

The Fourth part.

25 My soul doth cleave unto the dust,
  vouchsafe thou, gracious Lord,
 To quicken me as thou art just,
  and hast ingag'd thy word.
26 O Lord I have acknowledged
  my secret ways to thee;
 And thou thereto hast hearkened:
  thy statutes teach thou me.
27 Make me, O Lord, to see and search
  thy precepts perfect way:

Psalm cxix.

So shall I have thy wonderous works
  to talk of every day.
18 But now my soul doth melt away
  for heaviness, O Lord:
Vouchsafe to be my strength and stay,
  according to thy word.
29 The way of lying vanity
  from me, O Lord, withdraw:
And grant me very graciously
  the knowledge of thy law.
30 For I have chose the way most true,
  thy judgments are my aim:
31 Thy testaments I stuck unto,
  Lord, put me not to shame.
32 And I will run with full consent,
  the way thou giv'st in charge;
When with thy sweet incouragement
  thou shalt my heart inlarge.

The Fifth part.

33 Instruct me, Lord, to apprehend
  thy precepts perfect way:
And I shall keep it to the end,
  even to my dying day.
34 Make me, O Lord, to understand,
  and I shall keep thy law:
Yea to observe thy full command,
  my heart shall not withdraw.
35 Thy path-wayes let me never miss,
  but keep thy laws intire:
No other pleasure do I wish,
  nor greater thing desire.
36 Unto thy precepts bend my mind,
  as unto things of price;
And let me never be inclin'd
  to wicked avarice.

37 Avert mine eyes from vanity,
  the lure whereon they gaze;
And by thy spirit quicken me
  in thy diviner wayes.
38 And as thou hast ingag'd thy word,
  so ratify the same
Unto thy faithful servant, Lord,
  who vows to fear thy name.
39 The carnal fear of obloquy,
  from me, O Lord, repell;
For thou dost judge with equity,
  and therein dost excell.
40 Behold, Lord, with what eagerness
  thy precepts I pursue;
Vouchsafe then in thy righteousness,
  to quicken me thereto.

The Sixth part.

41 And now let thy compassion
  come unto me, O Lord:
And shew me thy salvation,
  according to thy word.
42 And so shall I enabled be
  to give reply most just
To him that thus reproacheth me,
  for in thy word I trust.
43 The word of truth Lord take not quite,
  out of my mouth, I pray,
Because thy judgments just and right
  are all my hope and stay.
44 And so shall I continually
  thy law for ever keep,
45 And I will walk at liberty,
  for I thy precepts seek.
46 Thy testaments will I recite:
  to kings, and fear no shame:

47 And in thy laws will I delight,
   for I have lov'd the same;
48 Lifting my hands to thy commands,
   which I have lov'd so well:
And for this cause will mind thy laws,
   which do so much excell.

The Seventh part.

49 Remember, Lord, the faithful word
   unto thy servant told:
And whereupon thou causedst me
   to build my hope so bold.
50 And only this my comfort is,
   in time of my distress:
Because thy word shall quicken me
   in all my heaviness.
51 Lo they deride that swell with pride,
   and scorn me very much:
Yet have not I declin'd thy law,
   for fear of any such.
52 I did record thy judgments, Lord,
   thy judgments wrought of old;
And meditating thereupon,
   took comfort and grew bold.
53 Yet horror great, like storms that beat,
   hath taken hold on me:
Because vile men forsake the law,
   which is ordain'd by thee.
54 Yet every-where thy statutes were
   my comfortable song,
In places of my pilgrimage
   as I have past along.
55 I did record thy name, O Lord,
   by night and kept thy laws.
56 And this I had by keeping them,
   and for no other cause.

The Eighth part.

57 Thou art my part and portion
 even thou, O Lord, alone.
 I said that I would carefully
 observe thy words each one.
58 Thy favour free I did intreat
 with my whole heart, O Lord,
 Then grant to me thy mercies free,
 according to thy word.
59 To thy decrees I turn'd my feet,
 when pondering my wayes.
60 Haft I have made, and not delay'd
 to keep thy holy laws.
61 And though the bands of wicked men,
 have made of me their prey:
 Yet have I not thy laws forgot,
 as careless of thy way.
62 At midnight I will wake and rise,
 to render thanks to thee:
 Because thy word and judgments, Lord,
 so just and righteous be.
63 With all that fear thy holy name,
 I am companion still:
 Of such as seek thy laws to keep,
 and precepts to fulfill.
64 Thy mercies great, O gracious Lord,
 the spacious earth do fill;
 Teach me the way how to obey
 thy statutes and thy will.

The Ninth part.

65 Thou hast dealt very well with me,
 who am thy servant, Lord,

66 Teach me good judgment in thy word,
   and knowledge of thy will:
 For thy commandements, O Lord,
   I have believed still.
67 Er'e thou didst touch me with thy rod,
   I err'd and went astray:
 But now I keep thy word, O God,
   and by it guide my way.
68 Lord, thou art good, and thou dost good,
   all graces flow from thee;
 Make then thy statutes understood,
   and practised by me.
69 For though proud persons did invent
   against me many a lie:
 Yet kept I thy commandement
   with hearts sincerity.
70 Their heart that never stands in awe,
   is like a lump of grease:
 But I delight me in thy law,
   and find a safer peace.
71 I count it very good for me
   chastised to have bin:
 That I may learn thy laws from thee,
   and shun the snares of sin.
72 The law of thy own mouth I hold
   far better unto me,
 Then many thousand pounds of gold
   and silver heaps can be.

The Tenth part.

73 Thy hands have made and fashion'd me,
   thy grace on me bestow:
 To know thy precepts what they be,
   and practise what I know.
74 Then all that fear thee shall be glad,
   when me they shall behold:

Because I have assurance had
in what thy word foretold.
75 Yet, Lord, I know and do confess,
how just thy judgments be:
And that of very faithfulness
thou hast afflicted me.
76 I pray thee let thy mercies kind
come to thy servant, Lord:
For comfort to my troubled mind,
according to thy word.
77 Thy tender mercies-bowels, Lord,
O let them come in sight:
That I may live and keep thy word,
for therein I delight.
78 But let the proud ashamed be,
for they without a cause
Have most perversly dealt with me,
but I will mind thy laws.
79 And now, O Lord, let every one
that truly feareth thee,
And all that have thy statutes known,
let them turn in to me.
80 And let my heart unto thy laws
be so sincerely fram'd:
That I may not have any cause
whereby to be asham'd.

The Eleventh part.

All people, *or,* O Lord, consider, *&c.*

81 My soul for thy salvation faints,
but in thy word is all my stay:
82 My failing eyes urge sad complaints,
when wilt thou comfort me? they say.
83 A wrinkled bottle set in smoke,
I rightly am compar'd unto:

Psalm cxix.

But lo the word which thou hast spoke,
  I have not yet forgot to do.
84 How many are thy servants days?
  when wilt thou righteous vengeance take
On persecutors of my wayes,
  and judge them for thy servants sake?
85 The proud have digged pits for me,
  which with thy law doth not accord;
86 For all thy laws are equity;
  they persecute me, help me, Lord.
87 They had consumed me almost,
  with cruel and injurious hands,
Here upon earths despiteful coast,
  yet I forsook not thy commands.
88 Thy loving kindness let be sent,
  to quicken up my fainting mind:
So shall I keep the testament
  which thy most holy mouth hath sign'd.

The Twelfth part.

89 The word which thou hast spoken, Lord,
  is permanent and sure:
And like to heavens constant course
  for ever doth endure.
90 All ages find thy faithfulness,
  which never slacks nor slides:
Like as thou hast established
  the earth, and it abides.
91 According to thy ordinance
  continuing to this day:
For all are servants unto thee
  and do thy word obey.
92 If in thy law and faithful word
  I had not found delight:
In my extream affliction, Lord,

93 Therefore I never will forget
   thy precepts to expreſs :
For thou thereby haſt quickened me
   in all my heavineſs.
94 Continue then to ſave me, Lord,
   for I am one of thine :
And I have ſought with diligence,
   thy precepts moſt divine.
95 Though wicked men laid wait for me
   to kill and to deſtroy :
Yet I conſider of thy laws,
   and think of them with joy.
96 For Lord, I ſee there is an end
   of all perfections here :
But only thy commandements
   far larger do appear.

The Thirteenth part.

97 O How I love the ſacred word
   which doth thy law diſplay !
It is my meditation, Lord,
   and ſtudy all the day.
98 Thou mak'ſt me by thy laws to be
   far wiſer then my foes :
For that thoſe laws abide with me
   and I abide by thoſe.
99 With all my teachers I compare,
   excelling them in skill :
Becauſe thy teſtimonies are
   my meditation ſtill.
100 In underſtanding I out-go
   the ancients (full of dayes:)
Becauſe I do not only know,
   but alſo keep thy wayes.
101 I have refrain'd my feet, O Lord,

That I may keep thy faithful word,
 and no time go astray.
02 And from thy sacred judgments, Lord,
 I never did depart:
For thou hast made thy heavenly word,
 to sink into my heart.

03 And Lord, in these thy words of truth,
 how sweet a tast I find:
Sweeter then hony to my mouth,
 thy word is to my mind.
04 Thy precepts do so well direct,
 and so much skill impart:
That all false wayes I do reject,
 and hate them in my heart.

The Fourteenth part.

05 Like as a lamp unto my feet,
 so doth thy word shine bright:
Both night and day it guides my way,
 and to my paths gives light.
06 And I have sworn most solemnly,
 and will perform it too:
That I will spare no pains or care,
 thy righteous laws to do.
07 I am afflicted very much,
 but quicken me, O Lord:
And let me be reviv'd by thee,
 according to thy word.
08 The free-will offerings of my mouth,
 I pray thee, Lord, accept:
And teach me now which way and how
 thy judgments may be kept.
09 My soul is ever in my hand,
 in danger to be lost:
Yet have I not thy law forgot,

110 And though the wicked secretly,
  their subtle snares did lay,
Yet am not I seduc'd thereby,
  to wander from thy way.
111 Thy statutes are the heritage,
  whereof I have made choice
To my last day, for those are they
  that make my heart rejoyce.
112 I have inclin'd my heart to keep
  the laws thou didst decree:
And will attend them to the end,
  even till I come to thee.

The Fifteenth part.

113 The foolish thoughts of vanity
  I do detest and hate:
But in thy holy law do I
  delight to meditate.
114 Thou art, O Lord, my hiding-place,
  and shield of my defence:
And in the word of thy good grace
  I put my confidence.
115 Depart from me ye wicked men,
  that other paths have trod:
And I will keep with freedome then
  the precepts of my God.
116 According to thy word proclaim'd,
  my soul in life uphold:
And let me never be asham'd
  of this my hope so bold.
117 Uphold thou me, and then shall I
  be very safely kept:

For their deceit will soon disclose
  the falshood of their way.
19 And all the wicked of the earth
  as drofs thou doſt remove:
Therefore the laws which thou ſet'ſt forth
  I do intirely love.
20 For I do tremble, Lord, to tell
  what vengeance thou wilt take:
Thy judgments are ſo terrible,
  They cauſe my fleſh to quake.

The Sixteenth part.

21 I have done right to other men,
  and followed righteouſneſs:
Then leave me not, O Lord, to them
  That would my ſoul oppreſs.
22 A ſurety for thy ſervant be
  engaged for my good:
And let proud mens oppreſſing me
  be by thy power withſtood.
23 But all this while mine eyes do fail,
  thy ſaving health to ſee:
Until thy righteous word prevail,
  to help and ſuccour me.
24 According to thy mercy, Lord,
  with me thy ſervant deal:
And the commandments of thy word
  to me, O Lord, reveal.
25 I am thy ſervant give me skill,
  and make me underſtand:
That I may know thy holy will,
  and practiſe thy command,
26 It's time for thee to work, **O God**,
  and not thy ſelf withdraw:
For wicked men have undertrod,
  and quite made void thy law.

127 Therefore I love thy statutes more,
    then gold dig'd from the Mine:
Yea, I preferre them far before,
    the gold that is most fine.
128 Therefore I judge all thy decrees,
    in all things to be right;
And all false wayes and heresies
    I hate as opposite.

The Seventeenth Part.

129 O Lord, how very wonderfull
    thy testimonies are:
And for this cause to keep thy laws,
    my soul doth take great care.
130 The very entrance of thy words,
    doth give thy servants light:
And maketh them though simple men,
    to understand aright.
131 My mouth I opened and did pant,
    with zeal as hot as fire:
Because that these thy just decrees,
    inflam'd me with desire.
132 Look on me in thy mercy, Lord,
    and grant me of the same:
As usually thou dost apply,
    tow'rds them that love thy name.
133 Order my foot-steps in thy word,
    and all my lusts controul:
And let no sin have entrance in,
    to lord it o're my soul.
134 Release me from oppression,
    and injuries of men:
And so shall I more chearfully
    observe thy precepts then.
135 And let thy gracious countenance,
    on me thy servant shine:

   And make me wife in myſteries,
     that truly are divine.
136 For, Lord, I weep Rivers of Tears,
     and 'tis my conſtant courſe:
   And all becauſe they break thy laws
     without the leaſt remorſe.

The eighteenth part.

137 O Lord, thou art a righteous God,
     a righteous God indeed :
   And upright all the judgments are
     which from thy mouth proceed.
138 The precepts, Lord, which thou doſt preſs,
     and giv'ſt us charge to do :
   Are perfect rules of righteouſneſs,
     and very faithful too.
139 My zeal hath quite conſumed me,
     it was ſo very hot:
   Becauſe my wicked enemies
     have all thy words forgot.
140 Thy word indeed is very pure,
     as ſilver try'd by fire:
   Therefore thy ſervant will be ſure
     to love it moſt entire.
141 And though I am of ſmall account,
     and ſcorn'd by carnal minds;
   Yet do not I forget thoſe laws
     to which my duty binds.
142 An everlaſting righteouſneſs,
     thy righteouſneſs muſt be :
   And, Lord, thy law can be no leſs
     then perfect verity.
143 Trouble and anguiſh very great
     on me have taken hold:
   Yet thy commandments unto me
     far greater joyes unfold.

144 Eternal are thy just decrees:
  to me vouchsafe and give
An understanding heart in these,
  and I shall surely live.

The Nineteenth part.

145 With my whole heart I cri'd to thee,
  O Lord, hear thou my prayer:
Thy statutes shall be kept by me,
  with diligence and care.
146 I cri'd to thee in my distress,
  Lord, save and succour me:
And I will keep with faithfulness
  the words of thy decree.
147 I did prevent the dawning day,
  so early was my cry:
I made thy holy word my stay,
  and waited patiently.
148 The watches of the night so late,
  my wakeful eye prevents:
That I might sweetly meditate
  on thy commandements.
149 O let my humble voice be heard,
  in loving-kindness free:
According to thy judgments, Lord,
  vouchsafe to quicken me.
150 Behold, O Lord, how near they draw,
  that wicked plots pursue:
But they are far off from thy law,
  in every thing they do.
151 But thou, O Lord, art near at hand,
  and rulest righteously:
Whatever things thou dost command,
  are truth and verity.
152 And as concerning thy decrees,
  I understand of old

Pfalm cxix.

That thou, O Lord, haſt founded theſe,
  eternally to hold.

The Twentieth part.

153 Conſider my adverſity,
  and now deliver me :
For I forget not careleſly,
  the word that comes from thee.
154 O plead my cauſe with equity,
  and reſcue me, O Lord :
Reſtore my ſoul and quicken me,
  according to thy word.
155 But ſurely thy ſalvation, Lord,
  from wicked men withdraws,
It is too far for them to ſeek,
  that do not ſeek thy laws.
156 Great are thy tender mercies, Lord,
  which in thy bowels ſtrive :
According to thy gracious word,
  my drooping ſoul revive.
157 Mine enemies are many, Lord,
  my perſecutors many :
Yet have not I ſwerv'd from thy word
  for ſlaviſh fear of any.
158 But I was greatly griev'd, O Lord,
  when I with ſorrow ſaw :
How theſe perfidious wicked men,
  would not obſerve thy law.
159 But as for me conſider, Lord,
  how much thy laws I love :
And in thy kindneſs quicken me,
  with favour from above.
160 For from the firſt to laſt, O Lord,
  thy word is true and ſure :
Thy righteous judgments every one
  perpetually endure.

The One and Twentieth part.

All people, &c.

161 Princes have persecuted me,
  maliciously without a cause:
 Yet stands my heart in fear of thee,
  so much thy word my conscience awes.
162 I have rejoiced at thy word,
  as one that finds the richest prize:
163 And I do love thy Law, O Lord,
  but hate and loath the way of lies.
164 Seven times a day I give thee praise,
  even for thy righteous judgments sake:
165 Great peace have they that love thy ways,
  and no offence they need to take.
166 Lord, I have hop't for thy defence,
  and thy command'ments I have done.
167 My soul hath kept thy testaments,
  and loves them dearly ev'ry one.
168 Thy precepts I have kept with care,
  thy testimonies I pursue:
 For all my ways and actions are
  before thee, ever in thy view.

The Two and Twentieth part.

169 O Lord, let my complaint and cry
  have quick access to thee:
 And give me knowledge graciously,
  as thou hast promis'd me.
170 O let my supplication,
  before thee be preferr'd:
 And grant me thy salvation,
  according to thy word.
171 And then my lips shall be prepar'd
  to utter thankful praise,

When

Pfalm cxix.

When unto me thou haſt declar'd,
  and taught me all thy wayes.
172 My tongue ſhall utter and expreſs
  the praiſes of thy word:
For thy commands are righteouſneſs,
  even all of them, O Lord.
173 Then let thy helping hand prevail,
  when perils do oppoſe:
For leaving other helps that fail,
  thy precepts I have choſe.
174 And I, O Lord, have long'd to ſee
  thy ſaving health and might:
And, Lord, thy law affecteth me
  with very great delight.
175 O let my ſoul in ſafety live,
  and it ſhall give thee praiſe:
And unto me thy judgments give,
  to help me all my dayes.
176 I went aſtray like wandering ſheep,
  O ſeek thy ſervant yet:
For thy commandements I keep,
  and do not quite forget.

II. *Metre.*

All People, *&c.* Or, O Lord conſider, *&c.*

♪ 169 To thee, Lord, let my cry come near,
  and graciouſly do thou afford
To give me underſtanding clear,
  according to thy faithful word.
♪ 170 The humble ſuit which I prefer
  Lord let thy gracious face accept,
And be my ſure Deliverer
  that promiſe may as ſure be kept.
♪ 171 Then ſhall I dare to promiſe thee
  my thankful ſongs of cheerful praiſe,

When thou hast fully taught to me
  thy statutes and thy holy wayes.
ת 172 Then shall my tongue thy truth express,
  and utter knowledge very much,
B cause thy lawes are righteousness,
  Yea all thy laws, O Lord, are such.

ת 173 Then let thy helping hand on high
  be powerfully for me display'd:
For I have chosen prudently
  thy righteous precepts for my aid.
ת 174 Thou know'st that I have long'd, O Lord,
  that I thy saving health might see,
Thy laws therefore I have preferr'd
  the chief of my delights to be.

ת 175 Then let my soul in safety live,
  and it shall give thee grateful praise,
And unto me thy judgments give,
  to help me on in all good wayes.
ת 176 Thy servant seek, though gone astray,
  like to a wandring sheep, by kind,
For I forget not all thy way,
  but bear thy precepts still in mind.

PSALM CXX.

I Cri'd in my extream distress,
  to God that heard my cries.
2 Save me from tongues deceitfulness,
  and lips inur'd to lies.
3 But what shall be thy share, thy fee,
  false tongue thus us'd to err?
4 Sharp shafts of his that mighty is,
  with coals of juniper.
5 O woe is me, that I am fain
  in Meshech to reside:
And must in Kedar's tents remain,
  and therein still abide.

Psalm cxx.

My soul hath much conver'st with such
as unto peace are foes:
Peace I would make, but when I spake,
they straight to wars arose.

II. *Metre.*

Ye Children, &c.

cry'd to God, in my distress,
Who did a ready ear address,
  to hear my prayer and send me aid.
Lord, save my Soul, I thee intreat,
From lying lips and tongues deceit:
  thus fervently to him I pray'd.
But ah! what shall be done to thee,
Thou tongue as false as false can be?
  what shall be given thee for thy part?
Sharp arrows of the mighty sure,
With burning coals of juniper;
  such shalt thou have, such as thou art.
But wo is me that must perforce
As far as Meshech have recourse,
  to be a tedious sojourner.
is banished from Israel,
That I must be constrain'd to dwell
  within the tents of Kedar here.
My soul hath dwelt this many a day
With him that hates a peaceful way,
  and is to quietness averse.
I am for peace I love no jars;
But when I spake they were for wars,
  and by disswasion grew more fierce.

PSALM CXXI.

Up to the hills I lift mine eyes,
  from whence my succour came.

2 My help from God the Lord doth rise,
    that heaven and earth did frame.
3 And not a whit will he permit
    thy foot to slide or fall,
  For surely he that keepeth thee,
    he slumbers not at all.

4 Lo, he that keepeth Israel,
    he slumbers not nor sleeps:
5 The Lord thy keeper shades thee well,
    at thy right hand he keeps.
6 That neither may the sun by day,
    have any power to smite:
  And hurt thee by malignity,
    nor yet the moon by night.

7 The Lord shall save thee from all harm,
    thy soul shall he secure:
  The Lord, I say, with powerful arm,
    shall keep thee safe and sure.
8 Thy going out is brought about,
    with safety by his power:
  Thy coming in secur'd by him
    henceforth for evermore.

PSALM CXXII.

Have mercy, &c.

1 Did rejoice that day
    when they to me did say:
  Unto the house of God let us
    together take our way.
2 The feet of all our train
    now shortly shall remain,
  In full resorts within thy courts,
    O thou Jerusalem.
3 Jerusalem's buildings are
    like to a city fair:

Psalm cxxij.

In form exact and all compact
  together every where.
4 The tribes to that place came,
  the tribes of God by name:
To th'oracle of Israel
  God's praises to proclaim.

5 For at Jerusalem,
  are set the thrones for them,
The judgment thrones, those royal ones
  of David's diadem.
6 Pray earnestly with me,
  Jerusalems peace to see:
O Salem such shall prosper much
  as bear true love to thee.
7 Let all tranquillity,
  be in thy walls, said I:
Also in these thy pallaces
  as much prosperity.
8 Now for my brethren here,
  and my companions dear:
Even for their sake this prayer I make,
  peace be within thee there.
9 And for the neighbour-hood
  of Sion, where hath stood
The blest abode of our great God,
  I'le alwayes seek thy good.

II. *Metre.*

Ye children, *&c.*

I did exceedingly rejoice,
  To hear the forward peoples voice,
    in offering of their own accord:
For in this manner did they say,
  Come, let us up, and take our way
    unto the temple of the Lord.

2 Within thy gates, Jerusalem,
  Our feet shall come and stand in them,
    to worship and to offer there.
3 Jerusalem is built so neat,
  Compact together and compleat,
    the like there is not any where.
4 Thy holy tribes with one accord,
  The tribes, I say, of God the Lord
    to Israel's testimony came;
Thither they went on solemn dayes,
  To worship, and to offer praise
    unto the Lord's most holy name.
5 For there are stately thrones erect,
  Erected there for this respect,
    for judgment and for equity:
Which thrones of right do appertain
  To David's house, which there must reign,
    to judge the people righteously.
6 O pray therefore and do not cease,
  But pray for our Jerusalems peace,
    they that love thee shall prosper well.
7 Peace be within thy walls, say I,
  I wish as much prosperity
    within thy palaces to dwell.
8 My brethren and companions dear,
  Make me now say, let peace be here,
    I wish it heartily to thee.
9 The temple of our God no less
  Makes me to seek thy happiness,
    as much as ever lies in me.

PSALM CXXIII.

To thee, O Lord, to thee alone,
  do I lift up mine eyes:
O thou the high and lofty one,
  that dwell'st above the skies.

Psalm cxxlij.

2 Behold, as servants look unto
  their lord and masters hand;
And as the eyes of maidens do
  their mistrisses attend:

So do our eyes attend and wait
  upon the Lord our God,
Till he do us commiserate,
  that here are undertrod.

3 Have mercy on us, O most high,
  have mercy on our woes:
For we are fill'd exceedingly
  with foul contempt of foes.

4 Our soul is fill'd exceeding much
  with scornings and contempt,
Of those that are at ease, and such
  as are most insolent.

II. Metre.

Give laud, &c.

To thee, O Lord, I rear
  a meek and humble eye:
O thou that dwellest there,
  above the starry skie.
2 Behold I stand,
  As servants do, attending to
  their masters hand.

And as a maidens eyes
  attend her mistris hands:
On our Lord God likewise
  our eye fast fixed stands,
    And in this case,
  We wait until it be his will,
  to shew us grace.

3 O Lord, now pitty us,
  extreamly fill'd with shame:

Just as a bird deludes the fowlers game
  And scapes away, right so it fares with us;
  The snare is broke, and we are scaped thus;
Our help is in the Lord our Saviour's Name,
Whose pow'rful word did earth and heav'n frame.

PSALM CXXV.

All they that trust in God shall prove,
  as firm as Sion hill::
Which never can be made to move,
  but standeth stedfast still.
2 As hills surround Jerusalem,
  so God is altogether,
About his people, guarding them,
  from this time forth for ever.
3 No sinners rod shall have command
  on just mens lot to lie,
Lest righteous men put forth their hand
  unto iniquity.
4 Do good, O Lord, do good to them
  that are good by thy grace:
And to the upright hearted men
  shew forth thy shining face.
5 But those whom wilful lust allures
  to sin and not to cease,
God shall lead forth with evil doers,
  but Israel shall have peace.

II. *Metre. To the Proper Tune.*

Whoever in the Lord confide,
  like Sion Hill shall firmly stand,
  And be removed at no hand;
For evermore it doth abide.
    So are believers sure
    For ever to endure.

And as the mountains huge and high
  are round about Jerusalem,
  So doth the Lord encompass them,
That are his flock and family:
    He will (as heretofore)
    Protect them evermore.

God shall restrain the sinner's rod
  from resting on the just mens lot;
  Lest work, which he approveth not,
Should draw the righteous from their God.
    Lord shew thy goodness then,
    To good and upright men.

But such as turn maliciously,
  to crooked wayes of their own hearts,
  The Lord shall give them their deserts,
With workers of iniquity:
    But peace on Israel,
    for evermore shall dwell.

PSALM CXXVI.

When as the Lord brought back again,
    the bondage most extream:
Wherein poor Sion did remain,
  we were like those that dream.
2 Our mouth was fill'd with laughter then,
  and singing fill'd our tongue:
Among amazed heathen men
  these speeches past along.
3 Great things for them and marvellous
  the Lord hath done indeed:
  Yea, God hath done great things for us,
  which makes our joy exceed.
4 Now, Lord, our thraldom turn again,
  as streams in southern parts:
5 For they that sow in tears, obtain
  to reap with joyful hearts.

5 Happy is he and free from shame,
  Whose quiver's furnisht with the same,
    in court and camp to foil his foes.

PSALM CXXVIII.

Blessed are all that fear the Lord,
  and walk as God commands:
2 For thou shalt eat the plenty stor'd
  by labours of thy hands.
All welfare shall to thee betide,
  and happy be thy life.
3 Like fruitful vine on thy house-side,
  lo, such shall be thy wife;
Thy children round about thy board,
  like plants of olive tree.
4 Behold the man that fears the Lord,
  thus blessed shall he be.
5 From Sion God shall prosper thee,
  and bless thee every way;
And thou Jerusalem's good shalt see
  unto thy dying day.
6 Yea, with great joy thou shalt behold
  a plentiful increase
Of childrens children (being old)
  and Israels stablisht peace.

PSALM CXXIX.

Many a time and oft have they
  distrest me from my youth,
Now Israel may speak and say,
  and speak it of a truth.
2 Oft from my tender infancy
  afflicted me have they:
Yet have they not prevail'd thereby
  against me any way.

3 The plowers on my back did plow,
  and made their furrows long.
4 The righteous Lord hath cut in two
  the wickeds cords so strong.
5 All Sions hateful enemies stop,
  confound, and overthrow:
6 Make them like grass on houses top,
  which withereth e're it grow.
7 Whereof the mower ne're receives
  so much as hands can gripe:
 Nor he that bindeth up the sheaves,
  a bosomful grown ripe.
8 Which never invites the passengers,
  at gathering of the same,
 To say thus much, God speed you sirs,
  we bless you in his name.

II. *Metre.* *Ye Children*, &c.

Many a time and oft have they
Afflicted me may Israel say,
  from my youth up unto this day.
Oft from my youth they did assail
And set me hard, yet did they fail,
  and could not possibly prevail;
The tyrants plow'd me like the ground,
My back with furrows they did wound,
  such bloody cruelty I found.
But the just Lord and most upright,
Hath cut their cords asunder quite,
  theirs that in wickedness delight.
And let them be confounded still,
And turned back that bear ill will
  and hatred unto Sion hill.
Like to the grass let them be made,
That on the houses top doth fade,
  and withers even in the blade:

Whereof

Whereof the mower ne're receives
A handful, nor a lapful leaves
   for him that bindeth up the sheaves.
Neither do they which there go by
Say, sirs, God speed you heartily,
   we bless you from the Lord most high.

PSALM CXXX.

Out of the depths I cri'd to thee,
2 Lord, hear my voice, said I:
And let thine ears attentive be
   to my request and cry.
3 If thou should'st mark iniquities,
   then who should stand, O Lord?
5 But there's forgiveness in thine eyes,
   that thou maist be ador'd.

5 I earnestly expect the Lord,
   my very soul attends,
In expectation of his word,
   whereon my hope depends.
6 My soul waits for the Lord, I say,
   more then the watch by night:
Yea, more then they that wait for day,
   and for the dawning light.

7 Let Israel hope in God alone,
   for with the Lord there is
Most plentiful redemption,
   and mercy for all his.
8 And this most gracious Lord shall please
   his Israel to redeem
From all their sins and trespasses,
   how great soe're they seem.

II.

Psalm cxxx.

II. *Metre.* Give Laud, &c.

Out of the depths of wo
  I cri'd to thee, O Lord,
Lord bow thine ear so low
  and let my voice be heard.
    O bow thine ear
Attentively unto my cry
      my prayer to hear.

If thou severe shouldst be,
  then Lord, who should be clear'd,
But mercy is with thee
  that so thou maist be fear'd.
    I wait, I tend
Upon the Lord, and on his word
      my hopes depend.

My soul waits for the Lord,
  more earnestly than those
That wait with great regard,
  till day the light disclose.
    Yea, more I say,
Desires dispatch than they that watch
      for break of day.

Let Israel hope in God
  for with the Lord is found
Mercy to spare the rod,
  redemption to abound.
    By him likewise
All Israel is redeem'd from his
      iniquities.

III. *Metre.*

The mighty God, &c.

Out of the horrors of the dreadful deep
Where fears and sorrows never cease nor sleep.

To

To thee, O Lord, I sent my woful cries,
Lord hear the accents of my miseries.
O bow thine ear with kind commiseration,
And please to hear mine earnest supplication.

O Lord, if thine inquiry should be strict,
To mark our sins, and judgments to inflict;
  who may abide it, or, when tri'd they are,
  Stand uncondemned at thy judgment bar :
But there is mercy with thee richly stored,
That thou with filial fear maist be adored.

My soul waits for the Lord, in him I trust,
Whose word is faithful, and whose promise just :
  On him I wait more earnestly than they
  That wait the comforts of the rising day.
Yea, more than those that have the day desired,
With tedious watchings of the night time tired.

Let Israel in the Lord alone repose,
For with the Lord abundant mercy flowes,
  And with the Lord (however sins abound)
  Is plentiful redemption to be found :
And by his grace shall Israel be acquitted,
From all his Sins whatever he committed.

PSALM CXXXI.

O Lord, I have no scornful eye,
  no proud or haughty mind :
I seek not things that are too high,
  but humbly am inclin'd.
2 My soul is like an infant wean'd
  even from his mothers brest.
3 And Israel so to be sustein'd,
  on God should alwayes rest.

II. *Metre.*

Give laud, &c.

No haughty heart have I,
  nor lofty scornful eyes;
Nor wade presumptuously
  into deep mysteries:
    I do not deal
In things that be too high for me,
  Lord, thou know'st well.

2 Surely I have contain'd,
  and shew'd my self as mild
As is the child that's wean'd,
  as is the weaned child.
    3 Israel therefore
Hope thou in heaven, henceforth and even
  for evermore.

PSALM CXXXII.

King David, Lord, remember now,
  and all his cares record;
2 How he did swear to God, and vow
  to Jacob's mighty Lord.
3 Surely, said he, I will not come,
  nor ever put my head
Into my house and lodging-room,
  to go up to my bed:
4 I will not give one wink of sleep
  unto my weary eyes:
Nor suffer slumber once to creep
  mine eye-lids to surprize;
  Until I do find out a place,
  a place wherein may dwell.
The mighty God of Jacob's race,
  the Lord of Israel.

6 The first news of his blest abode,
  lo, Ephratah did yield :
After, we found the ark of God
  plac't in the wood-land field.
7 Now therefore will we all go in,
  unto his dwelling-place :
And humbly we will worship him
  at foot-stool of his grace.
8 Arise, O Lord, and come at length
  into thy place of rest,
Thou and the ark of thy great strength,
  thy temple to invest.
9 O let thy priests be all arrai'd
  with righteousness throughout :
And let thy gracious saints be made
  for very joy to shout.
10 For David's sake thy servant known,
  O do not turn away
The face of thine anointed one,
  that unto thee doth pray.

The second part.

11 The Lord in truth to David sware,
  and will not turn from it:
Out of thy loins shall come thine heir,
  upon thy throne to sit.
12 If thy seed keep my covenant,
  and laws that I make known :
Thy children then shall never want
  heirs to enjoy the throne.
13 For God hath chosen Sion hill,
  desiring there to dwell.
14 This is my rest and dwelling still,
  for I have lik't it well.
15 Her meat I'le bless abundantly,
  wherewith she shall be fed :

Psalm cxxxiij.

And I will also satisfie
  her poor with store of bread.
16 And I will also clothe her priests
  with saving health and grace :
And with the voice of joyfulness
  her saints shall shout apace.
17 There will I make his horn to bud,
  even David's horn to spring :
I have ordain'd a lamp so good,
  for my anointed king.
18 His adversaries all of them
  then will I clothe with shame :
But on himself his diadem
  shall flourish with great fame.

PSALM CXXXIII.

Behold how much it doth excell,
  and what great joy to see,
When brethren do together dwell,
  in perfect unity.
2 It's like the precious ointment which
  was pour'd on Aaron's crown :
That to his beard and garments rich,
  even to the skirts, ran down.
3 Like pearly dew of Hermon hill,
  or Sion's silver showers :
Where God commands the blessing still,
  and life upon them poures.

II. Metre.

All People, &c.

Behold how good and full of bliss,
  And what a pleasant thing it is,
When brethren do most lovingly
  together dwell in amity.

2 It's like the precious ointment shed
  upon the top of Aaron's head:
Which drencht his beard, and from his crown
  even to his garments skirts ran down.
3 Like pearly dew of Hermon hills,
  or which on Sion mount distills:
Where God pours down his blessings store,
  blessings of life for evermore.

PSALM CXXXIV.

Have mercy, &c.

Behold ye here at hand,
  ye servants of the Lord,
Which in his house by night do stand,
  praise him with one accord.
2 Lift up your hands on high
  within his holy place:
And kneeling in humility,
  bless God, the God of grace.
3 The Lord (do ye say still)
  that made both heaven and earth,
Bless Israel out of Sion hill
  with favours thence pour'd forth.

II. *Metre.*

All people, &c..

Behold ye servants of the Lord,
  which in his house by night do stand,
Bless ye his name, his praise record,
  devoutly lifting up your hand.
2 I'th sanctuary bless his name;
  Then let the Levites thus reply,
The Lord that heaven and earth did frame,
  from Sion bless thee plenteously.

III. *Metre.*

A Praxis for the Tune of the 112 *Psal.* 2. *M. the same that was for* Our father, *&c.*

Behold ye servants of the Lord,
   which in his house stand night and day,
With rais'd-up hands his praise record,
   and in his sanctuary, say,
The Lord that made both earth and sky,
   From heaven bless thee bounteously.

PSALM CXXXV.

PRaise ye the Lord, praise ye the name
   of God with one accord:
O praise him, and extoll his fame,
   ye servants of the Lord.
2 O ye that are admitted thus
   within his house to stand,
And in the courts of our God's house
   are plac't by his command.
3 Praise ye the Lord, for he is good,
   sing praises to his name:
For it is sweet to be imploy'd
   his praises to proclame.
4 For God hath chosen to himself
   Jacob, of his own pleasure:
And hath elected Israel
   for his peculiar treasure.
5 For well I know the Lord is great,
   and that this Lord of ours
Transcends all gods, and hath his seat
   above all soveraign powers.
6 Whatever thing the Lord did please,
   he did effect and do,

 In heaven, in earth, and in the seas,
  and all deep places too.

7 He causeth vapours to arise
 from earths remotest ends:
 Lightnings, and rain, and winds likewise,
  he from his treasury sends.
8 Who smote the very first increast,
 throughout all Egypt land:
 All the first-born of man and beast,
  with his revenging hand.
9 Who sent his signs and wonders great
 into the midst of thee,
 O Egypt, upon Pharaoh's seat,
  and all his family.
10 Who did the mighty nations smite,
 and potent kings he slew:
11 As Sihon that strong Amorite,
 whom there he overthrew.
And next unto the Amorites,
 was Og of Bashan king.
And all realms of the Canaanites
 he did to ruine bring,
12 And the inheritance of their land,
 he gave it full and free,
Into his people Israel's hand,
 their heritage to be.
13 Thy name for ever doth endure,
 and thy memorial, Lord,
All generations shall be sure
 to keep on firm record.
14 For lo, the Lord is fully bent
 his peoples judge to be:
And of his servants punishment
 repent himself will he.

Psalm cxxxv.

The Second Part.

15 The idols of the heathen lands,
 are silver and of gold:
 They are the work of workmens hands,
 and such as men did mould.
16 They have a mouth, yet speak they not,
 and eyes, but want their sight:
17 Have ears, but never hear a jot,
 their mouths are breathless quite.
18 Such senseless stocks their makers are,
 that did these idols frame:
 And such is each idolater,
 that trusteth in the same.
19 But bless the Lord with one accord,
 O house of Israel:
 And all the praises of the Lord,
 let Aaron's house forth tell.
20 O bless the Lord, his praise confess,
 O ye of Levi's tribe:
 And ye that fear the Lord no less,
 due praise to him ascribe.
21 From out of Sion hill let them
 for ever bless the Lord,
 Who dwelleth at Jerusalem:
 his praise do ye record.

II. *Metre.*

Give laud, &c.

Give laud unto the Lord,
 and praise his holy Name,
His praises still record
 and spread abroad his fame,
 Ye that resort
To our great God and have abode
 In Sion's court.

His honour O proclame,
  for good and kind he is,
Sing praises to his Name,
  a pleasant work it is.
    Jacob hath he
Chose to himself and all his wealth
  must Israel be.

And this I clearly know,
  the Lord's a mighty one,
And that all Gods do owe
  subjection to his throne:
    For he brings forth
Whatever he please in deeps in seas,
  in heaven and earth.

He makes the vapours rise
  from earth's remotest ends,
And lightnings from the skies,
  with showers of rain he sends.
    The wind likewise,
Whatever it is he brings from his
  large treasuries.

The Second part.

Let God's high praise arise,
  that Egypts first-born smote,
Of man and beast likewise,
  who sent such signs of note:
    In mid'st of thee,
O Egypts, and on Pharaoh's land
  and family.

Who did great Nations smite,
  and mighty kings he slew;
King Sihon th' Amorite,
  and OG of Bashan too:
    and many a man
And kingdoms all both great and small

Pſalm cxxxv.

And gave away their land
  to be an heritage,
To's people Iſrael's hand
  He did the ſame engage;
    Thy Name, O Lord,
is ſtill the ſame, and thy known fame
  all times record.

For God is fully bent
  his peoples judge to be,
And of their puniſhment
  repent himſelf will he:
    And he will make
A quick redreſs by righteouſneſs
  for's ſervants ſake.

The Third part.

The Idols which they have
  in all the heathen lands,
Are gold and ſilver brave,
  the work of workmens hands:
    Blind dumb and deaf,
They move no jot, their mouths have not
  a puff of breath.

The vain Artificers
  are like thoſe Idols (juſt.)
Such are the worſhippers,
  and all that in them truſt:
    But bleſs the Lord,
O Iſrael's houſe, and each of us
  his praiſe record.

And Aaron's houſe muſt bleſs
  and magnifie his Name.
And Levi's tribe, no leſs
  muſt celebrate his fame.
    Yea, every one
That fears the Lord muſt ſtill record
  his praiſe alone.

Let every one of them
　　bless God from Sion hill,
Who at Jerusalem
　　hath habitation still:
　　　For there the Lord
Of Israel doth ever dwell
　　his praise record.

PSALM CXXXVI.

Have mercy, &c.

O Render thanks to God,
　　for he is very good:
His mercies sure do still endure,
　　and have for ever stood.
2 The God of gods proclaim,
　　with praises to his name:
His mercies sure do still endure,
　　eternally the same.
3 The Lord of lords most high
　　with praises magnify:
His mercies sure do still endure,
　　to all eternity.
4 To him who wrought alone
　　great wonders many a one:
His mercies sure do still indure
　　to ages all made known.
5 To him that prudently
　　compos'd the heavens high:
His mercies sure do still endure,
　　to perpetuity.
6 That did the earth extend,
　　the seas to comprehend:
His mercies sure do still endure,
　　and never have an end.
7 To him whose power divine
　　did make great lights to shine:

Pſalm. cxxxvj.

His mercies ſure do ſtill endure,
  not ſubject to decline.
8 The ſun to rule and ſway
  the motions of the day:
His mercies ſure do ſtill endure,
  and never fall away.

9 The moon and ſtars of light
  he made to rule by night:
His mercies ſure do ſtill endure:
  for they are infinite.

The Second part.

10 To him your thanks devote,
  who Egypts firſt-born ſmote,
His mercies ſure do ſtill endure,
  of everlaſting note.
11 Who from among them all
  brought Iſrael out of thrall:
His mercies ſure do ſtill endure,
  and are perpetual.
12 With ſtrong out-ſtretched hand,
  and arm of his command:
His mercies ſure do ſtill endure,
  and ſhall for ever ſtand.
13 To him that did divide
  the red ſea on each ſide:
His mercies ſure do ſtill endure,
  and evermore abide.
14 And Iſrael did tranſmit,
  thorough the midſt of it:
His mercies ſure do ſtill endure,
  and never fail a whit.
15 But on the red ſea-coaſt
  ſmote Pharaoh and his hoſt:
His mercies ſure do ſtill endure,
  unto the uttermoſt.

16 To him that led his own
   through deserts all unknown :
   His mercies sure do still endure
   as permanent alone. —

The Third part.

17 To him that smote and slew
18 Great kings, and famous too :
   His mercies sure do still endure,
   and ever so shall do.
19 King Sihon he did smite,
   that giant Amorite :
   His mercies sure do still endure,
   continuing day and night.
20 And Og great Bashan's king,
   he did to ruine bring :
   His mercies sure do still endure,
   an unexhausted spring.
21 And did their land ingage,
   to be an heritage :
   His mercies sure do still endure,
   out-wearing time and age.
22 That heritage befell
   his servant Israel :
   His mercies sure do still endure,
   times constant parallel.
23 Who thought on our estate,
   when low and desolate :
   His mercies sure do still endure,
   and bear eternal date.
24 Redeeming us from those
   that were our mortal foes :
   His mercies sure do still endure,
   a spring that overflows.
25 Who still provideth meat,
   whereof all flesh may eat :

Psalm cxxxvj.

 His mercies sure do still endure,
  for ever full and great.
26 The God of heaven therefore,
  with thankful thoughts adore:
 His mercies sure do still endure
  henceforth for evermore.

  II. *Metre.* *To the proper Tune.*

   Give laud, &c.

Give laud unto the Lord
 for very good he is,
The God of gods record
 and praise that Name of his,
  for certainly
His mercies shall endure to all
  Eternity.

Give thanks, O every one
 unto the King of Kings,
For he and he alone
 hath wrought such wondrous things:
  and certainly
His mercies shall, &c.

To him whose skill profound
 did make the heavens clear:
And set the seas their bound,
 and made dry land appear,
  for certainly
His mercies shall, &c.

To him that did display
 those great and glorious lights:
The sun to rule by day,
 the moon and stars by nights,
  for certainly
His mercies shall endure to all
  eternity.

The Second part.

Give thanks to God moſt high
   who ſmote with powerful hand,
In Egypt generally,
   the firſt-born of the land:
     for certainly
His mercies ſhall endure to all
   eternity.

And from them in that land
   brought Iſrael cleerly out,
With ſtretcht-out arm and hand
   that brought the work about:
     for certainly
His mercies ſhall, &c.

To him that did divide
   the red ſea into parts:
And there did Iſrael guide
   to paſs with joyful hearts:
     for certainly
His mercies ſhall, &c.

Amidſt it they did go,
   but Pharaoh and his hoaſt
The Lord did overthrow
   upon the red-ſea coaſt:
     For certainly
His mercies ſhall, &c.

The Third part.

Give God his praiſes due,
   and thankful thoughts expreſs,
Who led his people through
   the howling wilderneſs:
     for certainly
His mercies ſhall endure to all
   eternity.

Great kings the Lord did smite,
  and famous kings he slew,
King Sihon th' Amorite,
  and Og of Bashan too :
    for certainly
His mercies shall, &c.

And gave (in open view)
  the land where they did dwell
An heritage unto
  his people Israel:
    for certainly
His mercies shall, &c.

Who did remember us
  when our estate was low,
And hath redeemed us
  from the oppressing foe;
    for certainly
His mercies shall, &c.

To him give praises due,
  who gives all flesh their food,
O give ye thanks unto
  the God of heaven so good :
    for certainly
His mercies shall, &c.

PSALM. CXXXVII.

WHen as we sat in Babylon,
  and by the rivers side,
Remembring Sions sad estate,
  tears from our eyes did slide;
2 As for our harps and instruments,
  of musick us'd before ;
We hung them on the willow-trees,
  that grew upon the shore.
3 Where they to whom we prisoners were,
  did ask us eagerly,

Come, let us hear your Hebrew songs,
  and pleasant melody.
4 Alas! said we, who can dispose
  his sorrowful heart to sing
The praises of a loving God,
  under a forrain king?

5. No no, if ever I forget
  the thoughts of Sion hill,
Let my right hand forget her harp,
  and forfeit all her skill.
6 Yea, let my tongue cleave to my jaws,
  if that Jerusalem
Be not preferr'd in all my joyes
  above the chief of them.

7 Remember Edom's children, Lord,
  that in Jerusalem's day
Said, raze it, raze it to the ground,
  even to the ground, said they.
8 And thou, O daughter Babylon,
  thy ruine is design'd:
And happy shall that man be call'd,
  that serves thee in thy kind.

9 Yea, blessed shall that man be call'd,
  that takes thy little ones,
And dashes them with violence
  against the pavement stones.

II. *Metre.*

Hard by the brooks of Babylon,
  we sat down weeping there:
When Sion hill we thought upon,
  each thought inforc'd a tear.
2 Amidst it there green willows were,
  whereon our harps we hung:
For they that led us captives there,
  requir'd of us a song,

3 And they that wasted us that day,
   did ask and urge us thus,
  Sing one of Sion's songs, said they,
   and make some mirth for us.
4 How shall we ever tune our tongue
   to sing, at your command,
  The Lord Jehovah's sacred song,
   here in a forraign land?
5 If I forget thee in my heart,
   O Salem's sacred hill,
  Let my right hand forget her art,
   and forfeit all her skill.
6 Yea, let my tongue cleave to my jaws,
   if thou shalt be forgot:
  Yea, and above my chiefest joyes
   if I prefer thee not.
7 Lord, think on Edom's sons, we pray,
   whom we so spiteful found:
  That said in sad Jerusalem's day,
   rase, rase it to the ground.
8 Daughter of Babel, thou must be
   destroy'd and ruin'd thus:
  Happy is he that doth to thee
   as thou hast done to us.
9 He shall be blessed for his pains,
   that takes thy little ones,
  And dasheth out their infant brains
   against the pavement stones.

PSALM CXXXVIII.

I Will extol thee willingly
   with my whole heart in me,
 In presence of the Gods will I
   sing praises unto thee.
 I will adore thee bowing down
   towards thy holy place:

And give thy blessed Name renown
  for thy sweet love and grace.
And for thy faithfulness, O Lord,
  I will extol thy fame:
For thou hast magnify'd thy word
  Yea more than all thy Name.
The day whereon I cry'd to thee,
  thou didst, O Lord, reply:
And thou didst also strengthen me
  with comforts inwardly.
All kings on earth shall give thee praise
  when they shall hear and know
What promises thy word displayes
  where-e're the tydings go.
Yea, they shall sing triumphantly
  in God's most holy wayes,
Because our God's great Majesty
  deserves so great a praise.
Though God be high he likes the low
  the lofty he disdains:
And though I walk in midst of wo
  my quickning hope remains.
Thou shalt, O Lord, stretch out thy hand
  which shall for me engage:
And thy right hand for me shall stand
  against mine enemies rage.
What me concerns will God fulfil,
  so firm thy mercy stands,
Forsake not, Lord, but succour still
  the work of thine own hands.

II. *Metre.*

All people, *or,* O Lord, consider, *&c.*

With my whole heart I praise thee now,
  before the gods thy praise I sing,

Pſalm cxxxix.

2 Towards thy holy houſe I bow
  to praiſe thy name, O heavenly king.
 Even for thy loving kindneſs, Lord,
  and for thy truth ſo often tri'd:
 For thou haſt magnifi'd thy word,
  yea, more then all thy name beſide.

3 Thou anſweredſt me that very day
  wherein I did ſo call and cry:
 Thou ſtrengthened'ſt me and waſt my ſtay,
  my ſoul thou ſtrengthened'ſt inwardly.

4 All kings on earth ſhall give thee praiſe,
  when from thy mouth they hear thy words:

5 Yea, ſinging walk along thy wayes:
  ſuch fame, ſuch great fame is our Lords.

6 Though God be high above all things,
  the lowly he regardeth much:
 But on the proud contempt he brings,
  and afar off he knoweth ſuch.

7 Although I walk in dangers path,
  thou ſhalt revive me, and extend
 Thy hand againſt my enemies wrath,
  and thy right hand ſhall me defend.

8 The Lord will perfect my affairs,
  ſo firm and ſure thy mercy ſtands:
 Neglect not thou thy wonted cares,
  to keep the works of thine own hands.

PSALM CXXXIX.

O Lord, thou haſt me ſearch'd and known:
 2 Thou ſeeſt me ſit and riſe,
 My fartheſt thoughts thou know'ſt, each one
  whatever I deviſe.

3 Thou compaſſeſt my path, my bed,
  and all my wayes doſt note.

4 There's not a word my tongue hath ſaid,
  but thou doſt fully know't.

5 Behind, before, thou hast beset,
   and on me laid thy hand.
6 Such knowledge is too great to get,
   too high to understand.
7 Whither, O whither shall I go,
   and from thy spirit flie?
  Where shall I hide me high or low,
   from thy all-seeing eye?

8 If I should climb to heaven on high,
   or make my bed in hell;
  Thou art in heaven assuredly,
   thou art beneath as well.
9 If on the morning wings I fled,
   the utmost seas beyond:
10 There, by thy hand I should be led,
   and held by thy right hand.

11 And if I say, the darkness sure
   shall hide me from thy sight:
  The darkness which is most obscure,
   about me shall be light.
12 Yea, darkness hides not from thy sight:
   but night as day shines clear:
  To thee the darkness and the light
   do both alike appear.

13 For, Lord, my reins most secret room
   possessed is by thee;
  And in my mothers narrow womb,
   Lord, thou hast covered me.
14 I'le praise thee that hast made me thus,
   of rare and fearful frame:
  Thy handy-works are marvellous,
   my soul well knows the same.

15 My substance was not hid from thee,
   when secretly compos'd:
  And curiously thou formed'st me,
   in earth's dark caves inclos'd.

Psalm cxxxix.

6 Thine eye did see my substance rude,
  thy book nam'd every limb,
Which by degrees were fashioned,
  when yet was none of them.

7 How precious also unto me
  are thy sweet thoughts become!
O God, how very great they be,
  in gross and total summe!

8 If I should count them, they are more
  in number then the sand:
And I when I awake therefore,
  am still at thy right hand.

9 Surely thou wilt the wicked slay,
  O God, spare none of them:
Therefore from me depart, I say,
  O all ye bloody men.

o For lo, they utter all their spite,
  O Lord, in thy disdain:
Thine adversaries set thee light,
  and take thy name in vain.

1 Do not I hate thine enemies;
  and that for hating thee?
And those that do against thee rise,
  am not I griev'd to see?

2 Yea, Lord, I hate them perfectly,
  I count them my own foes.
3 Search me, O God, my conscience try,
  my heart and reins disclose.

4 And see if I do go astray
  in any course of sin:
Shew me the everlasting way,
  and lead me, Lord, therein.

Psalm cxxxix.

II. Metre.

All People, &c.

Lord thou hast search't and known me well
  Thou seest me sit, thou seest me rise:
My thoughts a far off thou canst tell,
  my path, my bed, and all my guise.
There's not a whisper in my tongue
  but thou dost fully understand:
Thou hast beset me all along,
  and lay'd on me thy mighty hand.

Such knowledge is too great, too high
  for me to apprehend and know:
For whither, whither can I fly
  thine omnipresence to outgo.
Climb I to heaven above my head,
  Thou dwell'st in that celestial sphere;
Or if in hell I make my bed,
  'tis all alike, for thou art there.

If on the mornings wings I ride
  beyond the seas that are so vast,
Even there thy hand shall be my guide,
  and thy right hand shall hold me fast.
If sure, I say, the dusky night
  shall cover me from thy survey,
The night about me shall be light
  as cleer as sunshine in the day.

Yea, darkness hideth not from thee,
  but night as day with glittering flame,
Are both of them alike to thee,
  darkness and light to thee the same.

The Second part.

O Lord, thou hast possest my reins,
  and clos'd me in my mothers womb:

I'le praise thee, Lord, by whose good means
   I did my native shape assume.
Thy workmanship that made me thus
   for dread and wonder doth excell:
Thy handy works are marvailous,
   and that my soul doth know right well.

My substance was not hid from thee
   when made i'th' womb before my birth:
Most curiously thou formed'st me,
   'as 'twere in caverns of the earth.

Thine eyes saw my rude substance there,
   thy book had all my members nam'd,
Which in continuance fashion'd were
   e're there was any of them fram'd.

The Third part.

How precious are thy thoughts likewise
   to me, O God! How great a summe!
If I should count to what they rise,
   the sands to no such number come.

When I awake I'm still with thee,
   and sure thou wilt the wicked slay,
Wherefore, I say, depart from me,
   ye bloody men, get far away.

For lo, they speak against thee still,
   and their discourse is all prophane,
Thine enemies in proud self-will
   do take thy sacred name in vain.

The Fourth part.

Do not I hate them, O most high,
   them that bear hatred unto thee!
Am not I griev'd exceedingly
   their bold impieties to see?

Those namely, those ungodly men
   that rise against thee, and oppose,
With perfect hatred hate I them,
   I take them for my greatest foes.

Search me, O God, and know my heart,
   Try me, and know my thoughts, I pray,
See if I ought from thee depart,
   and shew me th' everlasting way.

PSALM CXL.

FRom workers of iniquity,
   O Lord, be my defence:
Preserve thou me, and set me free
   from men of violence.
2 Whose hearts imagine villany,
   and gathered they are,
And do comply continually
   in purposes of war.
3 They whet their tongues as darts of death
   like to the serpent sly:
The poisonous breath of adders deaf
   under their lips doth ly.
4 Keep me, O Lord, from wicked hands,
   and from my furious foe:
Those fire-brands whose purpose stands
   my steps to overthrow.
5 A snare for me the proud did hide,
   and they have spread a net:
And cords they ti'd by th' high-way side,
   and grins for me they set.
6 Therefore unto the Lord, said I,
   thou art my God alone.
O Lord most high, attend my cry
   and supplication.
7 O God the Lord, thou dost bestead
   my soul with saving might:

And

And thou my head hast covered
  in day of bloody fight.
8 Grant not, O Lord, grant not a jot
  the wicked man's desire:
 O further not his wicked plot,
  lest that should lift them higher.
9 As for the head of all their throng,
  that compass me about,
 Let mischief sprung from their own tongue
  quite cover them throughout.
10 Let burning coals upon them fall,
  and cast them in the fire:
 And let them all in deep pits fall,
  whence they may not retire.
11 Let there be no establishment
  for leud tongues, here below,
 Evil shall hunt the violent
  unto his overthrow.
12 I know God will maintain, by might,
  the cause of the distrest:
 And will not slight the poor man's right,
  but help him, when opprest.
13 Surely the righteous every where
  thanks to thy name shall give:
 And all that bear a mind sincere,
  shall in thy presence live.

II. *Metre.*

Lord save me from the violent,
  and from the evil doer;
Whose hearts are bent with ill intent,
  my ruine to procure.
Continually for wars they throng,
  with adders sting they strike,
With sharp'ned tongue and poison strong,
  the subtle serpent-like.

Lord save me from my wicked foe
    and from the furious man,
Who would my goings overthrow,
    and aim it all they can.
Proud men have sought my soul to get,
    their cords and snares they ti'd,
They spread a net, their grins they set
    hard by the high-way-side.

But then unto the Lord, said I,
    Thou art my God most dear:
The voice of my request and cry,
    O Lord vouchsafe to hear.
O God the Lord (my saving might)
    Thou covered'st my head
In day of fight to stand upright,
    and save my blood unshed.

The Second part.

Lord grant not wicked mens desire,
    O speed not men in fault;
For wickedness that they conspire,
    lest they themselves exalt.
As for the head of all those men
    that compass me about,
Let the dire curses cover them,
    which their own lips gave out.

Let burning coals fall on their head,
    and cast them in the flame:
To be as people buried,
    no mischief more to frame.
Let th' earth afford no settlement
    for any wicked tongue:
Evil shall hunt the violent
    to ruine him e're long.

For sure I know God will maintain
    the cause of men opprest:

The poor man's right he will sustain,
  and have their wrongs redress'd.
And sure the just with great delight
  shall give thy Name the praise,
And in thy sight shall men upright
  live safely all their dayes.

PSALM CXLI.

To thee, O Lord, I call and cry,
  make hast and come to me:
And bow thine ear attentively,
  now when I cry to thee.
2 O let my prayer be now set out
  as incense in thine eyes:
And lifting up of hands devout,
  as evening sacrifice.
3 And set a careful watch before
  my hasty mouth, O Lord:
And of my lips keep thou the dore,
  against each evil word.
4 Incline my heart to no misdeed,
  with them that wicked are:
Nor let me ever dare to feed
  of their delicious fare.
5 But let the righteous smite me, Lord,
  for that is good for me:
And his reproof and sharpest word,
  a soveraign balm shall be.
Such smiting shall not break my head,
  for their reprocfs I prize,
And still my pray'rs are offered,
  in their calamities.
6 Their judges being overthrown,
  as on the stony street;
Then shall they hear my words each one,
  for they are very sweet.

7 But now about the graves they leave
   our bones, all scattered round;
  As wood which one doth cut and cleave,
   lies scattered on the ground.

8 But, Lord, mine eyes are unto thee,
   my trust is in thy grace:
  O God the Lord, then leave not me
   in so forlorn a case.

9 O keep me safely from the snare,
   they laid to take me in:
  And from the grins of those that are
   such practisers of sin.

10 And in their own devised net,
   Lord, let the wicked fall:
  Even in the net which they did set,
   whil'st I escape them all.

II. *Metre.*

All people, &c.

To thee I cry, O Lord make haste,
And hear me e're the time be past:
  As incense my devotions prize,
  Or as the evening sacrifice.

A watch before my mouth prefix,
And keep the dores of both my lips:
  My heart to no bad thing incline
  In wicked courses to combine.

Nor of their dainties let me eat,
That are allur'd by sins deceit,
  But let the righteous smite me, Lord,
  A kindness which I shall record.

For his reproof so meek and calm
Breaks not my head, but proves a balm:
  And I shall with like amity
  Pray for them in calamity.

When as their wicked leaders shall
Upon the rocks of vengeance fall;
 The rest (as warn'd) my words shall hear,
 And sweet my counsel shall appear.

But now alas our bones are found
As chips all scatter'd on the ground:
 Such inhumanity they have,
 They leave our limbs without a grave.

But though in darkness clos'd I lie
On thee, O God, I fix mine eye:
 In thee I trust, Lord hear my suit,
 Leave not my darling destitute.

O keep me from the cruel net
Which wicked men for me have set:
 Let them be snar'd in their own trap
 Whiles I escape so great mishap.

PSALM CXLII.

I Cri'd unto the holy one,
 with earnest voice and cry:
I made my supplication known
 unto the Lord most high.
2 I pour'd out my complaint and cry
 before his gracious face:
I shew'd before him readily
 my deep distressful case.
3 When, Lord, my spirit sunk in woe,
 my path was known to thee:
And in the way where I did go,
 they laid close snares for me.
4 I look't on my right hand and saw,
 but none would know me there:
Refuge did fail and quite withdraw,
 none for my soul did care.
5 I cri'd to thee, O Lord, and said,
 thou art my refuge then:

Thou art my portion and my aid,
  i'th' land of living men.
6 Attend my cry for I am low,
  and, Lord, deliver me
From them that persecute me so,
  and are too strong for me.

7 My soul from prison, Lord, set free,
  thy name to glorify:
The righteous then shall flock to me,
  when I thy bounty try.

II. *Metre.*

O Lord consider, &c.

With earnest voice and cries devout,
  to God the Lord I made request:
My deep complaint I poured out
  and shew'd the Lord my case distrest.
My spirit overwhelm'd and spent,
  my private path was known to thee,
How in the way wherein I went,
  they lay'd a secret snare for me.

The right hand-way I looked hard,
  but there was no man would me know:
All refuge fail'd, and no man car'd
  whether I scap'd with life or no.
I cri'd to thee, O Lord, and said
  thou art my refuge neer at hand:
Thou art my portion and my aid,
  while I am living in the land.

Attend unto my earnest suit,
  for I am brought exceeding low:
Save me from them that persecute,
  too hard for me, too strong a foe:
My soul from prison, Lord bring out,
  that I may render praise to thee:

The just shall compass me about,
 when thou deal'st bounteously with me.

PSALM CXLIII.

Lord, hear my prayer and humble suit,
 thy willing ear address:
And answer me in equity,
 in truth and faithfulness.
2 And into judgement or dispute,
 thy servant do not call:
For with thee can no mortal man
 be justifi'd at all.
3 My foes to death do persecute,
 my life to ground is trod:
My dwelling made in darksom shade,
 as men long dead, O God.
4 Therefore my burdened spirits shrink,
 my heart is desolate;
5 But wisely weighs the ancient days:
 thy works I meditate.
6 On all thy handy-works, I think,
 to thee I stretch my hands:
My soul in me thirsts after thee,
 as do the thirsty lands.
7 Lord, hear me soon, my spirits sink,
 hide not thy face from me,
Lest I should go to th' pit below,
 and like dead men should be.
8 Cause me to hear of thy kind love
 before the break of day:
Cause me to know what way to go,
 for thou art all my stay.
9 I lift my soul to thee above,
 Lord save me from my foe:
I fly to thee to shelter me,
 none other God I know.

10 Teach me thy holy will to prove,
 O God whom I confess:
  Thy spirit is good, be thou my guide
  to th' land of uprightness.
11 Lord for thy Names sake quicken me,
 and bring my soul from wo,
  So to express thy righteousness,
  and thy free grace to show.
12 And of thine own benignity,
 and for thy goodness sake,
  Cut off all those that are my foes,
  and vengeance on them take.
  Destroy'd and ruin'd let them be
  that do my soul oppress;
  For I serve thee religiously,
  with all submissiveness.

II. *Metre.*

All People, &c. Or, O Lord consider, &c.

1 Vouchsafe, O Lord, my prayer to hear,
And to my humble suits give ear:
 Answer me in thy faithfulness,
 And in thy perfect righteousness.
2 And into judgment do not call
Thy servant, Lord, no, not at all:
 For in thy sight severely tri'd,
 None living shall be justifi'd.
3 For th' enemy hath beset me round,
And trod my life down to the ground;
 Hath made me dwell in darkness deep,
 As those that in their graves do sleep.
4 Therefore my soul is sore opprest
And overwhelmed in my breast:
 My heart in this so sad estate
 Within me is most desolate.

The Second part.

5 I call to mind the dayes of old,
   I weigh thy wonders manifold:
     I muse with most intentive thought
     Upon the works thy hands have wrought.
6 To thee, Lord, I stretch forth my hands,
   My soul doth thirst as thirsty lands,
     It thirsts for thee, O Lord most high,
     7 Vouchsafe to hear me speedily.

My spirit waxeth wondrous faint,
Hide not thy face from my complaint:
     Lest I should be (by thy sad frown)
     Like them that to the grave go down.

The Third part.

8 Cause me of thy kind love to hear.
Before the morning doth appear:
     For in thee do I put my trust,
     Cause me to know thy way most just.
And how to walk, Lord, shew to me,
For I lift up my soul to thee:
     9 O save me from mine enemies,
     My soul to thee for safe-guard flies.
10 O teach me, for thou art my God;
To do thy will: thy spirit is good:
     Lead me, and let me find access
     Unto the land of uprightness.
11 Lord, for thy Names sake, cheer my mind,
Thy quickning comforts let me find:
     And for thy righteousnesses sake,
     My soul out of these troubles take.

12 And of thy mercy slay my foes,
Destroy them, Lord, destroy all those
   That vex my soul maliciously,
   For thy meek servant, Lord, am I.

PSALM CXLIV.

Blessed for ever be the Lord
   who is my strength and might:
Who taught my hands to use the sword,
   my fingers how to fight.
2 My goodness and my fort likewise,
   my shield of saving power,
My Saviour from mine enemies,
   and my exalted tower.

In whom I put my confidence,
   for he, and none but he
Subdueth to obedience,
   my people under me.
3 Lord, what is man that thou should'st take
   such knowledge of him here?
Or son of man that thou should'st make
   account of him so dear?

4 Sure man is like to vanity,
   his dayes decline and fade:
And pass away most hastily,
   like to a flitting shade.
5 Lord, bow the heavens and come down,
   the mountains gently stroke
Look on them with an angry frown,
   and they shall quickly smoke.
6 Cast forth thy lightning from the skies,
   and all thy foes disperse:
And to destroy thine enemies,
   shoot out thine arrows fierce.
7 Send from above thy hand that saves:
   rid me by thy command,

And free me from the mighty waves,
  and from strange childrens hand.
8 Whose mouth doth utter words devis'd,
  and fraught with falshood great:
  And their right hand is exercis'd
  in cunning and deceit.
9 New songs to thee will I present,
  my psaltery shall agree;
  And on a ten-string'd instrument
  will I sing praise to thee.
10 'Tis he that unto kings extends;
  salvations welcome pledge;
  His servant David he defends:
  from swords offensive edge.
11 Release and rid me speedily,
  from hands of sinners vile.
  Whose subtle mouths speak vanity,
  their right hand's full of guile.
12 That so our sons may thrive apace
  as plants in youth do grow;
  Like polisht stones of some fair place
  so may our daughters show.
13 Our garners full as they can hold
  with every kind of thing:
  And in our streets the flock and fold
  may many thousands bring.
14 Let not our labouring oxen faint,
  nor enemy invade:
  No leading captive, no complaint
  within our streets be made.
15 O blessed people, would we say,
  with such like blessings stor'd:
  Yea, rather blessed people they,
  whose God is God the Lord.

II. *Metre.*

The mighty God, &c.

Blessed be God my strength that taught me war,
   my hands and fingers how to fight the field,
My goodness fortress my DELIVERER,
   and my high tower my safety and my shield.
'Tis he in whom I trust for my protection,
Who brings my people under due subjection.

Lord what is man that thou shouldst knowledge take
   of one so far inferior unto thee,
What is the son of man, that thou shouldst make
   so high account of such a one as he?
Man's like to vanity, his dayes designed,
Are like unto a shadow far declined.

Lord bow thy heavens, and come down below,
   O touch the Mountains, Lord, & they shall smoke:
Cast out thy lightnings, and disperse the foe,
   shoot out thine arrows for a deadly stroke:
Thy hand send from above, O great Creator,
And rid and save me from the floods of water.

O save me from the hands of children strange,
   whose mouth speak vanity at every word:
Their hand, their right hand is a meer exchange
   of fraud and falshood, as thou know'st, O Lord.
New songs I'le utter with renown to raise thee,
With instruments of musick I will praise thee.

The Second part.

'Tis God that gives salvation unto Kings,
   his servant David saves he from the sword:
Lord save me from strange peoples quarrellings,
   whose mouth speaks vanity at every word:
And, Lord, their right hand, while their tongue is treating,
Is a right hand of falshood, & of cheating.

Lord

Lord make our sons as plants in youth upgrown,
 Our daughters as the corner stones to show
Of some fair palace, polish't (every one)
 with all the art the Carver can bestow:
Our garners with all sorts of store exceeding,
Our cattel thousands, and ten thousands breeding.

Our oxen strong to labour, and to toil,
 no breaking in, which with confusion meets;
No leading captive, while they take our spoil,
 no bitter lamentation in our streets:
Happy the people in this good condition,
Yea happy people who have God's tuition.

PSALM CXLV.

Thee will I praise, O God my King,
 and ever bless thy Name:
2 And all my days I will give praise,
 and still extol thy fame.
3 Great is the Lord in every thing,
 and greatly to be prais'd:
 His greatness still unsearchable,
 and past our reach is rais'd.
4 One age shall still be publishing
 to that which next succeeds,
 Thy worthy praise in all thy waies,
 and all thy mighty deeds.
5 And Lord I will discourse and treat
 what glory thou hast won,
 The fame of thy great Majestie
 that hast such wonders done.
6 Thy might likewise they shall repeat,
 and deeds of dreadful fame,
 Nor will I spare for to declare
 the greatness of thy Name.
7 The memory of thy goodness great,
 they largely shall express;

And

And shall in songs with joyful tongues,
 declare thy righteousness.

The Second part.

8 The Lord is kind and merciful,
 and shews compassion still :
To anger slow, and alwayes so,
 and bears us great good will.
9 The Lord is very good to all
 as all his creatures find :
For they do all in general,
 taste of his mercies kind.
10 Lord all thy works shall thee extol,
 and thee thy Saints shall bless :
11 They shall proclame thy kingdoms fame,
 and thy great power express.
12 To make the sons of men descry
 his mighty acts and deeds :
His kingdoms shining Majesty,
 and how his fame exceeds.
13 A kingdom of Eternity,
 thy kingdom is, O Lord,
And thy alone Dominion
 all ages shall record.
14 The Lord upholdeth powerfully
 all those that sink and fall :
He lifteth up all those that stoop,
 for he supporteth all.

The Third part.

15 The eyes of all things wait on thee
 and thou dost give them meat,
Thou giv'st it too, in seasons due,
 that all may have to eat.
16 God openeth his hand so free,
 and doth abundance bring

> To satiate the appetite
> of every living them.
> 17 Righteous in all his wayes is he,
> holy in all he doth:
> 18 And nigh to all that on him call
> in uprightness and truth.
> 19 Their hearts desire he will fulfill,
> whoever do him fear,
> He will likewise attend their cries,
> and save them every where.
> 20 Them that love him preserve he will,
> all them, in every place:
> But utterly he will destroy
> all the ungodly race.
> 21 My mouth shall speak God's praises still,
> and let all flesh indeavor,
> Still to proclame his holy Name
> forever and forever.

PSALM CXLVI.

> Praise ye the Lord, my soul give praise
> unto our heavenly King.
> 2 While life and breath prolong my dayes,
> His praises I will sing.
> 3 Trust not in Kings magnificent,
> nor in man's mortal seed,
> Whose power is not sufficient
> to help you in your need.
> 4 Because his breath doth soon depart,
> then turns he to his clay:
> And all the counsels of his heart
> do perish in that day.
> 5 O happy is that man and blest,
> whom Jacob's God doth aid:
> Whose hope upon the Lord doth rest,
> and on his God is staid.

6 Who made the earth, and heav'ns high frame,
  who made the swelling deep,
    And all that is within the same,
      who truth doth ever keep.
7 Who with right judgment still proceeds,
  for those opprest that be;
    The poor and hungry soul he feeds,
      and sets the prisoners free.
8 The Lord doth give the blind their sight,
  the bowed down doth raise:
    In righteous men he takes delight,
      and loveth them alwayes.
9 He helps the widows in distress,
  and strangers sad in heart;
    He doth defend the fatherless,
      and ill mens wayes subvert.
10 The Lord shall raign eternally,
  thy God, O Sion hill
    Shall raign to all posterity,
      O praise him, praise him still.

II. *Metre*.

All people, &c.

The Lord's due praise do ye proclame,
O thou my soul, do thou the same:
All my life long shall my glad tongue
Give praises to his holy Name.

I will unto my God sing praise,
While life and breath prolong my dayes:
Trust not in kings, nor mortal things,
Which cannot help you any wayes.

For quickly passeth forth their breath,
And they return to dust by death:
In that same day their thoughts decay,
And every project perisheth.

O blessed then, and happy one,
Who hath the God of Jacob known:
Whose hope is stay'd and firmly lay'd
Upon the Lord his God alone.

Which made the heaven, the sea, and shore,
The earth and all the numerous store,
Whatever hath bin, or is therein;
And keepeth truth for evermore.

Which worketh judgment righteously,
For men oppress'd with injury;
Food doth he find for th' hunger-pin'd,
And prisoners sets at liberty.

The Second part.

The Lord doth make the blind to see,
He raiseth them bow'd down that be;
The Lord above, just men doth love,
And strangers poor, preserve doth he.

The Lord relieves the Fatherless,
And aids the widows in distress:
But sinners path subverts in wrath,
And doth it utterly suppress.

The Lord shall reign eternally,
Thy God, O Sion rules on high;
Through ages still bear sway he will,
His Name forever magnify.

III. *Metre.*

Give laud, &c.

Praise God: Praise God, my soul,
   Praise to my God I'le give:
My song shall him extol,
   So long as I do live.

       No credit place
In earthly kings, or such vain things
    as humane race.
Breath fails, they fall to dust,
   that day their thoughts all fade:
But blest are they that trust
   in Jacob's God for aid.
      And hope in him
That made all these: Heav'n, earth, and seas,
   and all therein.

That keepeth covenant still,
   The righteous Judge is he,
He doth the hungry fill,
   and sets the prisoners free:
      Gives blind men sight,
Raiseth from ground the bowed down,
   and loves th' upright.
Strangers doth God secure,
   Relieves (in all their woes)
Orphans, and Widows poor;
   But leud mens wayes o'rethrows;
      Thy God, thy Lord,
O Sion, reigns while th' earth remains,
   His praise record.

PSALM CXLVII.

PRaise ye the Lord, for it is meet
   Our God's high praise to sing,
For the employment is most sweet,
   and praise a comely thing.
The Lord builds up Jerusalem,
   bring's Israel's out-casts home:
He healeth broken-hearted men,
   bindes up their wounds each one.

The number of the stars he tells,
   and doth their names recite,

Great

Great is our God, his power excells,
  his wisdom's infinite.
Poor humble souls the Lord doth raise,
  the wicked treads to ground,
Sing to the Lord our God, sing praise
  with harps harmonious sound.

Who with thick clouds o'respreads the sky,
  and rain on earth distills:
He makes the earth to fructify
  with grass on highest hills.
Both beast and bird he kindly feeds,
  young ravens cry to him,
He takes no joy in strength of steeds,
  nor in a strong man's limb.
But lo! the Lord's delight and joy
  is ever in the just:
In them that fear him faithfully,
  and in his mercy trust.

The Second part.

O praise the Lord Jerusalem.
  thy God, O Sion praise:
Who makes thy bars, and strengtheneth them
  wherewith thy gates he staies.
Thy children in thee he hath blest,
  makes in thy borders peace:
And fills thee with the very best
  of all the fields increase.

He sends out his command on earth,
  his word doth swiftly post:
The snowlike wooll he giveth forth,
  like ashes hoary frost.
His ice as morsels he sends out,
  his cold who can sustain?
His powerful word he sends about
  and melteth them again.

His

His power doth cause the wind to blow,
  whereby the water flows,
His word to Jacob he doth show
  his judgment Israel knows ;
He hath not dealt so lovingly
  with any land beside:
His law no heathen men descry,
  The Lord be magnify'd.

II. *Metre.*

All people, &c.

Praise ye the Lord, for it is meet
  the praises of our God to sing:
For the imployment is most sweet,
  and praise a very comely thing.
2 The Lord doth build Jerusalem,
  gathers th' out-casts of Israels bounds,
3 He healeth broken-hearted men,
  and bindeth up their bleeding wounds.
4 The number of the stars he tells,
  and all their names he doth recite.
5 Great is the Lord, his power excels,
  his wisdom is most infinite.
6 Poor humble souls the Lord doth raise,
  but treads the wicked to the ground :
7 Sing to the Lord our God, sing praise,
  praise him with harps harmonious sound.
8 Who with thick clouds o're-spreads the sky,
  prepared rain on earth distills,
And makes the earth to fructify
  with store of grass on highest hills.
9 He giveth to the beast his food,
  and feeds young ravens when they cry :
10 The strength of horse doth him no good,
  nor doth he in man's legs take joy.

11 The Lord doth take delight in them
   That in his faithful fear abide:
And taketh pleasure in those men
   that in his mercy do confide.

The Second part.

12 O praise the Lord Jerusalem,
   praise thou thy God, O Sion hill,
13 Why makes thy barrs and strengtheneth them
   to keep thy gates in safety still.
Thy children in thee he hath blest,
14 He maketh in thy borders peace,
He fills thee also with the best
   and finest of the fields increase.
15 He sends out his command on earth,
   his word doth very swiftly post;
16 The snow like wooll he giveth forth,
   he spreads, like ashes, hoary frost.
17 He casteth out his ice like crusts.
   his pinching cold who can sustain?
18 He sends his word and melt they must,
   and into water turn again:
His power doth cause the wind to blow,
   whereby the ragged water flows:
19 His word to Jacob he doth show,
   his laws and judgments Israel knows.
20 He dealt not so with other lands,
   as for the judgments of the Lord:
No heathen people understands,
   do ye therefore his praise record.

III. *Metre.*
Now Israel may say, *&c.*

Praise ye the Lord. A good work for good men,
   The solemn praises of the Lord to sing,
   For it is pleasant, and a comely thing:
                            The

The Lord doth build up his Jerusalem,
And Israel's out-casts gathers unto them.

To heal the broken heart he takes delight,
   He binds up all their wounds with gentle hand,
   He tells the stars, and names them as they stand.
Great is the Lord, great is his power and might,
His understanding is most infinite.

The Lord lifts up the meek men undertrod,
   He casteth down the wicked to the ground:
   Sing to the Lord with harps harmonious sound,
Sing praise, I say, with harp unto our God,
And with thanksgiving spread his praise abroad.

Who covers heaven with the cloudy sky,
   And on the earth prepared rain distills:
   He maketh grass to grow upon the hills,
Who giveth food the cattel to supply,
And feeds the hungry ravens when they cry.

The Lord delights not in the strength of horse,
   Nor taketh pleasure in a champions limb.(him,
   The Lord takes pleasure when men reverence
In those that count his fear the greatest force,
And those that to his mercies have recourse.

The Second part.

Praise thou the Lord, O Salem's sacred seat,
   Thy God, O Sion praise: since blest by him,
   Strengthening thy gates without thy seed within:
And in thy borders makes thy peace full great,
And fills thee with the finest of the wheat.

He sends out his commandement on earth,
   His word runs swiftly to the very full,
   He giveth snow like locks of gentle wool,
The hoary frost he also sendeth forth,
And scatters it as ashes on the earth.

He casteth out his clattering icy hail·
   Like little morsels as we may behold,
   And who can stand before his bitter cold?
He sendeth forth his word with gentle gale
To melt these morsels, and it doth not fail.

He gives commission for the winds to swell,
   And makes them at his pleasure for to blow:
   And by their storminess the waters flow,
His word to Jacob he doth shew and tell,
His judgments and his laws to Israel.

He hath not dealt such favours heretofore
   To any Nation of the world beside:
   As for his judgments, they were not descri'd,
The Heathens knew them not: Let us therefore
Applaud and praise the Lord for evermore.

PSALM CXLVIII.

1 PRaise ye the Lord, praise ye the Lord,
   even from the heavens high:
And from the heights his praise record,
   above the starry sky,
2 His angels all, his praise begin,
   and all his hosts of might:
3 Praise him both sun and moon, praise him
   O all ye stars of light.

4 Ye heaven of heavens lofty Sphere,
   him praise and magnify:
Ye waters also that be there
   above the heavens high.
5 O let them praise the mighty name
   of our almighty Lord:
At whose command all creatures came
   created at his word.
6 He hath establisht them to be,
   and that for evermore:
He hath ordained a decree,
   which they shall not pass o're.

7 Praise God from th' earth, all in your kind,
   dragons, and every deep:
8 Fire, hail, snow, vapour, stormy wind,
   his word that fully keep.
9 All hills and mountains, fruitful springs,
   all trees and cedars high:
10 All beasts and cattel, creeping things,
   and all the fowl that fly.
11 Kings of the earth and people there,
   princes and judges all;
12 Young men, and maidens every where,
   old men, and children small.
13 O let them praise the Lord's great name,
   for that excells alone:
   His glory is above the frame
   of earth and heavens high throne.
14 And he exalts his peoples horn,
   his people he doth raise:
   His dearest saints from Israel born,
   O give the Lord his praise.

II. *Metre.*

Give laud, *&c.*

The Lord of heav'n confess,
   On high his glory raise,
2 Him let all Angels bless,
   Him all his Armies praise.
3   Him glorify,
4 Sun, moon and stars, ye higher spheres,
   And cloudy sky.

5 From God your beings are,
   Oh therefore praise the Lord;
   You all created were
   when he but spake the word;
6   And from that place,
   Where fixt you be by his decree,
   you cannot pass.

7 Praise God from earth below,
  ye dragons and ye deeps :
 Fire, hail, clouds, wind and snow,
8 Whom in command he keeps.
9   Praise ye his Name
 Hills great and small, trees low and tall ;
10   Beasts wild and tame.

 All fowl, and creeping things,
  All people great and small,
11 All Judges, Princes, Kings,
12 Young men and maidens all,
   both young and old
13 Exalt his name, for much his fame
   should be extoll'd.

 O let God's Name be prais'd
  Above both earth and sky :
14 For he his Saints hath rais'd,
  And set their horn on high:
   Ev'n those that be
 Of Israel's race, near to his grace ;
   The Lord praise ye.

PSALM CXLIX.

Praise ye the Lord and sing new songs,
   God's praises to declare,
 O praise him in the thickest throngs,
  where saints assembled are.
2 Let Israel joy and triumph still,
  and of their maker sing :
 And let the sons of Sion hill
  be joyful in their king.
3 Let them extol his praise and fame
  in dances, when they meet,
 Let them sing praises to his name
  with harp and timbrel sweet.

4 For lo, the Lord's entire delight
   is in his people plac'd,
 And he will make the meek shine bright
   with his salvation grac'd.

5 O let the gracious saints rejoyce,
   whom glory doth invest:
 Let them sing praise with loudest voice,
   as on their beds they rest.
6 Let the high praises of the Lord
   be in their mouth contain'd:
 And let a double edged sword
   be put into their hand.

7 To execute great plagues and pains
   upon the heathen lands:
8 To bind their stately kings with chains,
   their Lords with iron bands.
9 To execute on them the doom
   found written in his word:
 This honour to all saints doth come,
   praise ye, praise ye the Lord.

PSALM CL.

Have mercy, &c.

Praise God, praise God most high
   within his sacred tower:
 I'th firmament of large extent,
   where he declares his power.
2 O praise him thankfully,
   for his almighty deeds:
 His praise forth shew according to
   his greatness which exceeds.

3 O magnify the Lord
   with stately trumpets sound:

With

Psalm cl.

With psalteries and harps likewise,
  that he may be renown'd.

4 Do ye his praise record
   among them in the dance:
  With timbrels, flutes, organs and lutes,
    his praises to advance.
5 Let the loud cimbals ring,
    his praise to magnify:
  Praise him upon the silver one,
    that soundeth loud and high.

6 Let every breathing thing,
    be ready to record
  The praise and fame of God's great name,
    Amen, praise ye the Lord.

II. Metre.

All people, *Or*, O Lord consider, *&c.*

Praise ye the Lord: Praise God on high,
Praise him within his Sanctuary:
O praise him in the firmament
Of his great power omnipotent.

2 O praise him for his mighty deeds,
After his power which exceeds:
3 Praise him with sound of Trumpet sharp;
Praise him with psaltery and harp.

4 Your timbrels in his praise employ;
And let your hearts even leap for joy:
Praise him with Instruments well strung,
And quavering Organs sounding long.

5 Praise him, O praise him cheerfully,
   With Cymbals sounding loud and high:
6 Let every creature that has breath,
   Applaud and praise the Lord till death.

FINIS.

www.ingramcontent.com/pod-product-compliance
Lightning Source LLC
Chambersburg PA
CBHW022107290426
44112CB00008B/577